THE LOTUS AND THE ROBOT

*the text of this book is printed
on 100% recycled paper*

The Lotus and the Robot

ARTHUR KOESTLER

Harper Colophon Books
Harper & Row, Publishers
New York

THE LOTUS AND THE ROBOT. Copyright © 1960 by Arthur Koestler. All rights reserved. No part of this book may be used or reproduced in any manner whatsoever without written permission except in the case of brief quotations embodied in critical articles and reviews. For information address Harper & Row, Publishers, Inc., 10 East 53rd Street, New York, N.Y. 10022.

This book was originally published by The Macmillan Company in the United States of America and is here reprinted by arrangement.

First HARPER COLOPHON edition published 1966 by Harper & Row, Publishers, Incorporated, N. Y.

Library of Congress Catalog Card No.: 61-6583

TO
VERRIER ELWIN

I am deeply indebted to Swami Age-
hananda Bharati (Dr. Leopold Fischer)
and Professor Herbert Passion, both at
the University of Washington, Seattle,
and to Professor Ivan Morris, Columbia
University, New York, for reading
through the manuscript and for their
patient criticisms, corrections, suggest-
ions and encouragement. I also wish to
thank two much maligned institutions,
the British Council and the Congress for
Cultural Freedom, whose representatives
in India and Japan provided much information and assistance.

Acknowledgements

THE publishers wish to thank the following for permission to quote from the works mentioned: Vedanta, Kerala, India, *Atma-Darshan* and *Atma-Nirvriti*, by Krishna Menon; Shree Shree Anandamayee Sangha, Varanasi, India, *Mother as Revealed to Me*, by Baiji, and *Jayanti Souvenir*, by Mahamahopadyaya Gopinath Kaviraj; The Hogarth Press, *The Twice Born*, by G. Morris Carstairs; Public Affairs Press (U.S.A.) and Beacon Press (U.K.), *Experiments with Truth*, by Mahatma Gandhi; Routledge and Kegan Paul (U.K.) and The Bollingen Foundation (U.S.A.), *Zen and Japanese Culture*, by D. T. Suzuki; Routledge (U.K.) and Pantheon Books Inc. (U.S.A.), *Zen in the Art of Archery*, by Dr. Eugen Herrigel; Charles Tuttle (U.S.A), *Understanding the Japanese Mind*, by Dr. J. C. Moloney; The Harvard University Press (U.S.A.), *The Psychiatric Hospital as a Small Community*, by William Coudhill; David Higham and Associates, *The World of Dew*, by D. J. Enright; Alfred Knopf Inc., *The Temple of the Golden Pavilion*, by Yukio Mishima, trans. by Ivan Morris; The Cresset Press (U.K.) and Alfred Knopf (U.S.A.), *The Western World and Japan*, by Sir George Sansom; The Yoga Institute, Bombay, *International Journal on the Science of Yoga*, by Mrs. Shri Yogendra.

Contents

Preface

ROME was saved in A.D. 408 by three thousand pounds of pepper imported from India as part of the ransom the Senate paid to Alaric the Goth; ever since, when Europe found itself in an impasse or in a questing mood, it has turned yearningly to the land of culinary and spiritual spices. The greatest influence during the Dark Ages was Augustine, who was influenced by Plotinus, who was influenced by Indian mysticism. Long before Aldous Huxley found in Yoga a remedy for our Brave New World, Schopenhauer called the Upanishads the consolation of his life; and the first generation of the Nuclear Age seems to have found a like solace in Zen. On the whole, the West's receptiveness to the voice of the East was limited to periods of spiritual emergency, to moods of futility and despair; its attitude to Asia was either that of the conqueror armed with his gun-and-gospel truth, or that of the pilgrim in sackcloth and ashes, anxious to prostrate himself at the guru's feet.

I travelled in India and Japan (in 1958–9) in the mood of the pilgrim. Like countless others before, I wondered whether the East had any answer to offer to our perplexities and dead-locked problems. I chose those two countries because they are at opposite ends of the spectrum: one the most tradition-bound, the other the most 'modern' of the great countries of Asia. I did not hope for any ready-made answer, but was anxious to look at the predicament of the West from a different perspective, a different spiritual latitude. The conclusions that emerged were rather unexpected and more reassuring than I had hoped; they are set out in the epilogue.

The book starts with the description of four very different contemporary Indian saints. This is followed by two chapters on the physical and mystical aspects of Yoga, and on recent research into its supernatural claims. The remaining chapters on India deal with the influence of an ancient spiritual tradition on the new State, and with certain lessons we may draw from it.

The second part of the book starts with impressions of the contradictory trends in modern Japan; in the chapters which follow I have tried to trace some of these trends back into the past. Much of it is permeated with the 'stink of Zen' – which is not a rude expression, but a phrase often used in Zen literature.

As a student, my interests were about equally divided between engineering and social engineering on the one hand, and the expanding universe of Freud, Jung, Eddington and Jeans, with its irrational and mystic undercurrents on the other. This tug-of-war continued in later life, and is reflected in the titles of earlier books, such as *The Yogi and the Commissar* – to which the present is, in some respects, a sequel. The respect for 'hard, obstinate facts' which a scientific education imparts, does not necessarily imply the denial of a different order of Reality; it does imply, however, the obligation to exhaust all possibilities of a natural explanation of phenomena before acknowledging that they belong to that different order. It could be said, then, that I went on my pilgrimage not so much with an open, as with an equally split, mind. What emerged is a mixture of pedantic detail and sweeping generalizations.

PART ONE

India

The world is pain
Its load all bearing past;
Never pine I, never thirst,
For its kingdom vain.
HYMN TO DURGA

Four Contemporary Saints

I. ACHARYA VINOBA BHAVE

The First Shock

THE sewers of Bombay had been opened by mistake, I was told, before the tide had come in. The damp heat, impregnated by their stench, invaded the air-conditioned cabin the moment the door of the Viscount was opened. As we descended the steps I had the sensation that a wet, smelly diaper was being wrapped around my head by some abominable joker. This was December; the previous day I had ben slithering over the frozen snow in the mountains of Austria. Yet, by the time we had crossed the reclaimed marshes of the seven islands on which Bombay is built, I had accepted the heat and was no longer aware of the smell.

An hour after leaving the aircraft, I was ushered into another air-conditioned environment: my hotel room. Its windows and shutters were hermetically closed against the outer atmosphere, its curtains drawn tight against the outer light. It was the peaceful interior of a bathyscope suspended in the sea. After a while I got accustomed to that too, and found it quite natural to live in an artificial atmosphere with artificial light, while the sun was blazing outside. However, each time I left my bathyscope and was hit by the steaming air with its heavy blend of smells, I felt the same shocked surprise as on the first occasion.

Late at night, on the day after my arrival, I opened the curtains, blinds and shutters, and walked out to the balcony. At this hour there were no pedestrians. My first impression of the deserted street was that a firing squad had passed through it, leaving the pavements strewn with corpses. The lifeless heaps of rags and bones, naked except for a loin-cloth, seemed to be lying in the position in which they had fallen when the bullets struck them. They were lying on the pavement amidst the red spittle, the dogs' excrement, the undefinable filth. But the idea of the firing squad did not really fit, for there was no atmosphere of heroism in the street; it had a look of resignation, rather like etchings of mediaeval towns in the grip of the Plague. I had read that out of the total population of three and a half million in Bombay, seven hundred thousand slept on the pavements – but these were abstract figures, and statistics neither bleed nor smell.

During my first week in Bombay, I was haunted by the corpse-like sleepers along the kerbs, on the stairs and passages of dilapidated Indo-Victorian houses. One late evening, visiting a friend, I actually stumbled over one of the lifeless shapes lying in the hallway. It did not stir. I lit a match and saw that there were actually five of them: their skins nearly black, their ribs sticking out like Christ's on the Cross.

The next day, I had an appointment with a physician working at a clinic. I went early in the morning before surgery hours: the gateway and courtyard of the clinic were a camp of human castaways – men, old women, children like twisted skeletons, sleeping among the refuse in the company of several pie dogs. Whenever, late at night, I tried to go for a stroll, I felt that I was walking over a battlefield combined with a refuse heap. Nobody in Bombay walks through the streets at night, except for some compelling reason.

My Indian acquaintances were puzzled by my obsession with the seven hundred thousand street-campers. It had always been like that, they explained, but perhaps with progressive industrialization under the third Five Year Plan . . . In actual fact, the third Five Year Plan does not even pretend to be concerned with the problem. As far as one can foretell, the situation, instead of improving, will get worse: the population increases at the rate of six or seven million a year; in the next ten years a figure larger than the total population of Great Britain will be added to its numbers. My Indian friends shrugged; after a while I stopped harassing them with questions. After another week, I took the huddled corpses for granted and actually no longer saw them – just as I was no longer aware of the beggars, cripples and legless deformities dragging themselves on naked buttocks along the pavement amidst the milling crowd.

Though I had read about it in books, the din and noise and profanity in Indian places of worship came as another shock. I found that there is more peace to be had in Manhattan than in any Indian town or village, temple or shrine. If the temple was an historic monument, the atmosphere was that of Brighton pier; if it was a modest local shrine, the scene was that of a family picnic. The voices were shrill and unrestrained; children would caper all over the place with mothers and sisters yelling after them; obeisance was shown to the idol, but no reverence; the feeling of sanctity was completely absent. I began to suspect that I had never encountered a people as un-contemplative as the nation of Yogis. At the same time I also suspected that something essential was escaping me, and that I must be mistaken.

But above all I felt that I had fallen into a chaotic ant-heap of ants of my size; gentle ants, mindlessly milling in all directions, falling over each other in the hot dust, some crippled, some starving, some hanging in grapes from ant-sized tramcars and liable to panic at any moment.

When it became too much, there was always an escape. I would retire to my air-conditioned bathyscope, close the shutters, and the ant-town would cease to exist. Instead, I would feel that I was sinking through an unreal world towards the bottom of the sea. My heart was sinking, my morale was sinking. I had almost forgotten what I had come for. It must have been some abstract, air-conditioned idea about spiritual values.

The Silent Avalanche

In May 1953, two years after Acharya Vinoba Bhave had set out on foot to solve India's problem by persuading the rich to give away their land to the poor, the Rajah of Ranka, province of Bihar, seized by the holy fever, donated 11,000 acres to one of his labourers and 2,500 acres to another. Vinoba asked the Rajah the reason why he had given four times more to the first than to the second. The Rajah shrugged respectfully and said he had given each labourer precisely the amount that he had asked for. Vinoba sucked in his cheeks as if sucking an acid drop, a habit of his when thinking: 'In this case, how much will you give me?'

'As much as you ask for,' said the Rajah.

'How much land do you have altogether?'

'A hundred thousand acres uncultivated and about seven thousand self-cultivated.'

'As a rule,' said Vinoba, 'I ask for one-sixth of the total. But in view of what you have just said, please make over to me the whole hundred thousand acres of uncultivated land and one-sixth of the cultivated.'

'As you wish,' said the Rajah, and as soon as it was drafted, he signed the deed.

The story, when narrated by a Westerner for Western ears, carries a ring of melodrama or fairy tale, which is as unavoidable as it is misleading; for such episodes were daily routine in the early years of Vinoba Bhave's Bhoodan campaign. During that tour through Bihar in 1953, the Rajah of Dhanbad donated one hundred thousand acres of good land; the Rajah of Ramgarh joined Vinoba's march, to persuade other princelings. The movement was growing like a slow, silent avalanche – without publicity, staff, or organization – an avalanche of dust stirred up by the old man's feet, stomping with piston-like precision round the country from village to village, at the rate of four miles an hour, twelve to fifteen miles a day, seven days a week, covering up to date[1] a total of twenty-five thousand miles.

In April 1954, on the third anniversary of the movement, a conference was held at Bodh Gaya, the city where the Lord Buddha had obtained enlightenment under the Banyan tree. Among the speakers paying homage to Vinoba were Prime Minister Nehru, the President and the Vice-President of the Republic, and the leader of the Socialist Party, Jayaprakash

[1] January 1959.

Narayan. The last-mentioned, one of the most revered figures in India, was at the time generally regarded as the likeliest successor to Nehru. On that historic occasion he alienated for ever thousands of his followers and electrified millions with a new and unexpected hope, for Jayaprakash announced quietly, almost shyly, his Jeevan-dan – his renunciation of politics and solemn pledge to devote the rest of his life to the service of the Bhoodan movement.

At the beginning of 1959, nearly eight years after the start of the movement, Vinoba had marched the equivalent of the length of the equator and collected nearly eight million acres of land. It seems a staggering figure, but it represented merely fifteen per cent of his original target of fifty million acres as a minimum solution of India's rural problem. Moreover, less than half of the donated land was in a cultivable condition, and owing to technical difficulties only a fraction of it had actually been distributed to the landless. Among the Indians to whom I talked before I met Vinoba, about one-third shrugged him off as a saintly crank, another third regarded him as a historic figure equal to or greater than Gandhi; the remainder hovered between rational scepticism and irrational hope.

I wanted to meet Vinoba in his natural habitat as it were – in a rural area in the backwoods untouched by modern life. I contacted one of the voluntary Bhoodan workers on leave in Bombay, and was told that Vinoba was expected on a certain date at a village called Raganathpur in Rajasthan.

I took the Frontier Mail to Dohad, in the vicinity of the border between Bombay State and Rajasthan, and from there had to travel by Land Rover a distance of 160 miles. It took some eight hours, a bone-shaking, occasionally frightening, but memorable experience. On my map, the best I could find in Bombay, this whole region was a blank; not a single village was marked on the virginal blot that stretches from Dohad to Udaipur – a distance of 120 miles as the crow flies. Only the Mahi River wends its muddy way across it in lazy loops like a child's scribble on blotting-paper. Stretches of metal road alternated with dirt tracks; often, for five or ten miles between two hamlets, there was no road of any description at all, and we lunged ahead cross-country over the stony desert, across gullies and banks of squelching reeds.

The villages we passed, and which do not appear on the map – Talud, Baswara, Sokusalya, Partapur, Gathi, Erdwala, Milula, Sagwala – seemed indeed to vegetate on the border of non-existence: a few ramshackle cubes of mud and straw dotted among the barren, archaic hills; shapeless, swaddled women with shapely jars on their heads standing rooted in the landscape or walking in a dream with eyes like buffaloes' gazing into the river; fly-encrusted infants sown indiscriminately into the dust like handfuls of cheap seed-corn from the bag of India's annual birth-surplus. The scraggy cows were rummaging in the refuse for what was left after the children and scavengers had their pick; the skinny goats looked like inmates of Belsen. The village well: a hollowed pumpkin serving as a bucket to scoop out the slimy ooze; a watermill of a model pre-dating the Mogul conquest; then bare existence, with its suspended heart-beat, faded again into non-existence. Looking back at Erdwala, I felt like holding a mirror over the village to see whether it was still breathing.

Here and there a trickle of water created an oasis or a vale of lush green; then more parched hills and more villages sunk in protoplasmic apathy, hiding their blue-faced octopus-armed idols, their unwashed saints and undusted gods. Even the cacti looked like phantom creatures with distorted limbs, and the occasional palm-trees stood irresolutely in the desolation like lone spinsters on Christmas Eve.

Raganathpur lies in a more fertile area than the places we had passed in the morning; it was larger and looked, by Indian standards, a shade more prosperous; by any other standards it was still unimaginably wretched and primitive. I passed an irrigation well: two oxen were yoked to a horizontal wheel which drove an upright wheel with earthenware jars attached to its rim; these scooped up the water from a hole and spilled it into a canal. The whole contraption, including cogwheels and bearings, was of wood with not a piece of metal in it; I remembered drawings of Egyptian wells three thousand years old which looked more modern.

But the village had awakened from its dazed slumber; it was teeming, buzzing with life. A large open space had been marked off as the assembly ground, and on it squatted and chatted a multitude of three or four thousand people. They had come from the surrounding hamlets, and were still flocking in from all directions, bare-footed down the hills. A wooden platform had been erected, covered by a bamboo roof; there were garlands, greetings painted on the earth, pavement-artist fashion, and even a kind of triumphal arch – two vertical poles and a cross-piece hung with flowers and bamboo leaves.

It was still too early for the meeting; I found Vinoba and his disciples billeted in the most prosperous house of Raganathpur – it had a narrow veranda and three or four rooms with practically no furniture in them. The white-clad voluntary workers, about fifteen in number, were resting on the floor of the largest room, their mats laid out in parallel rows, covering all the available space. Some were spinning on their small portable spindles, some asleep. Vinobaji, they informed me, was by himself in another room; it was his hour reserved for study – he was reading the Koran in Arabic for the sixth time from beginning to end. They made me feel welcome without fuss and gave me a mat; since I had only slept three hours in the train, I fell asleep at once to the sound of subdued chatter, giggling, and the hum of the spinning-wheels.

When they woke me up half an hour later, Vinoba and his retinue had just started for the assembly ground. He was marching across the village with his quick and precise step, his bare feet in tennis shoes, his long sinewy legs working like pistons. Whether he has to walk fifteen miles or fifteen yards, his gait remains the same, as unmistakably his own as one's voice or signature. He is of medium height, but when seated he looks smaller, when walking taller, due to his disproportionately long legs and to the impressive, bolt upright carriage of his body: he could be either a stern prophet or a gentle sergeant-major. At any rate, he did look more like an Old Testament prophet than a Hindu saint: silky white beard, short-cropped, dark hair, long face, bony nose, high forehead, grey eyes, twinkling smile. He wore a very finely woven white dhoti which looked as if it were silk, though it was, of course, cotton, spun and woven by himself; during one of his long sojourns in prison, he spun a length of yarn sufficient for a whole dhoti without once breaking the thread.

Now we were all seated on cushions on the dais. Vinoba had a white scarf wrapped like a hood round his head; he looked smaller and there was a great stillness about him – one could feel the ripples of stillness spreading around. The dense crowd squatting below was still chattering; the men to the left, women to the right, their gaudy saris a huge, undulating patchwork-quilt. Some children were sitting in front, others in their mother's lap; some were suckling, half buried in the saris, others toddled about, climbing over limbs and shoulders.

There were two or three fairly short speeches of welcome by local dignitaries, amplified by loudspeakers – the equipment travels ahead by jeep from village to village. Then the microphone was pushed unceremoniously in front of Vinoba who sucked in his cheeks and immediately began to speak, in an informal, business-like manner, as if continuing an interrupted conversation. He talked in a flat monotone without modulation or emphasis, almost too off-handedly, as if he were talking to himself and could not care less whether he was listened to or not; and, judging by the reactions of the crowd, this was indeed difficult to tell. They had heard legendary tales about Vinoba, they saw him for the first time, and some of them had walked more than twenty miles to get there. When Vinoba briskly climbed up to the dais and as abruptly seated himself on a cushion, their eyes were drinking him in, there is no other word for it – but whether their ears were taking in his words was another question. Most of the faces were devoid of expression, the women's almost painfully vacant. After a few minutes, some started fidgeting, more newcomers arrived and squatted down. Some others left unceremoniously, babies cried, girls giggled. Most of them seemed to be only half listening, yet their eyes remained fixed on the white-clad, hooded figure, babbling away in a soft, bored voice into his microphone.

I was puzzled and somewhat disappointed. I failed to understand how Vinoba had achieved the fantastic feat of obtaining nearly eight million acres for nothing, from some seven hundred thousand different donors, of influencing Government legislation and galvanizing a whole sub-continent. I could find in him no trace of magic, of hypnotic power, nor did I find any sign of the rapt attention such audiences were supposed to display. It was an amorphous, indifferent audience which became more fidgety as Vinoba talked on, and now hardly even pretended to listen – only their eyes kept feasting on him, returning every few seconds for another gulp.

Then it dawned on me that it was not the words that mattered. Most of them were probably acquainted with Vinoba's message. They sat at his feet as the disciples sit at the guru's feet in the ashram, reading, chatting, following their own occupations. It is not his words that matter, but his presence – they breathe him, they imbibe him, it is a process of acquiring merit by spiritual osmosis. He need not have the gift of the orator, nor specific learning, nor mystic insight. All he need have is the quality of being a guru: that curious gift of radiating peace which is physically felt like a laying on of hands; of making people feel enriched by his mere presence; of making the ascetic life seem enviable to the sybarite, and washing the master's feet a blissful privilege.

In Europe the gurus have died out, in India the tradition is still alive, though declining. It was the secret of India's greatness, the emotional yeast by which its great gurus, from Buddha to Gandhi, had kept the race in spiritual fermentation. Is also had its dangers: worship of the guru could degenerate into spiritual debauch – I had a taste of it in the south, about which later. But the scene I was witnessing – muddled, casual, confused – bore the stamp of authenticity.

Perhaps the audience of the Sermon on the Mount, peasants, shepherds and other illiterates, did not understand either what was being said and did not care whether they understood, staring with vacant adoration at their bearded guru and scratching for lice under their rags.

Another curious characteristic of authentic gurus is their unpredictability. When the restlessness of the audience became too much for Vinoba, he abruptly changed his tone, broke into a mocking peasant sing-song to berate them with clucking and chortling noises, made those who were standing sit down and stopped them moving about. After that, he chanted a line of a hymn three times and asked for a minute of silent meditation.

Now silence was complete; even the children became big-eyed and quiet, and angels seemed to move over the huge crowd. Then Vinoba broke the spell, re-established the atmosphere of a family picnic and ended his speech as it had started – flatly, conversationally. There was no flourish, his voice trailed off and nobody was quite sure whether he had finished, until he sucked in his cheeks and pushed the microphone impatiently in front of the last speaker.

Gandhi's Heir

At the appointed time, half an hour after the meeting, I was summoned to the little veranda of the house where the Bhoodan workers were staying, for a personal talk with Vinoba. We were seated on cushions with four or five disciples around us; I had prepared no questions and my mind was pleasurably blank. Vinoba opened the conversation by asking what purpose brought me to India. I said something vague about spiritual values and the perils of Western civilization. Vinoba, whose eyes seemed to be focused at some point half-way between himself and his interlocutor, which made his gaze appear outgoing and withdrawn at the same time, considered the matter for a moment and suddenly began to laugh with amusement. 'You say the spiritual values are in need of being "saved" and you still call this civilization?'

But he quickly relented, fearing that he might have hurt the visitor's feelings. He was not hostile to Western science, he explained, 'but science derives from the outer light, it must be complemented by the inner light. You have developed the head; the heart did not keep pace. With us it was the opposite. It is with the development of the heart we have been concerned in India, and still are concerned. That is the way of Bhoodan. The land which is given does not matter much in itself. It matters as a token of love. When land is given, both the donor and the receiver are changed. The spiritual value is in that change. There are half a million villages like this in India. I want them to come forward to lead the country and be its leaven.'

This first talk lasted for three-quarters of an hour, and most of what he said about Bhoodan was already known to me. Once more it was not so much what he said, but the way he said it which was so profoundly impressive: the complete lack of desire to persuade; the simple and direct persuasiveness which results from it; the circles of peace around him; the precise, almost faultless English alternating with archaic imagery: 'The earth is the peasants' mother. I give milk to the breast of the mother.'

The talk was continued on the next day, after another mass meeting at the town of Dungarpur. This time we were sitting indoors. I had participated in the early morning march from Raganathpur to Dungarpur, and this made the atmosphere more intimate. I asked Vinoba to recount how exactly the idea of Bhoodan had occurred to him. He answered with a good-humoured pun: 'So you want to hear about the *moving spirit* of the movement?' He then recited a kind of dehydrated account of his life, leaving out all dramatic highlights: there was no mention of his years spent in prison, or of his adoption by Gandhi:

'After I completed my college studies I left my family in search of truth and I was thinking of going to the Himalayas for meditation, but before going there I went to Benares where I thought to study for some time. But Bapu (Gandhi) had been there and all the people were talking of the speech he had made in Kashi about non-violent resistance. I wrote him a letter asking him some questions to which he replied, and thus our correspondence began to grow. Then he wrote that these conundrums which I put before him could not be solved by correspondence or mere discussion, only by practical action, and asked me to come to his ashram and lead my life there. This was in 1916 when I was twenty-one years old . . .'

In actual fact, Vinoba, whose real name was Vinayak, had at the age of nineteen burnt his college certificates in his mother's presence, and announced his decision to walk the path which leads to the liberation of the self and its unity with Brahma. His father, a Civil Servant of orthodox Brahminic views (he was the son of the village high priest), insisted that Vinayak should sit for the intermediate examinations in Bombay. Vinayak took the train to Bombay from his home State, Baroda, but on the way, at Sayak, he got out and headed for Benares, the Holy City, to study Sanskrit and the Vedic scriptures.

Benares, with its mixture of sanctimoniousness, beggary, rigid scholasticism and unholy stench, was a disappointment; he fell ill and went through a spiritual crisis. Then, at the solemn inauguration of the Hindu University at Benares by the Viceroy, with Annie Besant in the Chair and an audience stuffed with Maharajahs and Pundits, Gandhi caused a beautiful scandal by making a political speech and telling the Viceroy to go home: 'If for such plain speaking we are sentenced to death, let us go cheerfully to the gallows.'

This episode decided Vinoba's life. He had found the answer he had been searching for, the synthesis between saintly aspiration and service to society, between the spiritual and the practical, the crusading Yogi and the pacifist Commissar.

'This was in 1916, and from that time till Bapu's death in 1948 I was engaged in social work, especially in serving the people in the villages round the ashram, teaching students, and practising meditation for a few hours of the day. This went on till his death.'

In fact a lot more went on in those thirty-two years of Vinoba's life. For one thing, five and a half of them were spent in prison for his participation in various civil disobedience campaigns. Gandhi, who had adopted Vinoba as his spiritual heir, and conferred on him the title Acharya – preceptor – always singled him out to be the first to court imprisonment in the non-cooperation and quit-India campaigns from 1939 onward. After Vinoba's third arrest, he had become a national figure, and Gandhi issued a Press release in which he sang the praise of Vinoba's virtues as a scholar, itinerant teacher, social worker, menial worker, healer of lepers, and a propagandist for the educational and economic value of handicrafts: 'He has revolutionized spinning and drawn out its hitherto unknown possibilities. For perfect spinning he has probably no rival in India.'

Vinoba was scathing about his gaolers ('Have you ever been to a circus?' he asked a visitor. 'There men command the animals. Here it is just the reverse'), but in reality he took to prisons like a duck to water. He organized Sanskrit classes, scripture classes, spinning classes, and still had more time on his hands than at the ashram for meditation and the pursuit of his hobbies. He had three: Metaphysics, mathematics, and languages. 'Next to God,' he confessed, 'if I love anything best it is mathematics.' He speaks eleven or twelve languages, and in addition to that several Indian dialects; it takes him about six weeks to learn a new tongue. One of his former prison mates, Pyarelal Nayar (once Gandhi's secretary, later Keeper of the Gandhi Archive), told me in Delhi: 'I would rather share a prison cell with a criminal than with a saint. Vinobaji used to start his Sanskrit classes at 4 a.m., and since most of his pupils were blockheads, he yelled at them so that I couldn't sleep.'

Then came Independence, and in 1948 the assassination of Gandhi by Vinoba's namesake and caste-sake, Vinayak Godse. Both Vinayaks were Marathi Brahmins: the assassin embodying the extreme of fanaticism, the heir the extreme of tolerance, both inherent in the Hindu potential. Vinoba was now fifty-three:

'After Bapu's death, I felt the urge to come out of the ashram and to see the condition of the people of India with my own eyes. So I thought of travelling through India, but I felt that saving time and space by using high-speed vehicles won't help me much towards a solution of the problem of poverty by non-violent means, which I was searching for; so I decided to walk on foot. I started by presenting myself at the Sarvodaya conference, which was to be held in Hyderabad that year.

'While going there my heart was full of meditation. I had arguments with Communist leaders. I told them: you *talk* of Communism, but I want to *live* in communism, with God – because to live in communism with God is to live in communism with the poor.

'That is why I voluntarily adopted the life of the poor. In that way my heart and their hearts are so much intermingled. I went to the people and discussed with them how to get out of their difficulties by the power which is inherent in the soul. They felt that I was their mouthpiece, expressing the thought of their hearts. But then they began to think with their minds too, and in that way this revolution was brought about. They started to donate land to people even poorer than themselves, for in the beginning, it was the poor who came forward to share. But as this revolution grew, the hardened hearts also began to part with their land.'

Vinoba had telescoped the events of three years into one. After Gandhi's assassination, he had continued to live in retirement, occupied with social work at his ashram. In 1951, Sarvodaya Samaj, the Brotherhood for the Good of All, founded by Gandhi, held its third anniversary conference near Hyderabad. The atmosphere in the country was one of profound dejection. Independence had failed to bring the Kingdom of Heaven; it had brought instead the mutual massacre of Hindu and Moslem, a mud-flood of starved refugees, increased poverty, land hunger, and the threat of civil war. Gandhi was dead, his ideals trampled to dust. When Vinoba, who at first refused to attend the conference, was finally persuaded to do so, he went on foot. At the end of that three-hundred-and-fifteen mile march, his 'heart full of meditation', he had become fully awakened to the condition of his country; his thirty-two years of hiding in retirement had come to an end.

On the last day of the conference, Vinoba abruptly announced that he was going to tour the district of Telengana, where the Communist guerillas were fighting Government troops. Telengana was part of the Nizam of Hyderabad's five-million-acre state, controlled by a thousand families. In one of the first villages that Vinoba visited, a population of three thousand was living on a cultivable area of three thousand acres; these belonged to ninety families, the remaining five hundred families were landless. Vinoba summed up the situation: 'The rich have fathered the Communists.' It was in this God-forsaken district, in the village of Panchampalli, on 18 April 1951, that Bhoodan was born.

I asked Vinoba for the exact circumstances of how the idea had come to him. He looked bored and suggested that I start a Bhoodan in the British Isles. 'Yesterday,' he said resentfully, 'I told you that this spirit can also work in England.[1] You said that there is no comparable poverty in England. But I say there is poverty in the world; people in England should share their happiness with the world. You said, "this is too much to expect from human nature". I don't entirely agree with you. Human nature is not self-centred. It has a sense of love which no animal species has. That is how I feel, and that is why you have come here. Otherwise you have got your own country, you need not come here, but who is impelling you, compelling you to come here?'

I said: 'I came here, in the first place, to hear in your own words how the idea of Bhoodan had come to you. Was it in the morning or in the afternoon, at what precise moment? We both like mathematics.'

They all burst out laughing, including Vinoba; he was no longer evasive. On that historic day, in the village of Panchampalli, the Untouchables had come to him with their tale

[1] There actually exists, as an indirect result of this talk, a 'Friends of Bhoodan Committee' in England, under the joint chairmanship of Shri Jayaprakash Narayan and Professor Arnold Toynbee.

of misery. He asked them how much land they would need for bare subsistence. After some hesitation, their spokesman said: eighty acres . . .

'I considered that they ought to be given those eighty acres by the Government. But then I thought that perhaps a few men may obtain land that way, but it would not solve the problem. So I suddenly turned to the people of the village and asked whether there was somebody among them willing to give land to his brethren so that they may not die of starvation; and a man came forward and offered a hundred acres of land . . .'

The man was V. R. Reddy, a small land-owner, among whose relatives some had turned Communist.

'That night when I went to bed I could not sleep. I was thinking over the event. What has happened to me today? A man came forward and donated a hundred acres of his land without any compulsion. Is there a sign from God in this? As I am a mathematician, I began to work out how much land would be needed for all the landless people in India. I came to the conclusion that five crore, fifty million acres, will be required for distribution, that is, one sixth of all the cultivable land in India. I could not believe that people would offer that amount of land. The idea had come to me and attacked me, and my mind tried to resist because I was not ready to accept it. And so I hesitated. But a voice from within myself told me that if I doubt, if I do not put my faith in the power of love and God, then I must abandon my belief in non-violence and follow the violent way of the Communists. You can't sit quiet any longer. You must go either this way or that way. God puts the hunger into the child's belly and he also puts the milk into the mother's breast; so if you go begging in the name of God, you will get a response.

'But I had only a hundred acres of land in my hand, and this was a question of asking for fifty million acres. I did not consult any of my friends or any institution because they would have said that I may expect to get thousands of acres, but I could not expect to get millions. So I decided to go ahead by myself, to start begging for land and to see how people respond.

'The next day in the morning I started for the next village (Tongadpalli). The village people had prepared breakfast for me. I told them that I won't breakfast, I won't break my fast, while my countrymen are hungry; give me a few acres of land for my breakfast. And God's will was there and they gave me twenty-five acres.

'In this way the matter was decided, and I started to work in that Communist-infected area – although I feel that the Communists are also my brothers. Last year I marched to Kerala, and the Communist Prime Minister of Kerala State said: "I doubt whether you will succeed, but your movement may be an alternative to our movement – if you succeed." So now all depends upon the success.'

Crusaders on the March

'He is a Bhim – a Hercules,' Gandhi had once exclaimed, talking of Vinoba. At that time Vinoba had weighed ninety-eight pounds, and lived on bananas, milk and lemon. He was evidently the kind of person, to be found only in India, who takes to the ascetic life without frustration and self-righteousness. Gandhi renounced sex in middle age; Vinoba made his vow of chastity at the age of twelve. He was afflicted with chronic malaria, peptic ulcers, and was deaf in one ear – the result of a blow from a fanatic Brahmin, whose shrine Vinoba visited in the company of Untouchables. His diet, at the time of my visit, consisted of small cups of curd and molasses taken every three or four hours, a total of eleven hundred calories a day. Yet his body was all muscle and sinew, his skin had a healthy glow, his gestures were vigorous, and on the march he could outpace any of the younger disciples. He followed the same daily routine all round the week: reveille at 3 a.m., followed by ablutions and prayers; starting the march at 4 a.m., arriving at the next village between nine and ten; then a short rest followed by talks with the villagers and visitors till one. From one to three he would spin and read; at 3 p.m. the public meeting would start and last till five; from 5 to 7 p.m., more talks with the villagers and possibly a second, smaller meeting; 8 p.m. prayers; 8.30 to bed.

After the first talk with Vinoba in Raganathpur, I had to drive back to Dungapur where I spent the night. The next morning at sunrise I set out on foot towards Raganathpur to meet Vinoba's party half-way on the road.

The landscape was deserted. At first there was a metal road, then the usual dusty cart-track wending its way into the hills. I passed a gypsy encampment built of tins and rags, compared to which even the mud huts were palaces – poverty in India has unfathomable layers of depth. As the sky grew lighter, I met a few farmers who gave a solemn, unsmiling salute; a couple of tribesmen carrying swords on their loincloths and nothing else; then I saw in the distance a small group in a dust-cloud, wandering across the hills to meet Vinoba's procession. Peasant women stood in front of their mud huts, shading their eyes and staring into the distance; the land was still empty, but there was expectancy in the air. At a turn of the road three archways had been erected at intervals of a hundred yards. They were ingeniously built of columns of large earthenware jars set on top of each other, and held in place by bamboo poles. But there was nobody about, and the arches looked rather pointless in the deserted landscape.

I met the procession some five or six miles out of town. They approached at a kind of fast trot. In front, carrying a storm lantern, now extinguished, marched Ranishankar Maharaj – a patriarch of seventy-five and an expert spinner, who had walked with Vinoba for the last fifteen thousand miles and spun a hundred yards of yarn. Then came Vinoba in a white hood, dhoti and tennis shoes, vigorously treading the dust as if he were pounding corn, flanked by his two closest female disciples – Mahadevi Thai, elderly, energetic, with steel-framed spectacles, who had been with Gandhi and gaoled five times; and pleasant, round-faced Kusum, a former schoolmistress, who takes down all his speeches and conversations in long-hand. Behind them came Vinoba's secretary, a raven-haired young man, then a yellow-robed Japanese monk with a drum, and about a dozen more disciples and Bhoodan workers.

For about half an hour we marched in silence. Vinoba usually kept silence until around six. By the time we reached the first of the welcoming arches, about an hour and a half after I had passed it, there were rows of young girls lined up on the sides of the road, singing hymns; their leader presented Vinoba with a ball of raw cotton. Next came two rows of young boys, then two lines of women and two of men. From here on the landscape, which had been empty such a short while ago, began to fill up with people, and our procession grew. Vinoba was now chatting animatedly with any of the disciples who managed to elbow his way to the front. Occasionally he made a joke and then laughter rippled back through the whole procession though they did not know what the joke was about. A young man in a blue hood fought his way forward and slipped his hand into Vinoba's; for a while they marched in silence, affectionately holding hands, then the young man, satisfied, fell back into the crowd. A blind man, supported by a friend, stood in the middle of the road, his hands outstretched towards the approaching procession; when Vinoba, without stopping, had given him his blessing, he remained there, buffeted about by the procession, a boulder in the midst of an unruly stream. The Japanese monk was now beating his drum with all his might. As we walked on rapidly through the narrow path between the growing crowd on both sides of the road, I caught glimpses of the enraptured faces of women turned into mediaeval statues, and of old men, open-mouthed, with vacant expressions of wonder. At the third gate Vinoba abruptly halted, and a cup of milk-curd was served to him. He ate it standing, turning each spoonful several times round in his mouth with a rabbit-like chewing motion; then we marched on.

Our party, which originally had numbered about twenty, had now swollen to several hundred, and the fields on either side of the road were thronged with people. The people behind Vinoba were pushing and jockeying for position, and the crowd in the fields began to run parallel to the procession, outflanking it and threatening to submerge the thin line of orderlies who were trying to keep the road ahead clear. Women were pushed over into the dust and at moments the multitude seemed on the verge of hysteria; I was reminded that only a few days before at Nagpur there had been some five hundred casualties when a crowd of several thousand broke through a cordon to see its favourite film-stars.

At this stage Vinoba gave an astonishing display of what the irreverent Mr. Potter would call saintmanship: he abruptly left the metal road and began zig-zagging in a trot through the fields, pushing his way through the running crowd, putting them to shame and making them stop, all agape. Then, still at a run, leaving the panting disciples behind him, he returned to the road which now, as if by magic, was again clear. On two more occasions, when pushed from behind, he broke into a run, which had the immediate effect of making the procession slow down, with those in front bracing their backs against the onrush. It was superbly done, but his expression was unsmiling, almost grim.

The Lesson

'One spoonful of buttermilk is enough to turn a big pot of milk into curds,' Vinoba said in 1954 when he had received land gifts from three hundred thousand different donors. 'These three hundred thousand people will act exactly like a spoonful of buttermilk to convert the rest of the population.'

This prediction has not come true. Vinoba had set out to collect fifty million acres of cultivable land in five years; he had collected less than four million in nine years,[1] and only a fraction of the donated land has so far been distributed. In recent years his methods have become more adaptable and practical. He originally refused cash donations; he now accepts them gratefully, together with donations of seed-corn, cattle, equipment, wells. 'Bhoodan' has been

[1] It should be remembered that only half of the donated land was fit for cultivation.

complemented by 'Gramdan', a system under which the land donated by individuals or by a whole village is put to use in co-operative or collective farming. Yet in spite of this evolution towards new forms, the Bhoodan movement, measured in purely quantitative terms, can at best be called a partial success, at worst a noble failure.

But statistics represent only one aspect of reality – and, as far as India is concerned, the least important one. 'The Bhoodan movement,' Nehru said in 1954 in his inaugural speech at a Bhoodan workers' training camp, 'has unquestionably become a powerful factor in India. What is really important is not the actual acreage of land obtained, but the new spirit infused into the minds of the people. The movement has changed the atmosphere in India in regard to the agricultural question. Thereby it has not only helped directly to solve the problem to some extent, but indirectly it has also induced the Government to attempt some satisfactory solution.' That the Indian Government had been in need of an 'inducement' to tackle the most burning problem of the country was one of the disarmingly naïve admissions which Mr. Nehru from time to time feels compelled to make; but it was the strict truth and a measure of the impact of Vinoba Bhave on India's destiny.

In the critical year 1951, the appearance of the irascible saint had started the turning of the tide against the Communists in Hyderabad province, the heart of India. In the years that followed he had directly and indirectly influenced State and Government legislation, forced the politicians' attention on the country's most urgent problem, and created a phalanx of supporters, cutting across party and class divisions, from left-wing Socialists to dethroned Maharajahs, and including some of the most hard-headed and influential industrialists in the country.

Improbable as these achievements were, the real significance of the phenomenon Vinoba lies still on a different level. Bhoodan at its inception was, and to a large extent remained, a one-man show, the fantastic enterprise of a saintly ascetic who had always shunned the public eye (except when forced to court imprisonment) – until at the age of fifty-six, an inner compulsion set him on the road towards the greatest peaceful revolution since Gandhi. It galvanized the whole of India, filled millions of half-starved peasants and disillusioned intellectuals with a new hope, and made even the sceptics recognize that there may be other effective methods of action besides the blueprints of the rationalist planner and the voice of the soap-box orator. In other words, Vinoba Bhave has proved that even in the twentieth century a saint may influence history – at least up to a point, at least in India.

II. KRISHNA MENON ATMANANDA

Vinoba Bhave could be described as a Karma-Yogi – a person who seeks fulfilment by action, or, in Christian terminology, through Works. Krishna Menon (no relation to the Foreign Minister) belonged to a different category: his way was that of Dhyāna Yoga or Jnāna Yoga – the former meaning Union through meditation, the second through knowledge.

I had first heard of him in Europe where, among certain initiates, he was considered the last of the great, saintly Swamis after the recent death of Aurobindo and the Rama Maharashi. In Bombay, opinions had been more divided. The wife of a Hindu politician had, a few years before, spent a fortnight listening to Krishna Menon in Trivandrum and been so deeply impressed that she had returned every year since for a spiritual refresher course. Another lady, a Parsee, whom I met at the same reception, was even more devoted to him, whereas a third Hindu lady, a disciple of the late Maharashi, sounded more sceptical, without expressly saying so. This discussion took place at a soft-drink cocktail party in the house of a leading Parsee politician, and I could not help being reminded of New York society women discussing their psycho-analysts. There was the same partisan devotion, the same fervour, though unaided by alcohol and untinged by frivolity.

The Martial Saint

Trivandrum is the capital of Kerala, the only Indian State which, in 1959, was under a Communist Government. It was the first country under Communist rule that I had visited since I had left the Communist Party in 1938, for there was no Iron Curtain dividing Kerala from other Indian States, one needed no visa to get in, and no traveller was reported to have vanished there. It was a kind of tropical Marxist Ruritania, where Cabinet Ministers were known to consult their horoscopes to deduce the Party-line from the stars, and the Catholic missions, deriving from St. Francis Xavier, were still the most important cultural influence.

Nevertheless, it felt rather strange to land again, after nearly twenty-five years, in a Communist country, as the only passenger bound for Trivandrum in the Indian Airlines' little Dakota plane. Though it was January (Friday, the 13th of January, to be precise), the air was boiling, and the bungalow-like airport building looked deserted. As I showed my papers to the airport officials I expected some questions, but there were none. Had I been asked whether my visit had a political purpose, I would have truthfully answered, 'No, I came to see a holy man'; but I was quite prepared not to be believed. However, the two dark, gentle and sleepy officials were not interested, and while the Dakota took off for its next stop at Cochin, I got into the Airline bus and was driven, still the sole passenger, into Trivandrum.

The Communist State capital turned out to be the charming tropical suburb to a non-existent town, its low bungalows hidden among lush coconut-groves. It is true that there were a few huge concrete blocks in the usual Esperanto architecture – administration buildings, hospitals and clinics – but they stuck out like sore thumbs in plastercasts. The bazaars displayed mostly Woolworth idols and bicycle spare-parts; even spices were scarce. There was also a new sports stadium, with the giant cardboard figure of an athlete in the socialist-realism style. The odd thing about him was that he had a white skin, whereas the population of Kerala is dark-skinned.

I concluded that the figure must be a fraternal gift, mass-produced in a Moscow factory. The Kerala Government could of course have had it painted over, but that would have been too embarrassing, for the Indians are more obsessed with varna – colour – than German Nazis or American Negroes. The marriage advertisements praise the fair skin of the bride, the Brahmins take pride in their Aryan pallor, and even the old Hebrew community in Cochin has a colour-bar against dark Jews.[1] All this originated in the struggle between the fair-skinned Aryan invaders and the dark-skinned native Dravidians, and was perpetuated in the scriptural taboo on varnasankara, 'the mixing of colours' – one of the pillars of the caste system. The pillars show cracks, but they still stand firm; and that white-faced cardboard statue, put up by a dark-faced Communist Government, proclaims the triumph of irrationality over dialectics.

There was a garden in front of Krishna Menon's house, with a low stable occupied by several dwarf cows and calves. One shiny black cow was being bathed, buckets of water from the well were thrown over her, and she seemed to be blissfully enjoying it. Inside the house, the atmosphere was hushed and a trifle formal. The Swami's secretary, Bala Krishna Pillai, received me in a polite, worldly manner. He had been with Krishna Menon for thirty years; his head was almost perfectly spherical, covered with short-cropped white hair. He told me to come back at 4.30 p.m., when the Swami would receive me.[2]

I arrived a few minutes before the appointed time, and was ushered into a large room on the first floor, comprising the usual scant furniture. In the middle of the room stood an armchair of that curious Indian kind with arm-rests twice the normal length, giving the impression of a throne. Facing it was a row of five or six ordinary chairs, all empty. There

[1] They actually have three castes; the top caste claiming that their ancestors came to India in King Solomon's day, and kept the race pure by refusing to intermarry with later immigrants and coloured proselytes – the last being forbidden entry into the top caste's synagogue.
[2] Strictly speaking, the title 'Swami' applies only to monks, and Krishna Menon was not one; but in the South the title is applied more loosely.

was no opportunity for squatting, which made for a stiff, European atmosphere. A door opened, and Krishna Menon walked briskly in, a sinewy man in a dhoti, the naked torso of a very light brown, with a flush of pink. He went up to his large armchair with the gait of a soldier – before becoming a holy man, he had in fact served for twenty-five years in the Police Force.

The validity of first impressions is a controversial subject. But a holy man's holiness must somehow make itself felt – even to a sceptic – or else it is not present. Krishna Menon belonged to the long-headed, Brahmin type; he had a bony face with stern eyes and a soft, rather heavy mouth, the whole expressing a certain arrogance. His forehead was high and the receding white hair cropped. I was facing him across the room from my chair in the empty row. During the several hours that I spent with him, I never saw him smile.

Bala Krishna, the elderly secretary-disciple, hovered about in an anxiously helpful attitude. Krishna Menon opened the conversation by asking how long I intended to stay. I mentioned a week to ten days. He then turned to Bala Krishna, asked for the dates of his scheduled talks, and sounded somewhat annoyed that I could not hear them all. His next question was whether I had studied philosophy, for this would make it easier for me to understand him. I answered in a tone of appropriate modesty, which seemed to satisfy him, for he now launched directly into an exposition of his system. He talked for nearly half an hour, very fast, and with tremendous energy, owing to which and to his strong accent, I understood only half of what he said. But he gave me the two books he had written, and this enabled me later to fill in the gaps.

When he had finished, he invited me to ask questions. I asked whether he believed in the doctrine of reincarnation. His answer indicated that he did not. I then asked whether he believed in man's freedom of choice. He dismissed the question as a result of the Western habit of dualistic thinking: freedom and predestination did not constitute opposites. I asked about his daily routine. He said that he got up early and finished his ablutions and rites by 7 a.m., at which time the devotees 'are admitted into my presence'. My final question was how occidentals living in a mechanized world could find their way back to the right path. He answered that the only way was to find a sage to act as one's guru.

In the small dining-room of the Mascot, the only Western-style hotel in Trivandrum, my table stood at an arm's length from that of a visiting Soviet Trade Delegation – about a dozen burly, youngish men with bush-shirts and crew-cuts. I had once spoken Russian fairly fluently, but have almost completely forgotten it; nevertheless I had to make a strenuous effort to put on an aloof expression and not to appear to be eavesdropping. Again it occurred to me that if I had to explain to Comrade Gletkin of the OGPU that the purpose and timing of my visit to Kerala, and the position of my table, were purely coincidental, I would not have a chance of being believed; and, for entirely different reasons, I did not believe it either. I have always suspected that certain meaningful coincidences follow a causal law of their own whose equations are written in symbols other than those of physics. This one meant, apparently, that one cannot discard one's past any more than one's shadow.

This was driven home to me even more forcibly after dinner, when several young Malayalam writers – the language of Kerala – called with the request that I should address an anti-Communist meeting. They had been influenced by two of my earlier books on Communism, which had been among the first on that subject to be translated, among other Indian languages, into Malayalam. I tried to explain that I had given up writing or publicly talking about politics several years ago, and that I had really come to see Krishna Menon. They would not believe me; at any rate, would I at least speak to a small informal gathering? I had had my experiences of these 'informal gatherings' – which consisted of anything from fifty to three hundred people, solemnly seated in rows, two or three introductory speeches, and the garlanding of the guest in the expectation that he would talk for at least one solid hour – any shorter speech being considered a disappointment if not a discourtesy. When I refused, the young men did not hide their feelings. One of them, who described himself as 'an ultra-modern poet', with near-black skin stretched over an attractively ugly face resembling Hanuman the Monkey God, was refreshingly rude about it. 'We are busy fighting the Indian apathy due to mysticism and superstition,' he said, 'and here you come and go the opposite way.' However, we talked under the full moon till late into the night. They were thoroughly fed up with the corrupt Congress politicians who, by default, as it were, had brought the Communists to power; with a corrupt religion and a corrupt neutrality towards oppressors and oppressed. They were equally afraid of totalitarian state planning and of the 'shark teeth of capitalism'; they had no programme and no hope, except 'we need a new Gandhi'. But they were sceptical about Vinoba Bhave too, and it was obvious that they had an even poorer opinion of Krishna Menon. For the great Swamis of the past, however, they confessed a yearning admiration. They were convinced that religion is opium for the people, but did not seem entirely sure that opium was such a bad thing. This struck me as one of the basic differences between the disgruntled young men of India and of the West.

Another table in the Mascot's dining-room was occupied by an Egyptian gentleman in a pyjama-like attire, two middle-aged, prim-looking English ladies, and an English writer, all of them devotees of Krishna Menon. The next morning they invited me to their table for breakfast, and I learnt that the Egyptian was a former high-ranking Civil Servant who had become *persona non grata* under Nasser. The two ladies, who were eating cornflakes and porridge, and were making quite a fuss about the quality of the marmalade, came from London, where one of them was running a spiritualist group which the second was attending. Later in the day, I also met two young Latin Americans; they were

brothers and had travelled from Brazil to become disciples
of Krishna Menon, whose fame had spread to Rio de Janeiro.
The younger brother, a good-looking boy of about twenty
with a curiously innocent smile, spent most of his time in
Krishna Menon's garden, doing menial work, or sitting in
meditation, oblivious of the blazing sun.

On my second day in Trivandrum – which unexpectedly
turned out to be the last – I got up at six, and shared a taxi
with Peter, the English writer, to Krishna Menon's house,
where we arrived at 6.50 a.m. We had wanted to get there
earlier, but our taxi ran out of petrol. The driver-owners
are so poor that they only tank one or two gallons at a time,
paid out of the previous fare. Upstairs in the house, in a
room even larger and emptier than the one we talked in the
day before, Krishna Menon was sitting in his throne-like
armchair. Along the walls stood about thirty devotees. The
wall to the Swami's right was lined with Hindu women and
children; at the wall facing him were grouped the foreigners:
the two English women, the Egyptian, the two Brazilians,
Peter and I; along the wall to his left stood the Hindu males.

Proceedings started with Krishna Menon three times ener-
getically gargling, and spitting into a cup held by a little
girl. On the way up, Peter had told me regretfully that we
would miss the first part, when the devotees were allowed to
listen to the bathroom noises of the Swami's morning toilet.
The mouth-washing was the last part of it, performed in
public for the disciples' benefit. Next, the Swami's grand-
daughter, a little girl of about six, advanced, touched her
nose to his, then finger-kissed his feet. After that, a Hindu
woman sang hymns for about half an hour, each strophe ending with a chorus in praise of the guru. When she had
finished, Krishna Menon made a sign for the radio to be
switched on, and we listened to more hymns. While listening,
Krishna Menon fell asleep or into samadhi. He breathed
strongly and his hands, which were gripping the arm-rests,
looked unrelaxed; occasionally a slight tremor ran across
the lower region of his naked chest. Later the breathing
became shallower. After a few minutes he woke up, looking

dazed. Then we foreigners were dismissed, retreating crab-wise through the door, while the Hindus stayed behind. My companions looked transfigured. During the gargling cere-mony, I had watched the expressions of the two middle-aged English women, and felt rather repelled by the type of emotion reflected there.

'At the Ultimate'

After this second visit to Krishna Menon, I knew that I would never be able to establish a personal rapport with him. However, if people came from Egypt and Brazil to benefit from his teaching, there must after all be something in it; so during the rest of the morning, I read carefully through the two slim volumes he had given me. This was easily done, since each had only about thirty pages in very large print, some pages containing only one or two short aphorisms.

I shall quote from them at some length because they reflect the dominant trend of thought in Hindu and Buddhist philosophy, expressed in contemporary language. But I must put in a word of warning first – for that trend is so funda-mentally alien to Western philosophy that a strong effort of imagination is needed not to reject it in utter bewilderment. The traditional Eastern way of looking at things is to deny that there *are* things independently from the act of looking. The objects of consciousness cannot be separated from the conscious subject; observer and observed are a single, indivisible, fluid reality, as they are at the dawn of conscious-ness in the child, and in cultures dominated by magic. The external world has no existence in its own right; it is a function of the senses; but that function exists only in so far as it is registered by consciousness, and consequently has no existence in its own right either. The result of this stepwise dismantling of reality is that consciousness alone remains, and as the only object of consciousness, consciousness itself – the fullness of the void, the Brahma or atma. Traces of this type of thinking can be found in occidental philosophy, from Parmenides' 'Thought is its own Object', through Plato to Schopenhauer and Bishop Berkeley; but these were diluted versions of an acid philosophy which, in its concentrated form, acts as a dissolvent on Western conceptual thought. The excerpts which follow will serve to illustrate this.

The first booklet was published in 1946.[1] Its title is *Atma-Darshan,* and the subtitle *At the Ultimate.* Atma-Darshan is explained in the Glossary as 'perception of the Real Self, self-realization or the means of self-realization'. The frontispiece showed a photograph of Krishna Menon (the pen-name Atmananda means 'bliss of the atma'). The preface explained the identity of the individual soul, the Real Self, with Brahma, the collective, universal consciousness.

> 'Of the two lines of thought, namely those of bringing the individual under the universal and the universal under the individual, it is the latter that has been adopted here. It is the experience of all that, when viewed carefully, everything that is not oneself can exist only as the object of oneself, who is the subject. The object is also seen to have an inseparable connexion with oneself. There is no form without seeing; there is no sound without hearing. One views oneself as seeing and hearing, and thus takes the stand of the perceiver of these objects. In truth, seeing, hearing, etc., are themselves objects. When they are viewed as such, one's stand is in pure consciousness which is the perceiver. The idea of perceiver will also disappear there.
>
> Whenever the stand taken by the perceiver changes, the perceived also changes accordingly. Therefore by the analysis of the one, the truth regarding the other can also be arrived at . . .'

When reading works by Eastern philosophers, one often hesitates between literal and metaphorical interpretation, and wonders whether the author is engaged in stating a theory, or in providing images for meditation which should not be submitted to logical scrutiny. But throughout this book, and the second one, the Swami leaves the reader in no doubt that he is meant to be taken literally. Thus we read:

[1] Sri Vidya Samiti, Tiruvannamalay, 1946.

'18. *Thoughts and Objects.*

I. The attribution of reality to things which rise in thoughts is the cause of all bondage.

II. Form can exist only as the object of seeing and never independently of it. This rule applies alike to all sense-objects.

III. Objects have themselves no connexion with each other – their connexion is always with thought alone.

IV. An object cannot exist for a moment unless cognized by thought. When thought changes, the object changes also.

V. Thus they are inseparable and therefore one. The truth is that One thing is kept divided by mere words.

VI. Therefore even to hold that a thing rises in thought is mere delusion. There is thought only and the content of thought is Consciousness.

VII. If this truth is always kept alive thought will soon vanish and Consciousness reign. Then comes liberation from all bondage.'

'19 *Two aspects of Consciousness.*

I. Samvit (Consciousness) has two aspects: conditioned and unconditioned. It is the former that illumines objects of Consciousness. The latter is pure Consciousness . . .

IV. Observing carefully, one can see every thought rise and set in pure Consciousness alone.

V. What is not Consciousness is all thought-form. Pure Consciousness can never bear witness to it.

VI. It is no argument to say that memory – itself a thought-form – stands changeless watching all thoughts in succession.

VII. It is common experience that when there are other thoughts memory is not there with them. How then can memory call up past thoughts?

VIII. If memory cannot do it, it is no memory at all. Memory is therefore a meaningless word.

IX. It cannot but be admitted that it is always memory that calls up past thoughts.

X. If memory is non-existent, it follows that other thoughts are non-existent also, there being no witness to prove their existence.

XI. Therefore it can be clearly understood that what appeared to be conditioned is also pure unconditioned Consciousness.'

The following and last section of the book establishes in a similar manner that just as objects, thoughts and memory cannot logically exist, so dreams also cannot exist:

'If a man seen in dream was unreal, his mind must be equally unreal. His thoughts, seeing, hearing, etc., will likewise be unreal. In the same manner the subject in the dream-state, who is also a product of the dream, cannot but be unreal . . . The question then arises: who had the dream? To this the correct answer is that no one had it and there has never been a dream state. The world of the waking state also, if examined in the like manner, will be found to be non-existent.'

The second book, *Atma-Nirvriti (Freedom and Felicity in the Self)*, was published six years later, in 1952, 'with the collaboration and helpful co-operation of the Superintendent and staff of Government Presses in Trivandrum'.[1] The author's preface, printed in facsimile, explains: 'In many places this book goes beyond Atma-Darshan and expounds Truth from a higher level. A study of this book will be of considerable help to those who have gained knowledge of Truth from Atma-Darshan, to make that knowledge steady and thereby obtain lasting peace.'

If the first volume left any doubts in the student's mind, the second dispels them. Thus section 9 consists of seven points, of which the first three are:

'9. *Knowledge is not the name of a Function.*
I. All objects dissolve in knowledge. They are therefore none other than consciousness.

---

[1] Vedanta Publishers, Trivandrum.

II. A pot (when broken) dissolves into earth because it is of earth that it is made. It cannot dissolve into anything else.

III. So the statement "I know the thing" when properly examined, will be found to mean only that the thing has dissolved in knowledge.'

Sections 12 to 15 I shall quote in full. The footnote and note appear in the book.

'12. *The Non-existence of Objects.*

I. Before the seeing, there is no "seen" (drishyam)[1] and there is no "seen" after the seeing. There can be no doubt about it.

II. When this truth is clearly understood, it will be evident that there is no "seen" even at the time of seeing. And then ceases all bondage.'

'13. *The Non-existence of Thought.*

I. Thought is subtle: it cannot come into contact with a gross object nor can it have any connexion with it because they are in different planes.

II. This being so, one can never think of a gross object, and to say one can, is wrong.

III. The idea that subtle objects can take their rise in thought will also be found on careful examination to be untrue.

IV. There is no doubt that a subtle object is itself a thought-form. One thought can never exist in another.

V. A thought can therefore never have an object, gross or subtle. It cannot then be called a thought.

VI. This objectless thought is one's real domain, formless and changeless. It is this that is pointed to by the word "I".

VIII. There was no bondage before, there is none now and there will not be any hereafter, since thought has no existence.'

[1] *Drishyam* is an object seen, with the accent not on the thing which has no existence by itself, but upon the seeing as a result of which the thing comes into existence.

'14. *Past being Past, where is Bondage?*

I. A past action cannot come back again, nor can a past thought.

II. There is no thought in an action and no action in a thought; they have no connexion with each other.

III. Though a thought may occur after an action, that thought cannot be related to it since the action is not present when the thought occurs.

IV. Though one thought may follow another, there can be no connexion between them either.

V. A past thought is one that has ceased to exist; how then can such a thought come into contact with a new one?

VI. Two or more thoughts can never occur simultaneously. For this reason also, thoughts can never have any connexion between themselves.

VII. This clearly proves that action and thought exist independently of each other.

VIII. This being so, how can they be the cause of bondage? To think that bondage is caused by them is clearly an illusion.'

Note: —In this Section the word 'action' is used to denote only bodily activities.

'15. *The Subject and the Object are one in Myself.*

I. Experience and knowledge are inside. How can their objects be outside?

II. It follows that there is nothing outside: all is within.

III. What is within is myself, and therefore the experiencer and the experience are one and the same, that is Myself.'

The book ends with three essays by Krishna Menon which he particularly recommended me to read. The first is called 'I' and is meant to clinch the argument about the Real Self.

'. . . The pain I experience in the dream is confined to the dream state, and does not affect me in the waking state.

And the pain I experience in the waking state is likewise confined to that state, and does not affect me in the dream state. Therefore, it is clear that the experiences I am having in particular states do not go into my being . . .'

The second essay is called 'Witness'; it starts with the unqualified statement: 'No object can exist without getting recorded in my knowledge', and consists of repetitions of previous statements.

The third essay is called 'World', and its last paragraph concludes the book:

'. . . Objects are not different from, but one with perceptions. These perceptions not being outside, what is called the world cannot also exist outside . . .'

I have quoted about one-fourth of the repetitive contents of these two booklets because, as I said, they are representative of past and present Indian thought. Every line and every image can be traced back to their origins in Hindu and Buddhist scriptures,[1] whose intent is rendered in the sharp, uncompromising language of a mystic with twenty-five years experience in the Police Corps. It is the undiluted acid, extracted from the mythological symbols of Eastern Philosophy: the Wheel, the Veil of Maya, the secret of the golden flower. And that precisely is the trouble: Eastern philosophy cannot be de-mythologized and conceptionalized. Every attempt to distil its essence produces an unpalatable acid; and every attempt to translate it into the verbal concepts and categorical structure of Western language leads to logical monstrosities.

It is one thing to say that the world is a dream; it is another to 'prove' logically that because the dreaming mind in sleep is unaffected by bodily pain (which is blatantly untrue) therefore the body does not exist. It is one thing to say that the world is a veil of illusions around an ultimate reality of

---

[1] This is equally true of the only non-repetitive passages that I have left out – those dealing with samadhi and Nirvana – which will be discussed in another chapter.

which, in exceptional moments, mortal minds may gain some intuition; and it is another thing to 'prove' that two thoughts cannot be simultaneous, therefore memory does not exist, therefore thinking does not exist, and so forth. The genuine mystic is entitled to state experiences and affirm convictions which contradict logic, science and common sense. But he is not entitled to borrow words which have a precise meaning in science or philosophy, and roll them around in a game of Wonderland croquet with mobile hoops.

But here an interesting difference arises between European and Asian mysticism. The Christian mystic was steeped in the conviction that in Christ the *logos* had become flesh to play the role of mediator between human and divine reason; his thought was moulded and patterned by the Aristotelian, Neoplatonic and Pauline heritage, with its sharply defined categories and concepts. This imposed a verbal discipline, an acute, painful awareness of the impossibility of communicating his experiences, and led eventually to the division of the realms of the Light of Reason and the Light of Grace. Eastern thought, on the other hand, did not crystallize into concepts, its categories remained fluid, its grammar elusive, and its reasoning indifferent to contradiction. The Eastern mystic was under no restraint, the realms were never divided, symbolic and literal meaning never separated, mysticism and reasoning never parted ways.

There is no *hubris* in making this distinction between Eastern and Western thought. Admittedly, 'when Aristotle drew up his table of categories which to him represented the grammar of existence, he was really projecting the grammar of the Greek language on the cosmos'.[1] That grammar has kept us to this day ensnared in its paradoxa: free will and determinism, mind and body, ends and means: it made the grandeur and misery of two millennia of European thought and action. It may even be admitted that the categorical structure of Western thought acts as a screen between the mind and reality. And here lies the profound attraction of the

[1] Sidney Hook, 'Conscience and Consciousness in Japan', *Commentary*, New York, January 1959.

Eastern attitude – the Buddha's smile lends a transparency to that opaque screen.

But I also felt, while reading *Atma-Darshan* in the Swami's garden under the sympathetic stare of the black calves, that further than that I could not go. When it comes to words, doctrines, philosophical systems, the East has no cure to offer for our perplexities. Western thought cannot return to a pre-conceptualized state, a vertebrate cannot evolve into an invertebrate. The excerpts which I have quoted may strike the reader as particularly crude or extreme examples of Indian philosophy, but they are not (as other samples will show); they are typical of the basic difference in the structure of thought.

That apparently was the reason why I had felt unable to respond to Krishna Menon. The misplaced concreteness and dogmatic rigidity of his teaching had acted as a screen. On the other hand, some of his devotees whom I met in Bombay and Trivandrum undeniably derived a spiritual benefit from his courses. Peter, for instance, and the young Brazilian in the garden, had that quality of stillness and inner peace which I envied.

To some extent his influence could be explained by the nature of his message, which satisfied both mystic yearnings and the need to be rationally convinced – 'the world does not really exist, so why worry – and moreover I can prove it to you by strict logic'. This combination of mystic assertion and pseudo-rational proof is as old as the world, but it does not mean that the teacher is a charlatan, for his proof may rest on bona fide self-delusion – as in Krishna Menon's case it no doubt did.

But clearly the main influence was not the content of his teaching but his personality, which acted as a catalyst. And if he was capable of acting as a catalyst on people who were sincere in their spiritual aspirations, then there must be a core of genuineness in him beside the undeniable element of showmanship. This taught me the main lesson of this frustrated encounter, a lesson childishly obvious once one has learnt it, which saved me a lot of doubt and uncertainty. I never again tried to decide whether a holy man, a Yogi or a prophet was a saint or a charlatan, but rather to find out the relative percentage of the genuine and the other elements. It saved me from disappointment and cynicism, for nobody is a saint for twenty-four hours a day; not even in India; not even Gandhi, who always travelled in a third-class carriage but did not object to having air-conditioning installed, and the carriage to himself.

Back at the Mascot Hotel I found that I had been evicted from my room. The manager had in fact said that I could have it for one night only because my telegraphic reservation had never arrived, and the room had been booked in advance by another customer; but he had not been very emphatic about it and I had trusted that things would somehow work out. After some argument, an iron bedstead was put into the public lounge on the first floor and I tried to settle down to work there. The hotel was built in the bungalow style, with a balcony running around it which gave access to the bedrooms and lavatories. The lounge I occupied was at the end of the building and opened on three sides to that balcony; it had no doors, screens or curtains. The heat was stifling; I lay down on the bed under the churning ventilators and tried for a nap, but there were always about a dozen people staring in from three sides through the windows and open doorways. I felt like a rare animal in the zoo, except that the latter can usually be viewed from one side only; and I realized how deep-rooted the European need for privacy is, and how alien to the Asiatic. I also began to wonder whether my hotel reservation had really gone astray or whether the manager of the hotel, which was run by the Government of this Communist Ruritania, had contrived to turn me into a public exhibit as a dialectical joke. If so, the laugh was certainly on me.

I got up and tried to work under the watchful gaze of my spectators. A toothless Brahmin in a loin-cloth, who had been leaning on the arm of a big-eyed youth with thick lips and a simple-minded face, walked in and, after a dignified *namaste,*

hung a garland round my neck and asked me to autograph a
book which he had brought along. When this was done, he
beckoned to the youth who stumbled into the room with
signs of great agitation and squatted down on the floor at a
few feet from my chair, while the old man made to go. I
asked the youth what he wanted, but only got an incoherent
stammer out of him. The old man then explained with a
sweet smile that his son wanted nothing in particular, merely
to spend an hour or two in my room and thus acquire merit
and spiritual benefit from being in the presence of the
learned visitor.

More guests filed in from the balcony. A lawyer, who gave
me his card; an old man who just wanted to shake hands; a
reporter from a local paper. I explained to the latter that I
would not talk about politics, and the dialogue went thus:
'What do you think of Communism?' 'No politics.' 'What
do you think of Marxism then – that is a philosophical
question?' 'No politics.' 'Will there be a third World War –
that is a prophetic question?' 'No politics.' 'Is Nehru right
in recommending Realism to writers?' 'No politicians should
tell writers how or what to write.' 'But if he is a writer himself?' 'Then even less.' 'If you won't talk about politics then I
have no more questions,' said the reporter, and we parted in
mutual detestation.

All this time the young man squatting on the floor never
took his large Bambi-eyes off me. They drank in my sweat-
dripping countenance, they drained me, they sat on me like
electro-magnetic leeches. Whether I smiled or scowled, wrote
or gargled, made no difference to him; it was all spiritual
enrichment; he was feeding and feasting like a tick in a dog's
fur. I had read about Yogis living in Himalayan caves with
their gurus who, for fifteen years, never spoke a word to
them – but only now, under the rapt gaze of that boy did I
suddenly grasp the symbiotic nature of the relationship
between disciple and master, and I found it rather awe-
inspiring.

I left Trivandrum on the same day. Krishna Menon's books
and personality held out no further promise, and my

glass-cage made work impossible; so I decided to cut my losses and caught the afternoon plane to Madras.

This sudden departure led to a grotesque episode. A local newspaper reported that I had been 'hounded out' of Trivandrum by being refused a hotel room, which was not strictly true, and other papers took the story up. The Kerala Government issued a statement declaring that it was all my fault because I had not officially notified the Government of my arrival, and denied as 'wholly unfounded and mischievous' Press reports that I was 'not accorded a cordial treatment by the State Government'; this was followed a few days later by a second statement partly contradicting the first. In reply I expressed my earnest belief that the misadventure was due not to political reasons, but to an unfavourable constellation of the stars. This elicited a third statement from the Kerala Government, to the general merriment of readers of the Indian Press, and there the matter ended.

But after I had left India, friends wrote to me that they had inquired into the matter and discovered that the hotel manager had been right: the travel agency had simply forgotten to make the reservation. I mention this episode because it was yet another odd coincidence, and also because it shows how, in the overcharged atmosphere of India, trivial events can acquire a high-voltage load which makes them appear as symbolic pointers.

Shri Krishna Menon Atmananda died the following year; a short time later the Communist Government was ousted from office.

III SANKARACHARYA OF KANCHI

I was anxious to meet a religious leader occupying a position of authority, from whom I could learn the orthodox view. But Hinduism is split into countless sects, and it has of course no Church hierarchy in the Western sense. The nearest to an authoritative position, I learnt, was attributed to the five Sankaracharyas, leaders of an important Traditionalist sect, all of them descendants in direct spiritual lineage, as it were, from Sankara Acharya, the great religious reformer in the eighth century. Sankara combated idolatry, taught a purified version of pantheism, and tried to create a unified system of orthodox Hindu belief. Each of the subsequent Acharyas appointed his own successor, and in the present generation His Holiness the Sankaracharya of Kanchi Kamakoti Peetam wielded the highest spiritual authority. He had succeeded in unifying two large, previously divided sects, and was considered to be the originator of the current of religious revival noticeable mainly in the South. He was described to me as a very holy man, far advanced on the path towards final enlightenment. He was staying near Madras when I visited him.

The audience had been arranged by Professor Raghavan, who holds the Chair of Sanskrit at the University of Madras. His book, *The Indian Heritage* (with a Preface by the President of the Republic), was published in 1956 by UNESCO, and I am much indebted to it as an authoritative source-book for Sanskrit literature, which will be often quoted in subsequent chapters.

The first time I met Dr. Raghavan at his office at the University, he wore European clothes and behaved with the somewhat harassed courtesy of a busy don. The second time, when I picked him up in the evening for our appointment with the Sankaracharya, he emerged from his house and got into the car, dressed only in a loin-cloth. There are, of course, a number of pilgrims and beggars similarly attired in the streets of Madras; nevertheless, a middle-aged professor reclining on the leather upholstery of a limousine, naked down to the navel, is an unusual sight. I asked him whether he, and a mutual friend, had been influenced by the Sankaracharya. He said: 'To the measure of our success we are his pupils, to the measure of our failings we desert him.'

We drove to a suburb, stopped at a dark street-corner, got out of the car and of our shoes, and were greeted by another middle-aged gentleman in a loin-cloth, whom the Professor introduced as a Madras publisher. The publisher explained that he was spending every evening from six to eleven in attendance on His Holiness.

We entered a small and dilapidated house next to a temple. Facing us there was a dark, narrow corridor, blocked by an ancient palanquin painted white, with long, hard-wood poles sticking out front and back. A small room, rather like a police cell, opened from the corridor, and there we squatted down on a mat in the company of several others. After a few minutes of whispered conversation, a young man approached the palanquin, bent over it and murmured some words. A brown rug inside the palanquin, covering what looked like a shapeless bundle, began slowly to heave and stir, and finally His Holiness scrambled out of it, wrapping the blanket round his head and bare torso in the process of emerging. Tall and lean, but not emaciated, he looked dazed as he squeezed past the palanquin in the corridor and entered the little cell. He sat down cross-legged, facing me on the mat, while the others moved out into the corridor, leaning in through the open door to hear better. One of the devotees was a compulsive nose-picker, such as one finds in every Indian crowd. A Professor of Philosophy, from the Vivekananda College in Madras, acted as interpreter.

His Holiness remained silent for about half a minute, and I had time to study his remarkable face. Its features had been reduced to bare essentials by hard spiritual discipline. It was dominated by the high, smooth, domed forehead under the short-cropped, white hair. The brown eyes were set so deep that they seemed to be peering out from inside the skull, with soft dark shadows underneath. His firm, curved lips, framed by a trimmed white beard, were surprisingly mobile and expressive as they carefully formed each word. He was emerging from sleep or trance, his eyes only gradually focusing on those present. I was told that he managed an average of three hours' sleep a day, in short fits between duties and observances, always huddled in the palanquin; and that the devotees were often unable to tell whether he was asleep or in samadhi. He asked me gently why I had come to India:

'Is it merely to observe the country and the people, or is it to guide them in some healthy manner?'

This was an allusion to certain Press comments, concerned with earlier books. I answered that I had come to see and learn, and with no other purpose.

H. H.: 'One's passive interest, too, exerts an influence. Even without any specific activity, the angle from which you approach a problem or country produces a shakti – an active force.'

I said that I was sorry this should be so, but nobody could avoid throwing a shadow.

The Sankaracharya answered: 'But one's sincere sympathy throws its own radiance'; and as he said that, a smile transformed his face into that of a child. I had never seen a comparable smile or expression; it had an extraordinary charm and sweetness. Later, on my way back, I wondered why in Western paintings of saints entranced, blessed or martyred, I had never encountered anything like that enchanted smile. Since all mystics agree that their experience cannot be put into words, perhaps their expression also eludes representation by chisel and brush. However much I admired a Last Supper or a scene from Calvary, I have never felt that Jesus of Nazareth really looked like that. On the other hand, certain sculptures of the Gupta period and of the early Indian Baroque do convey an idea of that peculiar smile.

My first question was whether His Holiness thought that it was necessary to adapt the doctrines and observances of Hinduism to the changing social structure of India.

The Sankaracharya's answer, according to the stenographic transcript (which I have slightly compressed) was as follows:

'The present is not the only time when there has been a social revolution. Changes have been taking place even in the remote past, when revolutions were not so violent as they are now. But there are certain fundamentals which have been kept intact. We compare the impact of a social change to a storm. It is necessary to stand firm by the fundamental values and to keep affirming them. We may note the deterioration in moral values and standards. When Alexander came to

India, Greek observers wrote that there were no thefts in this
country. One cannot say that this standard has been kept up
in subsequent times. But we cannot say either that because
the situation with regard to morality has changed, teachers
should adapt themselves to present-day standards. In the same
way, adaptations have no place in the standards of spiritual
discipline.'

Question: 'Is there not a difference between spiritual
values and religious observances? Assuming a person is working in a factory or office. He has to be at his working place at
9 a.m. To perform his religious observances he must start at
five in the morning.[1] Would it not be possible to shorten the
prescribed ritual?'

H. H.: 'If a man cannot perform his prayers, rites and
obediences in the prescribed way, he must feel regret and
penitence. He can do penance and still perform his duties in
the proper way on holidays or at other times of the day when
he is less busy. Once concessions are made in the way of
shortening observances, there is no limit, and this will lead to
their gradual dwindling and extinction.'

Question: 'If the full discharge of the rites is, in modern
society, beyond the average person's capacity, may it not be
harmful to make him feel constantly guilty and aware of his
failings?'

H. H.: 'If a person feels sincere repentance, that sincerity
has its own value.'

In view of his unyielding attitude, I changed the subject.

Question: 'In the West, in the days of the Pythagorean
Brotherhood, and again during the early Renaissance, the
great savants were also great mystics and considered the
pursuit of Science as a form of worship. This was also true of
Einstein, who was a deeply religious man, or of Max Planck,
the founder of the quantum theory; and Kepler, the father of
modern astronomy, regarded Science as an approach to the
ultimate mystery. How does this approach relate to Indian
thought?'

[1] The orthodox Hindu purification rites, prayers and observances require
several hours a day.

H. H.: 'The more Science develops the more does it confirm the fundamental truths of religious philosophy. Indian Science, far from being opposed to religion, had a spiritual origin and a religious orientation. It is significant that every science in India is called a Sastra – a system of thought with a spiritual purpose. In our temples, for instance, all sciences and arts are pressed into the service of religion. Architecture, music, dance, mathematics, astronomy, all have a spiritual and religious significance.'

Again I felt that the saint and my humble self were talking different languages. The Sankaracharya's reference to the sciences being pressed into service in the temples implied approval of the debasement of astronomy into astrology, of mathematics into mystic number-lore, which had brought Indian science to a standstill some fifteen hundred years before. I again changed the subject, and brought up the din and noise in Indian temples. Was this the reason why Indians with a meditative disposition had to resort to the solitude of the mountains, or bury themselves in lonely caves?

H.H.: 'The case is just the reverse. Because solitude and a secluded spot have been prescribed, from oldest times, for contemplation, temples do not have to serve that purpose. Our temples are not organized as places for meditation, nor for congregational worship. The purpose of a temple is different. We enjoy the goods of life such as house, food, clothing, ornaments, music, dance, etc. We pay a tribute in the form of taxes to the King – now the Government – for making it possible for us to enjoy them by giving us their protection. The King-protector is provided with a palace and other paraphernalia of royalty. Even as we render homage to the king for the enjoyment of these things, we are bound to tender our gratitude to God who has primarily given us the good things of life. We offer a part of these good things as a token of our gratitude to Him in the temple. We first offer to Him all that He has given to us, in the shape of food, clothing, jewels, music, flowers, lights, incense, and so on, with the grateful consciousness that they are His gifts to us; and we receive them back from Him as His *prasada*. The temple is the place where these offerings are made on behalf of the collective community where it is situated. Even if people do not go to the temple, it is enough that these offerings are made to God on behalf of the community. The duty of the people at the place is to see that these offerings are made in a proper manner. There have been people who would not take their day's meal till the temple bell announced that the offering to God of food for the day had been done. Then only do they take their meal as God's prasada.'

Question: 'Where, then, can an individual meditate in silence and enjoy the feeling of being alone with his God?'

H. H.: 'In almost every Hindu home, and in riverside structures, there is a place of daily worship. We can obtain in it the seclusion and silence needed for meditation.'

It would have been impertinent to contradict the saint by telling him that I had visited some of those 'riverside structures' and private shrines in Hindu houses. About the former – the ghats and shrines of Benares, for instance – the less said the better; the latter are usually the size of a larder, or simply a corner in a bedroom. There would be a small figure of Krishna or Durga with some wilted daisies in front of it, and some oil-prints of the Monkey God on the wall. But in the average cramped and crowded Indian habitation, that shrine offers no privacy whatsoever. A saint, of course, will feel at peace in the midst of any din and noise. But I was concerned with the average person.

I asked His Holiness whether the doctrines of Hindu religion are meant to be interpreted literally or as symbols. He answered:

'Every such idea must be understood literally and not symbolically.' He then went on to explain that 'a comparative study of Hindu and Christian doctrines revealed that the fundamental philosophical truths of Hinduism appear in Christian religion as dogmas based on a misunderstanding of their original meaning'. Thus the 'Adam' of the Scriptures is to be traced to Atma, which in the original Sanskrit was Ad-ma, and 'Eve' corresponds to Jiva (the individual self). In the Upanishads there is a reference to two birds sitting on the same tree. One bird eats the fruit of the tree. The other simply looks on without eating. The bird which eats the fruit is Jiva – Eve. The bird which simply looks on is the supreme Atma – Adam. The tree on which the two birds are seated is the pippal, which is akin to the Biblical apple. It is also known as the Bodhi tree, or the Tree of Knowledge. It was while sitting under it that the Buddha got enlightenment. Adam and Eve ate of the Tree of Knowledge. But in the transition of the idea from India, the real significance of the Upanishadic motive was lost.'

I suspected that few students of comparative religion would agree with the Sankaracharya's theory. But time was running short, and I turned to a subject on which he was an unquestioned authority.

Question: 'I had several talks with Hindu psychiatrists in Bombay. They all agreed that spiritual exercises greatly help to effect medical cures. What bothered them was the absence of criteria to distinguish between insights gained in mystic trance on the one hand, and hallucinations on the other.'

His answer was short and precise: 'The state of hallucination is a temporary one. A person should learn to control his mind. What comes after such mental discipline is mystic experience. What appears in the uncontrolled state of mind are hallucinations. These are caused by the wishes and fears of the ego. The mystic's mind is a blank, his experience is shapeless and without object.'

Question: 'Can a mystic experience be artificially induced by means of drugs?'

H. H.: 'You ask this because you think of the experiments of Aldous Huxley.'

A. K.: 'No, I was thinking of bhang.'[1]

H. H.: 'Bhang is used among the people in some parts of India to induce certain states of mind. It is not a habit in the South. Such an artificially induced state does not last long. The real mystic condition is more permanent.'

---

[1] Bhang is a narcotic distilled from hemp, similar to hashish. It is used to induce trance-like states.

Question: 'How is an outside observer to distinguish between the genuine and the not-so-genuine?'

H. H.: 'Of course, sometimes people mistake a pseudo-Yogi for a real one. But the behaviour of the man who has disciplined his mind, who is a true Yogi, will be different. When you look at him you will see that his face is serene and at peace. That will discover and differentiate him.'

He spoke without a trace of self-consciousness; it evidently did not occur to him that the description applied to himself.

I felt that my time was up, though the Sankarcharya denied with great gentleness that he was tired; in India, it is the visitor who is supposed to bring the audience to an end, which sometimes leads to embarrassing situations. I waited for H. H. to get up, but he made no move. There was a silence; only the nose-picking disciple kept up his activities. So I embarked on an anecdote – about the Jesuit priest who was asked how he would reconcile God's all-embracing love with the idea of eternal Hell, and who answered: 'Yes, Hell does exist, but it is always empty.'

I suppose my motive in telling the story was to make him smile again. He did, then said, still smiling: 'We have no eternal Hell in Hinduism; even a little practice of *dharma* will go a long way in accumulating merit.' He quoted a line from the *Gita* in Sanskrit.

That was the end of the conversation. I found at last the courage to get up first, and the Sankaracharya, after a very gentle and unceremonious salute, quickly took the few steps to the palanquin and vanished into its interior. The room was suddenly dingy and empty, and I had a feeling of a personal loss.

Such were the views of an orthodox religious leader in contemporary India. The remarkable thing about them is that they bore no relation to contemporaneity. Equally striking was the contrast between his gentle, saintly personality, lovable and loving, peaceful and peace-giving, immersed in contemplation 'without shape or object' – and the rigidity of his views on Hindu doctrine and religious observances. If one tried to project him onto the European scene, one would have to go back several centuries to find a Christian mystic of equal depth and stature; yet in his views on religious practice he compared with the rigid ecclesiastics of the nineteenth century.

Indians call the Sankaracharya a Jnāna Yogi with a strong inclination toward *bhakti*-Union through devotional worship. The last of my 'four saints' is a woman who relied on shakti – the earthly manifestations of divine power, which usually have an erotic tinge.

IV. ANANDAMAYEE MA

The Saint and her Clown

Krishna Menon received his devotees in his house in Trivandrum, but did not run an ashram. Shri Shri Anandamayee Ma has ashrams in eighteen different places in India, including Delhi, Calcutta and Benares, some of which have schools attached to them. Long before I visited her, I saw her striking portrait in colour-print displayed in the homes of people from varied walks of life, including a Professor of Benares University and a foreign Ambassador. Her devotees call her Mother or Ma, and consider her of divine origin, an incarnation of Kali, Durga or Saraswati.

There are two ways of looking at Anandamayee Ma, the psychiatrist's and the mystic's, and the two need not be mutually exclusive. From both points of view, she is an extraordinary personality. Though she was nearly sixty-three when I visited her, she gave the impression of a gypsy beauty in her forties. Her earlier photographs show a dark, slim, ravishing girl with the grace of a wildcat and a face to tempt St. Anthony. The atmosphere she creates among her devotees is illustrated by the following passages from *Mother As Revealed To Me*, a biography written by her favourite disciple, Bhaiji.[1] He was a saintly person who died of

[1] Tr. G. Das Gupta, Benares, 1954.

consumption at the age of forty, after twelve years of devoted service to Ananda:

'On one occasion Mother came to our house. In the course of our talk I said casually – "It appears, Ma, that to you hot and cold are the same. If a piece of burning coal fell on your foot, would you not feel pain?" She replied, "Just test it." I did not press the point further.

After a few days, taking up the thread of our previous conversation, Mother placed a piece of burning coal on Her foot. There was a deep burning sore. For one month it did not heal up. I felt very upset about that silly suggestion of mine. One day I found Her sitting on the veranda with Her legs stretched out and Her gaze fixed on the sky. Some pus had gathered on the sore. I bowed down at Her feet and licked the pus up with my tongue and lips. From the following day the sore began to heal up . . .

On another occasion, I observed Mother striking the ground with a bamboo chip when a fly was accidentally killed by a stroke. With great care and concern Mother picked it up and kept it in Her closed fist. Many persons were present. Four to five hours passed in conversation. Mother then opened Her fist and said to me, "Can you do anything for the good of this fly which has passed on to the other world?" I said, "I have heard people say, there is heaven inside the body of man." So saying, I swallowed the fly.'

Bhaiji was a kind of saintly, tragic clown to Ananda.[1] They were about the same age. Ananda, by her real name Nirmala Devi, was born in 1896 in the village of Kheora, into an old Brahminic family. One of its members is reported to have mounted the funeral pyre of her husband 'chanting hymns merrily'. As a child, her parents believed her to be mentally retarded, because she had a habit of talking to trees, plants,

[1] Although 'Ananda' is masculine in gender, it is currently used in Bengal in referring to Anandamayee Ma.

and invisible beings. At the age of twelve she was married to Ramani Mohan Chukravati, known afterwards as Pitaji, who also came from a well-known family of Brahmins. He seemed to have been considerably older, and without any particular profession. Ananda stayed, however, only a few months at her husband's house. During the next fifteen years she was constantly on the move, living now with one relative, now with another, and spent altogether only five or six years with Pitaji.

'From the seventeenth to the twenty-fifth year of Her life, various supernatural phenomena began to manifest in Her. At times She would become mute and motionless while chanting the names of Gods and Goddesses. During Kirtans [the devotional singing of hymns] Her body got stiff and benumbed. After visiting a Temple Her behaviour did not appear to be normal . . . Her limbs spontaneously formed into various Yogic poses . . . Fearing that Her body might be possessed by some evil spirit, the help of some *sadhus* and exorcists was sought. It was of no avail; on the other hand, when these men tried to give Her treatment, they were forced to withdraw in fear and amazement. It was only by praying for Her mercy that they could recover their balance.'

Towards the end of this period, when, for the first time, she was continuously living with her husband, she was stricken by muteness which lasted for three years. After fifteen months she left him and went to live in Dacca (now East Pakistan), but the condition continued for another twenty-one months. It was in Dacca that she met Bhaiji.

Bhaiji, too, was a Brahmin. In his book, he devotes less than a single page to his own childhood:

'I lost my mother when I was but a small boy. I have heard my relations say that my eyes used to swim in tears whenever I heard infants babbling out "Ma, Ma" with their soft shrill voices; and that I would soothe my heart by lying on the floor and weeping silently . . . In 1908 I had my initiation in shakti mantra from our family Guru. On that account I had to worship the Mother Divine; and when I could pour out all my devotional fervour with "Ma, Ma", during my prayer time, I found great relief and happiness . . . There was an over-powering desire in me to find such a Living Mother who, by her loving glances, could transform my storm-tossed soul. I approached many saintly persons and was desperate enough even to consult astrologers for an answer to this query – "Shall I have the good fortune to meet such a mother?" All held out high hopes.'

He was working as a Government official in Dacca when he learnt about Ananda, and went to see her. She was then twenty-eight:

'One morning I went there in a prayerful spirit, and was fortunate enough to see Mother . . . It sent a thrill into my heart to see Her serene Yogic posture along with all the modesty and grace to be met with only in a newly married lady. It at once flashed upon my mind that the Person for whom my heart had yearned for so many years, and in whose search I had travelled to so many sacred places, stood revealed before me.

My whole being was flooded with joy and every fibre of my body danced with ecstasy. There was an impulse to throw myself prostrate at Her feet and to cry out in tears – "Mother, why have you kept me away from you all these long, long years?" . . . I had come with a load of thoughts struggling for expression, but all were hushed into silence under the spell of Her soothing grace. I sat there speechless and dumb. Mother, too, spoke not a word. After a little while, I bowed to Her and left the place. I could not touch Her feet though I had a strong desire to do so. It was not through fear or delicacy; some mysterious power pushed me away from Her presence.'

He did not go to see her again for seven months. He was torn by a great conflict: 'a strong desire to see Her and a sharp pain at Her aloofness – if She would not draw me close to Her like my own Mother, removing Her veil, how could I clasp Her feet to my bosom?' The fulfilment of his desire to touch, clasp or kiss Ananda's 'lotus-feet', which returns like a *leitmotif* in various passages of the book, was denied to him throughout his life – except on that one occasion when he was allowed to lick the pus off her wound.

When I visited Anandamayee in her Calcutta ashram, before having read Bhaiji's book, the first thing that struck me were her beautifully formed feet, which she conspicuously displayed while squatting on a dais in her white sari; and while we talked, she kept playing with them, rubbing the interstices between her gracefully mobile toes.

During these seven months of indecision, he would lurk around her garden wall to see her from a distance without being noticed. At last he made up his mind, and brought Ananda to the house where he lived with his wife and child: 'An intense joy thrilled my whole being to meet Her after such a long time. But it was not permanent. When she was about to leave my house, I bowed down to touch Her feet, but She withdrew them. I felt as if pierced by a smarting pain.'

At that time Ananda was in the habit of wearing a golden nose-ring. Bhaiji sent his wife to her 'with a large silver plate, some curd, flowers, sandal paste, and one diamond nose-ring, and with great delight and respect she offered them at Her feet.' One feels sorry for the wife, because, a few days later, Bhaiji decided to live henceforth as brother and sister with her. Ananda had said to him: ' "Remember you really are a Brahmin; and there is a very subtle close spiritual link between this body and yourself". From that day I tried to keep my body pure in all respects.'

But still he was not sure whether Ananda was human or whether, as the devotees said, she was a Goddess incarnated. One day he asked her:

' "Mother, pray, tell me, what are you in reality?" She laughed out loudly and said with all affection: "How could such childish queries arise in your heart? I am what I was and what I shall be; I am whatever you conceive, think or say. But it is a supreme fact that this body has not come into being to reap the fruits of past karma. Why don't you take it that this body is the material embodiment of all your thoughts and ideas. You all have wanted it and you have it now. So play with this doll for some time. Further questions will be fruitless." I said, "These words of yours, Mother, do not satisfy my yearning." Hearing this She spoke with slight vehemence, "Say, say, what more you desire" and immediately a dazzling flood of heavenly light shone forth from Her face. I was struck dumb with awe and wonder. All my doubts were laid at rest.

About fifteen days later, I went to Shah-bag one morning and found the door of Mother's bedroom closed. I sat down in front of it some 25 to 30 cubits away. The door opened all at once. I found to my bewilderment, the figure of a divinely beautiful goddess as genially bright as the sun at dawn, illumining the whole interior of the room. In the twinkling of an eye She withdrew all the radiance within Her body and Mother was there, standing and smiling in Her usual manner . . . I realized at once that Mother had revealed Herself in response to what I had said a few days back. I began to recite a hymn and prayed to Her.

After a little while Mother advanced towards me. She picked a flower and a few blades of durba grass and placed them on my head, as I fell at Her feet. I was beside myself with joy and rolled on the ground at Her feet. From that moment a deep conviction began to take root in my mind that She was not only my mother but *the Mother* of this universe . . .'

By stating as a 'supreme fact' that her body did not come into being as a result of past karma – that is to say, that she was not, as mortals are, attached to the wheel of re-birth – Ananda had implied that she was an avatar, a deity incarnate: 'You all have wanted it and you have it now,' But she never expressly said so, either to Bhaiji or to others. 'I am what I was and what I shall be; I am whatever you conceive, think or say.' Questioned by a famous sage – the late Swami Dayananda – she gave a similar answer: 'You want to know what I am. I am what you consider me to be – not more, not less.' This might be taken for diplomacy – but it is also the authentic language of Hindu mysticism. And, whatever the virtues and failings of Anandamayee, diplomacy was not one of them.

Nor did she claim supernatural powers, except of one kind which she ascribed to others too: the omnipotence of the will. 'Whatever you seek can be obtained, provided the thirst for the object of your desires pervades every fibre of being.' Her three years' muteness is closely related to this belief, for it seems to have been voluntarily provoked: 'If you merely want to abstain from speech, it is a different matter altogether. But if you desire to observe real silence, your heart and mind must fuse so closely into one thought that your whole nature inwardly and outwardly may freeze, as it were, into the condition of an inert stone.'

This power of mind over matter, which the mystic takes for granted as the mathematician takes an axiom of Euclid for granted, she believed to be within the reach of all. At the beginning of the association, when Bhaiji asked her whether he had a chance to attain to a higher spiritual level, she had answered: 'Your hunger for such a life is not yet strong enough.' But a few months later, she visited his house and, as he came downstairs to see her off, filled with despair about being deprived of her presence, 'the car did not move though the driver had started it. She was looking at me, Her face beaming with a laugh.' Again a few days later, he did not go to his office because of her, but his offence remained undetected because the chief's car broke down. 'When Mother heard the story, She said with a laugh – "Is that anything new to you? The other day you threw out of gear the car in which I was to leave".'

Most of the 'miracles' reported by Bhaiji are of an equally

naïve nature: he dreams of Ananda, and in the morning finds the wet prints of her lotus-feet on the floor. But Bhaiji's naïveté is equalled by his sincerity; and some of the episodes which he relates, about Ananda's remarkable faith-healing powers, carry a ring of truth. Thus, for instance, a girl suffering from paralysis was brought to Anandamayee. She first asked the girl to roll on the floor, but the girl 'could not move at all, she could not even turn round'. Ananda was cutting up betelnuts into small pieces for devotional purposes. She suddenly threw some nuts at the girl, sharply ordering her to catch them. The girl, to her own surprise, caught them. The family left. The next day, the girl was lying as usual in her bed when 'she heard the rumbling noise of a passing car; she suddenly jumped out of bed and ran to the window'. Evidently, if Ananda was able to paralyse her own vocal cords, she was equally capable of reversing what appears to have been a hysterical conversion symptom of a like nature in another person. Any skilled psychiatrist could probably have performed the cure; but Ananda's intuition was derived from more ancient sources.

According to Bhaiji's account, there existed a telepathic rapport between Ananda and himself; he claims that he was able to tell the colours of the sari she wore while he was away, or that she was sleeping in her bed with her head in a direction opposite to that which she was accustomed to. 'On other occasions, I saw to my surprise the full image of Mother appearing on the wall opposite like a film picture'. Another phenomenon is equally familiar from the literature of mysticism: the perception of a sudden dazzling radiance around the worshipped person. Whether we call it a vision, or the hallucination of an exalted consumptive, is irrelevant; the curious fact is the uniformity of reports of this kind.

Though none of it can be regarded as evidence, I must confess that I found Bhaiji's narrative in most parts convincing. Partly because the whole story reflects a very humble, saintly and simple-minded person; and partly because he does not claim to have witnessed any supernatural feats beyond the kind of thing that I have mentioned. There are only two exceptions to this: a single phrase which runs: 'We have seen many instances when by a mere glance Mother stopped rain, or by a gentle smile or loud laughter put an end to all disputes and display of ill-will amongst Her devotees.' But this, as the context shows, is perhaps not meant to be taken literally. The second is a photograph showing Ananda sitting in Yogic posture and Bhaiji standing behind her, with the caption 'Mystic Image of Bhaiji on a Photo taken of Mother alone'. It is obviously a practical joke of the photographer, who copied two plates together – either to tease or to please the simple-minded saint.

A Taste of Hindu Theology

If Bhaiji was of a naïve and loving disposition, others, more sophisticated, believed not only in Ananda's genuineness, but in her supernatural origin. One of the most astonishing documents about her is an article by Mahamahopadhyaya Gopinath Kaviraj, M.A., D.LITT., Late Principal, Government Sanskrit College, Benares (the leading theological University in the country), written for a memorial booklet on the occasion of Anandamayee's sixtieth birthday.[1] The following quotation from it may convey an idea of Hindu academic theology.

'There was a difference of opinion at that time [1928] concerning the precise status of Mother. Some held that She was a Goddess in human form – Kali according to some, Durga according to others, Sarasvati or Radha according to others still. Some thought that She was a human aspirant, who had attained perfection in this life after a series of births during which Her spiritual progress had been continued. Others again entertained the view that She was a Brahmavadini as of yore, or perhaps an Incarnation of the Divine come down to earth to relieve its sufferings. She was identified with Sukadeva by some and with Shri Krishna Himself by others. People of worldly

---

[1] *Jayanti Souvenir*, published by the Anandamayee Ashram, Benares; no date, presumably 1956.

nature used to think that some higher spiritual entity, human or celestial, was in possession of Her body and utilized it as an instrument to serve its own ends . . . During succeeding years I was privileged to come in closer touch with Her and to know Her more intimately.'

The learned theologian then proceeds to his own deductions concerning Ananda's origin. His starting point is the fact that she received no diksa (guidance, initiation) from any guru. But - 'in the History of mysticism it is recognized everywhere that in exceptional cases illumination is possible and this takes place even when an external source is lacking. We know of the Pratyekabuddha who neither received his wisdom from any previous Buddha nor communicated it to others'. In such cases illumination is directly due to Divine Grace descending on the soul of man. This Grace, or shakti, is of three different kinds: intense, mild and dull. Each of these three varieties is again sub-divided into three classes, so that there are altogether nine degrees in all.

Apart from the Pratyekabuddha type, there are two other categories which might fit, according to the author, Ananda's case because they also do not need gurus. Firstly, the so-called Swayam Siddha Sants, 'or persons who are saints from the very birth and not due to the accident of knowledge from an external source . . . These great Souls descend from transcendent regions, specially from the Divine World, beyond the Cosmic Mind and the Great Void. And when embodied, their centres of consciousness never come down below the middle of the two eyebrows'. Secondly, 'we know of cases of souls which are always perfect and which dwell permanently on the Divine Plane as eternal associates of the Divine Person to whom they are related . . . As a matter of fact they are never required to come down to earth except in company with the Supreme Lord during His descent or at other times as directed by Him. Such souls considered from the standpoint of spiritual status and attitude are varied in nature . . . However,' proceeds our theologian, 'it would be unfair to place Mother in this category'. The reason is that while such souls are *intimate* with the Divine Person, they are not *identical* with Him, whereas Ananda's 'integral self-awareness never tolerates even in the slightest degree the idea of separation, or distinction from, the integral Central Being. Her confession concerning Her consciousness of identity with the Cosmic and the Supercosmic existence and with all the powers and attributes associated with it, is a clear argument against the inclusion of Mother in this category'.

Nor can she be placed in the other categories of the Pratyekabuddha or the related Swayam Siddha Sants, because a Pratyekabuddha is 'in his blissful seclusion indifferent to the fact of universal misery, [whereas] Mother is too keenly sensitive to the sorrows of the world to remain contented with an isolated existence'.

Lastly, 'the view which accepts Mother's personality as a case of Avatara may be dismissed with a few words of comment. The question of Ansa or Kala may be left aside, but it seems to me that even the possibility of a Plenary Avatara is excluded in Her case. The fact is that every Avatara, unless he is of the plenary type, represents an aspect of the Divine Power and can never represent the Divine Essence or even the Divine Person *in toto*. In several cases the Avataras are self-forgetful Divine emanations whereas in others in which self-consciousness is retained, integral consciousness seems to be always lacking. In case of the Plenary Avatara also, if there be any, unbroken consciousness of his plenary nature does not appear to exist. A careful study of Mother's utterances and a critical attitude towards Her life and activities would perhaps reveal the fact that Her case is altogether different. She Herself has confessed to some that She never loses Her supreme self-consciousness. Samadhi or no samadhi, She is where She always has been. She knows no change, no modification, no alteration; She is always poised in the self-same awareness as a supreme and integral universality, transcending all limitations of time, space and personality and yet comprehending them all in a great harmony.'

Thus Ananda does not fit any of these categories because they are too limited and rank too low in the spiritual hierarchy. Where, then, does she fit? Though he is cautious in his formulations, the author leaves us in no doubt about the conclusions that he reached:

'. . . That Mother is untouched by Karma of any kind need not therefore be an enigma. There being no previous Karma the origin of Her body is to be explained by the play of the Supreme Power, either in itself or as reacting to the collective aspirations of humanity. As to why the Supreme Power should have expressed itself in a particular human body is a question to which an ordinary man is not in a position to reply.

. . . She is too near us to be seen in Her proper perspective and as for ourselves we too shall have to rise up to the height and attain to the broad outlook in which an attempt may be made to study Her properly. What is really needed is to feel that She is Mother and we are Her children and that as mere children we cannot be expected to know Her as She is but only as She shows Herself to us in response to our cravings. It really becomes us to behave as infants crying out in the night and invoking Mother with an inarticulate language for Her actual descent and benediction.'

The Clinical Side

The long quotations were meant to serve a double purpose. Firstly, as already said, I wanted to give the reader a taste of Hindu academic theology. In Europe, scholasticism went out of fashion in the sixteenth century; in India, the angels are still dancing on the point of the needle.

Secondly, the writings of the learned Principal, so different in every respect from the humble Bhaiji's, further illustrate the extraordinary hold which Ananda had on the most varied people. Particularly impressive appear to have been Her trance states, which sometimes lasted several days.

'On some days while walking about or sitting in the room after casually entering it or after laughing and speaking a few words, Her eyes became wide open with a vacant stare and all Her limbs relaxed in such a supernatural way that Her body seemed to melt down on the floor as it were.

We could observe then that like the soft golden disc of the setting sun all the brightness of Her normal manners and expressions faded away little by little from Her countenance into some mysterious depths. A short while later Her breathing slowed down, sometimes stopping altogether, Her speech ceased completely, Her eyes remained closed. Her body grew cold; sometimes Her hands and feet became as stiff as logs of wood; sometimes they hung down loosely like pieces of rope – falling flat in any direction one would place them . . . Thus passed some ten to twelve hours and then efforts were made to bring Her back to the physical plane with kirtan [hymns] and the like, but all in vain.

I myself failed to rouse Her from that state of self-absorption. There was no response whatsoever when rubbing Her hands or feet hard, and even pricking them with sharp points. Her consciousness came back when the proper time arrived. It did not depend on any external stimulus.

When Mother came back to physical consciousness, Her breath returned and became deeper and deeper; along with it revived all the movements of Her limbs. On certain days, a short while after such an awakening Her body relapsed once more into its former inert condition and tended, as it were, to freeze again into the state of samadhi. When the eyelids were opened with finger-tips, there was a vacant unresponsive stare in Her eyes, and the lids soon closed again automatically.'

At other times, however, the trance was preceded by violent seizures, with symptoms easily identifiable in clinical textbooks:

'As the kirtan progressed many changes became visible in Mother. She sat up very straight, then Her head gradually bent backwards till it touched Her back; hands and feet twisted and twined till the whole body fell flat on the floor.

In concord with Her breath, Her body was thrown into rhythmic surges like waves and with Her limbs stretched out it rolled on the ground in time to the music . . . Many tried to stop Her without any success. At last Her movements ceased and She remained motionless like a lump of clay. She appeared to be steeped in all-permeating, all-pervading Bliss.'

On another occasion:

'Her breath was almost suspended; She stretched out Her hands and feet and lay on the ground with Her face downward. Then She rolled on nimbly in a wavelike motion. After a while, like one overwhelmed by a great upward urge, She rose from the ground slowly, without any support and stood upon Her two big toes, barely touching the ground . . . Her hands were lifted up towards the sky; Her body had only very slight contact with the ground, Her head was bent backwards touching her back, the eyes were directed towards the mid-sky with a glowing stare. As a wooden doll moves about under the pull of a hidden string held by the operator behind the screen, She stepped along . . .

Her body appeared to be so full of ecstatic joy that even the roots of the hairs on Her body swelled, causing them to stand on end. Her complexion turned crimson. All the self-initiated expressions of a Divine state appeared to be crowded into the narrow frame of Her body and they manifested all the exquisite beauties of the Infinite in countless graceful and rhythmic ways.'

I said at the outset that Anandamayee could be judged both from the mystic and the psychiatric point of view, and that the two do not necessarily contradict each other. She had, however, still other symptoms which belong to the pathological domain alone. She had always lived on very small amounts of food; from the age of twenty-eight onward, for an undefined number of years, she was unable to feed herself.

'Whenever She tried to carry food to Her mouth, Her grasp slackened and a large part of the food slipped through Her fingers. At that time it was arranged that the person who used to feed Her should once during the day and once in the night give Her only as much food as could be grasped by the tips of two fingers.'

After four or five years of this, she was persuaded to try taking food with her own hand: 'But after putting a pinch of food into Her mouth, She gave some to others and rubbed the rest on the floor . . . After this nobody ever asked Her to eat with Her own hands'. There were, however, occasions when, at the sight of an Untouchable eating rice, or a dog devouring garbage, she would begin to cry plaintively, 'I want to eat, I want to eat.' On yet other occasions, she had fits of ravenous overeating. Though she always referred to her body as 'this doll' or 'this lump of clay', she evidently did not object to others making a cult of it: dressing her up as the Lord Krishna, mouth-feeding her, and licking the pus from her feet.

'People flock round Her from early morning till late at night. Some are painting Her forehead with vermilion drops, others dressing Her hair, yet others offering to give Her a bath, or to wash Her face and mouth, or to clean Her teeth with tooth paste. Some may request Her permission to change Her sari, others express a desire to put some sweets or a slice of fruit into Her mouth, some whisper their secret requests into Her ear . . . She sits up, hour after hour, day after day, in Her exquisitely peaceful manner in the midst of all this noise and bustle, rush and tussle; She remains steady and firm with a face brimming over with cheerfulness . . .'

She was prone to weeping, and to laughing fits which often lasted over an hour. She liked to tease her devotees and to display a kittenish behaviour, though sometimes her playfulness could more appropriately be called cruelty. When Bhaiji was ill, she did not visit him for several months, and on

certain occasions during his convalescence she expressly forbade that food be sent to him. But Indians are accustomed to
their cruel female deities.

At the height of the mystic romance between the saint and
her clown – though their roles often seemed to be reversed –
Bhaiji, 'for a full three years', would rise from bed at 2 a.m.,
finish his ablutions and prayers by 4.30 a.m., and set out for
Ananda's ashram to be the first person to see her. He always
entered the ashram when a nearby clock struck five. If he was
too early he would sit and wait at the gate; and he was frequently early 'having confused the two hands of my watch'.
When Ananda was ready, he went for a walk in the fields
with her, or rather a few steps behind her, both in complete
silence. Around midday he went to his office. He never sat
in her presence; 'when I was asked by anybody to sit down, I
felt quite embarrassed'.

One early morning, an old babu came to join them on
their walk. 'He said to Ananda: "I have come, not to see you,
Mother, but to meet your pet lamb and to observe with my
own eyes how he comes to you so early every morning regardless of cold, heat, or rain and how he follows your every foot-
step in mute silence. The very sight gives me great delight."
I told him, "Kindly bless me so that I may pass the rest of my
life in this manner." The old man clasped me to his bosom
and said, "You are already a blessed fellow".'

Ananda in person

When I visited India, Bhaiji had been dead for more than
twenty years; but at Ananda's ashram in Benares I met some
other 'blessed fellows' of that rare kind whose peaceful personalities are true oases in the desert – and in Benares, more
than anywhere else, the traveller is in dire need of an oasis.

Benares is a holy inferno. The lepers have been banished,
but the streets around the Golden Temple and the steps to
the bathing ghats are still bedlam, and the impact of the filth,
stench and din is terrifying. The only escape is to change
from the bicycle-rickshaw – whose half-starved operator must
pedal single-legged up to four passengers up and down the

steep, sewer-like streets – to a river boat. There, at a safe distance, transformed into a pukka sahib, one can enjoy the bizarre and chaotic backdrop of temples and shrines, Victorian façades and neo-Mogul palaces, rising tier by tier, without a single gap, in a promiscuous medley; while down in the muddy water there is an equally promiscuous hotch-potch of pilgrims, animals, babes riding on their mother's hip and old hags with bared udders, all jostling and bobbing and dunking and praying.

Not far from the bathing ghats are the sites where the corpses of the dead are being burnt and their ashes strewn into the river. I watched one of these cremation places, where fire, water and cooking fat combine to dispose of the body, while the soul is already on its way towards its next incarnation. The corpses are wrapped in cotton sheets which look as if they were bloodstained because they are printed in pink and white patches, like Army oilskins used for camouflage. They are carried to the river on bamboo poles and put down near the fire, on which another corpse is sizzling away, to await their turn. Each time the queue advanced, the pink-and-white bundles were picked up and put down again closer to the fire. A few spectators were sitting around, looking bored, and the smoke rose calmly to the houses in the neighbourhood where a housewife would occasionally lean out of a window and watch the proceedings. When, at last, the corpse is put on the fire – by the oldest son, if there is one – it is covered up with logs, and the smoke gets blacker for a while. There is no religious ceremony of any kind, and the handful of spectators, who are presumably relatives, loll around smoking cigarettes. I could not help thinking of the crematoria at Auschwitz. But, our smiling oarsman explained, a dead body is just like the clothes one has shed, or a lizard's skin. With children, holy men, and the victims of certain diseases, the procedure is simpler: they are thrown into the water without being burnt.

Farther down the river, on the outskirts of the town, the scenery became more peaceful, and animals abounded on the shore. The donkeys seemed to have the majority – shaggy,

sturdy, stolid-eyed. Crows have a preference for perching on
their backs. All along the river there were goats, pie-dogs,
pigs, doves, camels, monkeys, and occasionally a battered-
looking elephant.

Ananda's ashram overlooks the Ganges from the inside
of a curve. It is a derelict building with loggias and a courtyard. From the loggias open small, cell-like rooms and one or
two larger ones. Mother herself, I was told, had left the day
before for Calcutta, but I had a recommendation to one of
her devotees who had lived for the past eight years in this
ashram. Brother N. – he had shed his original name –
received me indeed like a gentle, older brother. He had a
sparse body and a gaunt, passionate, rabbinical face – he
came from an Alsatian orthodox Jewish family, and had been
brought up to become a rabbi, but took a medical degree
instead. He had practised in the South of France, but after
a spiritual crisis left for India, where he eventually met
Ananda and joined her Benares ashram.

We were talking in his small, almost completely bare, and
not too clean cell. There was no furniture, not even a book
– only a sleeping-mat on the floor and a primus-cooker, on
which he boiled his rice himself. When I asked him about
the ultimate purpose of spending his life in this fashion, he
answered with a single word: 'Self-realization.' I asked him
what came afterwards. He answered: 'If one dreams that one
shall soon wake up, one does not ask oneself what one will
do in waking life.'

He showed me round the ashram. It was inhabited by
about twenty, mostly elderly, men and women. They were
meditating alone in their cells, or jointly in one of the two
larger rooms; some were reading, some chatting quietly on
the balcony overlooking the river. They all had a peaceful,
childishly gay manner; in spite of the austere and rather
dirty surroundings, they seemed to be leading a happy and
contented existence. In the courtyard there were some
children, for the ashram has a school attached to it. They
were less noisy than children normally are, but they also
seemed to be quite happy there.

About a week later I met Anandamayee in her Calcutta ashram. After the peaceful hours spent at her Benares place, I was favourably prejudiced and eagerly looking forward to the meeting.

The ashram is in a walled-in compound in a suburb. It looked a little cleaner than the Benares ashram, and was in a grander style, but also more noisy. I was led into a spacious hall in the main building, which was completely bare except for a low wooden platform on which stood, side by side, a kind of dais and a bed. Both were as yet unoccupied, but about fifty people were squatting in rows on mats facing the platform, men on the right, women on the left. Two Juno-esque ladies in saffron robes had been placed in the front row on the men's side, presumably as a special honour. I was told in a whisper to sit down next to them, and my guide informed me that they were 'the Finnish sisters from Los Angeles'. Whether that was their nationality, or name, and whether they were really sisters, I did not find out, for, like everybody else in the room, they were both engaged in silent meditation. In front of us, before the empty platform, a man in a dhoti lay prostrate on his face, asleep or in a trance.

Some twenty minutes passed like this, in a silence inter-rupted only by an occasional murmur. Yet I was unable to enter into the spirit of the silence, and wondered why. The ugliness of the bare room, with its dirty and peeling plaster-walls, might have had something to do with it, and also the bed with its greyish, creased sheet, standing in lieu of an altar on the platform. It lent the atmosphere an ambiguous physical intimacy. In this unresponsive mood I was called by a young woman with a calm, nun-like face, to be led into Ma's presence.

I followed her through the door out into the corridor, and thence into the room adjoining the hall. There, on another raised dais squatted Shri Shri Ananda, the Mother of the Universe. She was dressed in a white silk sari which exposed her lovely feet; they caught my eyes at once for she was play-ing with them, rubbing the spaces between her mobile and expressive toes, which had a life of their own. Her beautiful gypsy face with its wilful and wistful eyes, had a commanding and rather intimidating expression; yet it also had a quality of girlishness, or rather hoydenishness, hidden beneath the surface like the half-effaced writing on a palimpsest. She seemed restless, and was chewing *pan*; as I was shown in, she sized me up in a single quick glance, pointed at the mat beneath the dais, on which I squatted down, then seemed to lose interest in me.

The nun-like girl invited me to ask Mother any question I liked. I learnt later that she had been a brilliant research student, a botanist who, at the age of twenty-seven, had suddenly given up her promising career to become Ananda's disciple and permanent attendant. Yet I felt no magic coming from Ananda's person, and no particular emotion. Thus my question came out rather flat, and it was the wrong question to ask: 'Does Mother approve of what has been written about her, claiming that she was of divine origin?' While the question was being translated by the botanist nun, Ananda continued her conservation with another woman in the room; then she snapped impatiently: 'Everybody sees in me what he likes.'

With that the conversation came to an end; Ananda kept chatting to the woman and chewing pan, ignoring my squatting presence at her lovely feet. After five minutes, the botanist made a gentle sign; Ananda gave me a brief smile and two tangerines out of a basket, and I was led back through the corridor to the assembly room. A moment later, Ananda herself entered by a communicating door giving directly onto the platform. She was followed by a very old woman with the face and skull of a head-hunter's shrunken trophy. The old woman sat on the bed while Ananda squatted down on the dais, carefully arranging her sari and playing with her toes.

The devotees now came forward one by one, made obeisance, and presented their offerings: flowers, fruit, rice, sweets. She rewarded each of them with a couple of tangerines or a flower, a garland or a sweet, but not all of them with a smile. Then there was an incident. An old woman came forward, prostrated herself, and begged Ananda to intercede for her son, a soldier reported missing after a clash in the border area. Ananda kept chewing pan, ignoring her. The woman began to shout and sob in near-hysterics. Ananda said harshly, 'Go away,' brushing her aside with a single gesture, and the old woman, still crying, was led from the room.

The obeisances having been completed, Ananda made a speech. The moment she began to speak, her ageing weathered gypsy face became transparent, as it were; the little-girl expression lurking under its surface broke through and took hold of the entire personality. She wriggled and giggled as she spoke, and from time to time laughed out aloud as if marking the points of a funny story. She was evidently in her playful mood, and I wondered why nobody else laughed, until an old man – probably Pitaji, her husband, but I was not sure – made a sign to her to stop, and translated what she had said into English. It turned out to be an admonition to meditate for at least a quarter of an hour every day, and always at the same hour.

Ananda then resumed her speech in the same kittenish manner, wriggling and giggling. I watched the effect on the audience: the Finnish sisters in their saffron robes listened with their faces buried in their hands; the middle-aged, lawyer-like man squatting on my other side sat with his mouth open, shaking his head and smacking his lips in wonder, his eyes shining, his expression reverting to infancy. Another youngish man, a portable harmonium in his lap, with a short-cropped black beard and steel-rimmed glasses, was swaying with closed eyes. It again seemed to me that, as with Krishna Menon, I was the only one left out in the cold.

When Ananda's speech was finished, the bearded young man, still swaying, burst into a hymn, thus preventing the translation. The text of the hymn, which he accompanied on his instrument, consisted of three words, repeated forty-two times in Hindi and then forty-two times in English: 'O my Mother – O my Mother – O my Mother', and so on. The whole scene – the woman with the shrunken skull on the bed, Ananda in her white sari, rubbing her toes, the young man with the lachrymose voice accompanied by the belly-belches of his harmonium – gave me a feeling of acute distress, and I began to tip-toe towards the door. But I was intercepted by several indignant devotees and made to pick up the two tangerines which I had left behind. They were sticky and dirty, but sanctified by Mother's touch, and I gave them to some urchins in the street, hoping they would derive from them a darshan that, for one reason or another, was denied me.

Yoga Unexpurgated

THE word Yoga means Union. The aim of all Yoga practices, as defined in the *Yoga Sutras of Patanjali*, is the ultimate absorption of the subject in his 'real self', in pure consciousness without object. When this is attained, individual consciousness merges into cosmic consciousness, and the real self dissolves in the universal self –'as sparks issued from the same fire are destined to return to it', or 'as the dewdrop, trembling on a lotus, slips into the shining sea'. Then the Yogi's detached alone-ness becomes transformed into the experience of all-oneness; both expressions are derived from the same root, and the Sanskrit word atma covers both.

The Rise of Hatha Yoga

Patanjali's Yoga Sutras,[1] which probably date from the second or third century B.C., are a profoundly seductive, if somewhat obscure treatise on a mystic philosophy of much earlier origin. Yoga began apparently in the form of Raja Yoga – as a journey towards the primal verities, the Royal Union with the Absolute, by way of meditation. But it was gradually superseded by Hatha Yoga – literally 'forced Union'– a discipline with its main emphasis on physiological techniques. Hatha Yoga is at least a thousand years old, and seems to have remained basically unchanged throughout that period. It is the only form of Yoga still practised on a large scale, taught by individual gurus or approved Yoga institutes, and propagated in the Western world. But of the doctrine on which it is based only bowdlerized versions are made available to Western sympathizers. These give the impression that Hatha Yoga is merely a superior system of gymnastic exercises, designed to relax the body and mind by adopting a

[1] *Patanjali's Yoga Sutras,* tr. V. Raghavan, *op. cit.*, pp. 141-149.

85

suitable posture, a natural way of breathing, and thus to facilitate a meditative attitude. At the same time, it is usually denied that there is anything 'mysterious' or 'occult' about its doctrines.

In fact, every Indian-born practitioner of Hatha Yoga, from the Himalayan hermit to the Bombay insurance clerk who spends an hour a day at a Yoga institute, knows that Hatha Yoga does promise the attainment of supernatural powers; and he also knows that every posture and exercise has both a symbolic meaning and a physiological purpose related to the tenets of ayurvedic medicine, and not considered a fit subject for discussion with foreigners.

The following summary of Hatha Yoga doctrines and practices is based partly on the primary sources, and partly on information obtained from various Indian Yoga Institutes, Research Centres and individual practitioners. The primary sources are: the *Hatha Yoga Pradipika,* apparently the first standard work on the subject, probably written in the twelfth century, but based on a much older tradition; the *Siva Samhita* and the *Gheranda Samhita,* which are compendia of a somewhat later date. All three have been translated into English, but are rather difficult to obtain.[1]

Cleansing Practices (dhautis and bastis)

The eight steps, or limbs, of Yoga according to Patanjali are: (1) and (2) abstentions and observances (such as non-violence, chastity, avoidance of human company, dietary rules); (3) postures; (4) controlled breathing; (5) and (6) sense-withdrawal and concentration; (7) meditation; (8) samadhi – the complete absorption of the mind in the atma.

The *Hatha Yoga Pradipika* opens with the statement that its purpose is to serve 'as a staircase' for those aspirants who, confused by the multiplicity of methods recommended by various sects, are unable to master Raja Yoga. The steps of

[1] Sinh, Pancham, tr., *Hatha Yoga Pradipika,* 2d. ed. Allahabad, pub. by Lalit Mohan Basu, The Panini Office, 1932.
Vidyarnava, Rai Bahadur Srisa Chandra, tr., *Siva Samhita,* 2d. ed. Allahabad, pub. by Sudhindra Nath Basu, The Panini Office, 1923.
Vasu, Sris Chandra, tr., *Gheranda Samhita,* The Tatva-Vivechaka Press, Bombay, 1895.

the staircase are bodily exercises. In the original system of Patanjali, these were contained under headings (3) and (4): posture and breathing, and were discussed only briefly, in general terms. About the first he merely says that it is preferable to adopt a posture 'in which one can continue for long and with ease'; about breathing he is equally laconic.

In the *Hatha Yoga Pradipika,* however, no less than eighty-four postures are mentioned, most of them consisting of twists and contortions, and the control of breathing is carried to the gruesome length to be presently described. Some of the postures, such as the various headstands and spine twists, serve gymnastic purposes, but the more elaborate ones have a different function.

Before he is allowed to practise the advanced techniques, the adept must learn to master the various cleansing practices. Foremost among these are purifications of the alimentary tract. The stomach is cleansed by three principal methods: (*a*) by thrusting a stalk of cane slowly down the gullet and drawing it out; (*b*) by swallowing as much tepid water as the stomach will hold and vomiting it up; (*c*) by swallowing a cloth about four inches wide and twenty-two and a half feet long, and then pulling it out. The last method is considered the most effective, and is still vigorously practised, for instance, at the approved Yoga Health Centre at Santa Cruz, Bombay. It takes about a month or two to learn to swallow the seven-and-a-half yards of surgical gauze in about ten minutes, and it is supposed to 'cleanse the waste matter coating the walls of the stomach'.

I now must enter upon the painful subject of the Hindu obsession with the bowel functions, which permeates religious observances and social custom. I quote from the *Gheranda Samhita*:

'14. Dhouti is of four kinds, and they clear away the impurities of the body . . .

VATASARA-DHOUTI

16. Contract the mouth like the the beak of a crow and drink air slowly, and fill the stomach slowly with it, and

move it therein, and then slowly force it out through the lower passage.

17. The Vatasar is a very secret process, it causes the purification of the body, it destroys all diseases and increases the gastric fire.

VARISARA-DHOUTI

18. Fill the mouth with water down to the throat, and then drink it slowly; and then move it through the stomach forcing it downwards expelling it through the rectum.

19. This process should be kept very secret. It purifies the body. And by practising it with care one gets a luminous or shining body.

20. The Varisara is the highest Dhouti. He who practises it with ease purifies his filthy body and turns it into a shining one.

AGNISARA or FIRE PURIFICATION

21. Press in the navel knot or intestines towards the spine for one hundred times. This is Agnisar or fire process . . .

BAHISKRITA-DHOUTI

24. . . . standing in navel-deep water, draw out the Sakti-nadi (long intestines), wash the Nadi with hand, and so long as its filth is not all washed away, wash it with care, and then draw it in again into the abdomen . . .'[1]

The reverse procedures are known under the term basti or 'Yoga enemas'. Jala-basti consists in squatting in a tub of water navel-high and sucking the water up through the rectum. At a more advanced stage, the adept also learns to suck liquids up through his penis (vajroli mudra). These achievements presuppose, of course, considerable training, particularly the exercises known as uddiyama and nauli (the isolation and independent control of the straight and trans-verse abdominal muscles) and asvini mudra (control of the anal sphincter and of certain visceral muscles). By these methods it becomes possible to reverse peristalsis, and to create suctional effects in the digestive and urinary tracts.

[1] pp. 2-4.

The remarkable thing is that these techniques are still recommended and practised in precisely the same form in which the *Gheranda Samhita* and *Hatha Yoga Pradipika* taught them a millennium ago. Thus in *Yoga Hygiene Simplified*,[1] a booklet published by the above-mentioned Yoga Institute in Santa Cruz, it is asserted that practice of the methods just described leads to results 'which could not be accomplished by any modern device known to science'.

The Vital Breath

Pranayama occupies a central position in the doctrine of Yoga. Prana means 'life breath', in the physical sense of air, and in the wider sense of vital spirit, comparable to the Greek *pneuma* and the Hebrew *ruakh*.

Patanjali has only this to say about pranayama: '50. The regulation of breath is exhaling, inhaling and storing within; is governed by place, time and number;[2] and is long and subtle. 51. A fourth form of the control of breath is its storing up with attention on an external or internal object. 52. By breath-control, the afflictions that shroud the luminous quality are annihilated; 53. and the mind becomes fit for steady contemplation . . .'[3]

Thus originally the control of breathing, like that of bodily posture, was meant to facilitate a peaceful, meditative state of mind. By the time the *Hatha Yoga Pradipika* came to be written, it had become not only an all-cure for every form of disease, but also a means for acquiring supernatural powers.

The opening passage of the chapter on breathing in the *Pradipika* is significant: 'When the breath moves, the mind also moves. When breath ceases to move, the mind becomes motionless. The body of the Yogi becomes stiff as a stump. Therefore one should control the breath.'

'Control' means, chiefly, holding the breath locked in the body as long as possible to induce the trance state of samadhi.

---

[1] Bombay, 1957.

[2] 'Place' in this context means the minimum distance from the subject's lips at which a feather will remain undisturbed by his quiet exhalation; 'time', the duration of holding the breath locked in, and 'number', the rhythm.

[3] *Patanjali's Yoga Sutras*, tr. Raghavan, *op cit.*, p. 146.

The first step in the training is the cleansing of the nadis –
the channels or pathways through which the vital forces of
the body are supposed to move. This is achieved by various
techniques, such as bhastrika (bellow-breathing), or inhaling
through the right nostril and exhaling through the left nostril
at a fixed rhythm. The classic timing is 1 : 4 : 2 for the duration of inhalation, retention, and exhalation respectively; for
instance: 2 seconds, 8 seconds, 4 seconds. After a few months
of these preliminary exercises, the nadis have been purified,
and the proper breathing practices can begin.

Their main purpose, as already said, is to suspend the flow
of breath by locking in the air. This is achieved by various
mudras and bandhas (locks, seals, restraints), which serve to
seal all bodily orifices. Some examples of these are:

Jalandhara mudra, or chin lock. It consists in contracting
the throat and pressing the chin firmly into the jugular
notch, while simultaneously contracting the abdominal
muscles and drawing in the anus. The eyes and mind are
focused on the space between the eyebrows. 'This causes the
mind to swoon and give comfort. For by thus joining the
mind with the atma, the bliss of Yoga is certainly obtained.'[1]

Maha mudra and maha bandha ('the great binding') consist
in a combination of the chin lock, the drawing in of the
abdominal viscerae towards the spine, and the drawing of air
into the small intestines by contractions of the anal sphincter.
The air is kept locked in by pressure of the heel of the left
foot against the anus and perineum. I ought to remark here
that in most of the advanced postures the left foot is used
for the same definite purpose, that is, for sealing the anal
orifice, with simultaneous pressure on the genitals.

Maha-vedha ('the great piercing') is a variation of the
previous, but the Yogi 'resting both hands equally on the
ground, should raise himself a little and strike his buttocks
against the ground gently', then exhale the locked-in air
through the rectum.[2]

One of the most important practices is khecari mudra,
because it is supposed to confer the gift of levitation. It is

[1] *Gheranda Samhita*, V. 82.   [2] *Pradipika*, iii, 25-31.

described at great length by the *Hatha Yoga Pradipika*; a
shorter version is given in the *Gheranda Samhita*:

'Cut the lower tendon of the tongue, and move the
tongue constantly; rub it with fresh butter, and draw it out
(to lengthen it) with an iron instrument. By practising this
always, the tongue becomes long, and when it reaches the
space between the eyebrows, then Khecari is accomplished.
Then (the tongue being lengthened) practise turning it
upwards and backwards so as to touch the palate, till at
length it reaches the holes of the nostrils opening into the
mouth. Close those holes with the tongue (thus stopping
inspiration), and fix the gaze on the space between the
eyebrows. This is called Khecari. By this practice there is
neither fainting, nor hunger, nor thirst, nor laziness.
There comes neither disease, nor decay, nor death. The
body becomes divine.'[1]

This technique is often called the King of the Mudras. It
is still actively practised. The best documented report of a
European initiated into the higher techniques of Yoga is
Hatha Yoga, a Report of a Personal Experience by Dr. Theos
Bernard.[2] His account of learning khecari mudra is as follows:

'The process itself is simple enough. I started by "milking" the tongue. This was accomplished by washing it and
then catching hold of it with a linen towel . . . I pulled it
straight out and then from side to side as far as it would
go. This I did regularly twice a day for ten minutes. After
a couple of weeks I noticed that the fraenum was beginning to give way because of being drawn over the incisor
teeth; but I wanted to encourage the process, so I resorted
to a razor blade. Each morning I delicately drew the blade
across the fraenum until blood appeared. There was no
pain, and the bleeding stopped before I finished milking the

---

[1] *Gheranda Samhita*, iii. 25-28.
[2] London, 1950. Dr. Bernard studied under various gurus in India and
Tibet (he was killed in Tibet in 1947). The thirty-six plates in his book
showing him performing the various *asanas* are probably the best photo-
graphic documentation on Yoga.

tongue. The following morning the wound had begun to heal and a light tissue was beginning to form, which I scraped off; then I repeated the process of the preceding day.

I was also taught a practice supplementary to milking the tongue. In order to get the tongue down the throat, it is first necessary to loosen the soft palate. The most convenient way is to bend the end of the handle of an ordinary teaspoon enough to form a hook. Insert this in the back of the throat and draw it forward until it catches on to the palate ridge. When a firm grip has been secured, repeatedly pull the palate towards the front part of the mouth. In time this membrane will become so flexible that it will be almost possible to touch the teeth with the soft palate. I practised this daily for ten minutes after milking the tongue.

Success depends upon the amount of time spent in practice. I was able to accomplish it in about four months by working an average of ten minutes a day . . . To elongate the tongue so that it can be placed between the eyebrows requires several years,[1] but it is not necessary to achieve this goal at once. It is sufficient to acquire the ability to swallow the tongue and to use it to direct the breath into the desired nostril or shut it off completely . . .

In the beginning I was permitted to help the tongue down the throat with the fingers, but after a time this was not necessary. As soon as I placed the tongue behind the palate, the saliva began to flow in a constant stream. In this way I was supposed to determine the condition of the body fluids. At first it was thick, heavy, and slimy; eventually, it became thin, clear and smooth.'[2]

Dr. Bernard further reports that blocking both cranial holes of the nose seemed to inhibit the breathing reflex. He

[1] *Op. cit.*, pp. 67 f.
[2] Sris Chandra Vasu, the translator of *Gheranda Samhita*, writing in 1894, remarks: 'It takes about three years to cut away the whole tendon. I saw my Guru doing it in this wise. On every Monday he used to cut the tendon one-twelfth of an inch deep and sprinkle salt over it so that the cut portions may not join together. Then rubbing the tongue with butter he used to pull it out. Peculiar iron instruments are employed for this purpose.' (p. 21.)

had progressed to a state of proficiency where he could hold his breath for four minutes, but that was his limit. At this stage he learned khecari mudra, which enabled him to hold it for five minutes in ten consecutive breathing cycles; while 'for a single aspiration I could hold my breath several minutes longer'. However, to acquire supernatural powers, the texts prescribe a suspension of at least an hour and a half.

The Vital Fluid (bindu)

Apart from breath control, khecari, the king of the mudras, serves another, more important purpose related to one of the traditional ideas of Yoga and Hindu medicine. It is the belief that a man's vital energy is concentrated in his seminal fluid, and that this is stored in a cavity in the skull. It is the most precious substance in the body – variously called bindu, soma-rasa, nectar, vital fluid, etc. – an elixir of life both in the physical and mystical sense, distilled from the blood; it is supposed to take forty drops of blood and forty days to make one drop of semen. A large store of bindu of pure quality guarantees health, longevity and supernatural powers; it is also held responsible for that radiant glow of the body, ascribed to Yogis and all Brahmacharis – men living in continence. Conversely, every loss of it is a physical and spiritual impoverishment. Losses occur not only in sexual intercourse, but also through suspicious discharges of the ears, nose, and other body openings; they all consist of spoiled bindu.

By blocking his windpipe, gullet and nostrils through khecari mudra, the adept is supposed to prevent the loss of vital fluid through its dripping down into the lower centres, and to absorb it back through his tongue. Jalandhara mudra, the chin lock, incidentally also serves that purpose, but less effectively. Hence the *Hatha Yoga Pradipika*:

'If the hole behind the soft palate be stopped with khecari by turning the tongue upwards, then bindu cannot leave its place even if a woman were embraced. If the Yogi drinks somarasa by sitting with the tongue turned backwards and mind concentrated, there is no doubt he

conquers death within 15 days . . . As fire is inseparably
connected with the wood and light is connected with the
wick and oil, so does the soul not leave the body full of
nectar exuding from the Soma [cavity in the skull] . . . He
who drinks the clear stream of liquor falling from the
brain . . . by applying the tongue to the hole of the pendant
in the palate . . . becomes free from disease and tender in
body, like the stalk of a lotus, and that Yogi lives a very
long life. On top of the Meru [spinal column], concealed in
a hole, is the somarasa . . . the essence which, leaving the
body, causes death in men. It should, therefore, be stopped
from shedding. This [khecari mudra] is a very good instrument for this purpose . . .'[1]

An even more drastic instrument, serving the same purpose, is vajroli mudra, which I have briefly mentioned before.

'Even one who lives a wayward life, without observing
any rules of Yoga, but performs vajroli, deserves success
and is a Yogi. Two things are necessary for this, and these
are difficult to get for the ordinary people – (1) milk[2] and
(2) a woman behaving as desired. By practising to draw in
the bindu discharged during cohabitation, whether one
be a man or a woman, one obtains success in the practice
of vajroli. By means of a pipe, one should blow [i.e., draw]
air slowly into the passage in the male organ. By practice,
the discharged bindu is drawn up. One can draw back and
preserve one's own discharged bindu. The Yogi who can
protect his bindu thus, overcomes death; because death
comes by discharging bindu, and life is prolonged by its
preservation. By preserving bindu, the body of the Yogi
emits a pleasing smell. There is no fear of death, so long
as the bindu is well established in the body. The bindu of
men is under the control of the mind, and life is dependent
on the bindu. Hence, mind and bindu should be protected
by all means.'[3]

---

[1] *Op. cit.*, iii 41-50.
[2] Milk is believed by Hindus to be an aphrodysiac.
[3] *Hatha Yoga Pradipika*, iii 82-90.

The pipe mentioned in the quotation is used in the first stage of the training, until the adept has learnt to aspire fluids through the urethra, as he has previously learnt to do through the colon. To Hindus brought up in the traditions of ayurvedic medicine – which applies to the vast majority of the nation – the procedure may seem complicated, but perfectly logical. Thus in *Hatha Yoga Simplified,* published by the Yoga Institute, Santa Cruz,[1] the author explains that sexual intercourse in itself is not harmful: only the loss of vital fluid which it entails. Therefore vajroli mudra is to be highly recommended.* After explaining the various stages of training – the aspiration through the urethra first of water, 'then of liquids of higher specific gravity, e.g. milk, honey, and sometimes even mercury' (the latter, however, only under expert supervision), he concludes:

'The highest technique of vajroli . . . consists in successfully withholding the ejaculation of sex secretions prior to or during . . . orgasm under sexual excitement and thus cause their resorption through the lymphatics. In case the secretions happen to be ejected, the Yogi is advised to withdraw the secretion from the vagina where it may have become deposited, with the aid of Madhavadasa vacuum [part of the vajroli technique] . . . The scientific theory may be simplified thus: that instead of mere passivity, it is preferable and hygienic to engage in normal sexual activities when necessary – for this certainly causes less strain and lesser energy waste than what has to be actually expended in self-denials and repressions – remembering that there should be no physiological loss. This loss, to be sure, is inevitable if the secretions escape from the body. The Yogi, therefore . . . suffers no corresponding loss. On the contrary, he gains much through healthful reactions and resorption of the extra fresh fluids otherwise not available . . . It is thus . . . an excellent hygienic ideal and – *if only* the process of vajroli could be made available to and brought within the practice of one and all – solves

[1] Bombay, 1958.

incidentally the most-discussed topic in modern eugenics, namely family planning through birth control . . .'[1]

The author is the head of an Institute which enjoys Government support.

Even level-headed Englishmen, if they have lived long enough in India, seem to succumb to these ideas. Thus Mr. Ernest Wood, the author of the latest popular book on *Yoga*[2] who had a long and distinguished career as an educationalist at the Universities of Bombay and Madras:

> '[It should be] remembered that the semen draws its material from all over, and transmits something from every part of the body to the succeeding generation, and that waste of this fluid, or excessive generation of it, depletes the body all over, and on the other hand conservation of it is highly beneficial to the whole body. It appears that this is the one function of the body which does not work for the benefit of the body, but draws from it for the sake of another or others, and therefore its non-use does not harm the body but on the contrary is beneficial to it. This is at the back of the universal belief of the yogis in favour of continence and celibacy.'[3]

We shall see that this preoccupation with continence in the strictly physiological, seminal meaning, is not restricted to Yogis, but is to be found in every region and in every social stratum in India.

The Serpent Power (Kundalini)

The ultimate aim of Hatha Yoga is to awaken the vital force in man slumbering at the base of his spine in the shape of a coiled serpent – Kundalini. When Kundalini is awakened, she must be forced to ascend through a narrow canal in the spinal cord, through various gates and stations,

[1] *Op. cit.*, pp. 101-103.
[2] Penguin Books, 1959.
[3] p. 176.

to the top of the brain, and there consummate her symbolic union with Shiva, her spouse. She then returns to her former abode. When this union becomes permanent, the Yogi is liberated and enters into his final samadhi.

The process of awakening and moving the Kundalini serpent has a physiological and a symbolic aspect – the former grotesquely unappetizing, the latter beautiful and profound. Both are derived from the archetypal erotic imagery which permeates Hindu religious art and ayurvedic medicine.[1]

The serpent Kundalini 'lies coiled three and a half times' around the base of the spine, clothing the sushumna with its mouth. The sushumna is a narrow canal in the centre of the spinal cord, through which the serpent must be forced to go upward.

The awakening of the serpent is done by one or the other combination of the various air-locks and bowel gymnastics which have been described. Essential to most is asvini mudra, the rhythmic contraction and dilation of the anal sphincter. One recommended variant is yoni mudra, the closing up of all orifices – ears with the thumbs, eyes with the index fingers, nostrils with the middle fingers, lips with the remaining fingers, rectum and member by the heel of the foot. This is combined with mental concentration and repeating certain mantras – invocations. The effect is that the serpent begins to suffocate, awakens with a hiss and 'becomes straight like a snake struck with a stick'. In order to make her enter the narrow channel in the cord, violent bellow breathing is recommended for a few minutes. After that various abdominal muscle contractions are applied for periods of an hour and a half at a time, accompanied by mantras, to force her gradually upwards through the channel.

The serpent must force her way through three 'gates' and past six chakras, or centres. These six centres are of great importance in the Hindu concept of the human body. The first is at the base of the spine, the second at the genitals, the third near the navel, the fourth near the heart, the fifth near

[1] cf. A. Avalon (Sir John Woodruff): *The Serpent Power* (new edition, London, 1958).

the throat, the sixth between the eyebrows; a seventh, at the very top of the brain, forms a category apart.

Each of the chakras (literally, wheels) has a padma or lotus-flower attached to it, with varying numbers of petals. Whereas the greatest number of petals in the lower centres is sixteen, the top of the brain displays a thousand-petalled lotus.

Each time Kundalini passes through one of the centres, its lotus, whose petals had previously been pointing downward, now turns and faces upward. The flower is said to have become 'cool'; its attention has been diverted from the nether impulses of the body, towards the seat of the God where the union with the life-snake is going to take place. Kundalini's painful journey, assisted by visceral acrobacies and respiratory intoxication, is one of the most ancient symbols for the sublimation of the libido.

Apart from its lotus, each of the centres has a symbolic animal, a colour, a male divinity with his shakti and an invocatory mantra associated with it. Thus the chakra at the base of the spine is associated with Brahma and the Goddess Dakini, with the colour yellow, and the four-petalled lotus; its animal symbol is the elephant and its invocatory mantra the syllable *lam*. The highest of the six centres, between the eyebrows, is called the ajna chakra. Ajna means 'command'.[1] Here Shiva resides; his symbol is the lingam, or phallus, which the Shaivites display painted on their foreheads. His seat in the command centre is always represented by a triangle enclosing the lingam, the crescent moon and a dot. This dot has a multiplicity of symbolic meanings. The Sanskrit word for it is bindu, signifying dot or drop; but also semen; and also the dot on the 'm' in the mantra *oṁ* – the highest invocation of God – which makes the sound of the 'm' trail and reverberate like a slack cord.

All the symbols are here crowded together: the lingam and the seed, the God, the point representing the infinite void. Kundalini's journey comes to an end at the seventh

---

[1] I am indebted to Swami Aghananda Bharati for the following comment: 'The word *ajna* indeed means "command" and this is how many scholars render it in the context. This interpretation, however, is wrong, for *ajna* here is a compound of the prefix *a* plus *jna* and means something like "inceptive intuition" '.

chakra somewhere under the crown of the skull – the seat of the thousand-petalled lotus. It is here that her union with Shiva is consummated; after that she returns, 'no longer a maiden but a young widow', to her home at the base of the spine. On her return journey, the lotus-flowers in the various centres are again made to face downward, and the residing divinities cohabit with their female shaktis, thus lending new vitality to each centre.

However, when the Yogi reaches ultimate samadhi, the snake will remain permanently united with Shiva in the form of an ardhanarishwara – a god half male and half female – a motive often encountered in Hindu sculpture.

The location of the cavity in which the bindu is stored is somewhat dubious; sometimes it is said to be located on the left, or lunar, side of the brow-chakra, sometimes above it, sometimes just above the top of the spine.

Samadhi, the ultimate end of the hard and devious road of Yoga, will be discussed in the next chapter. But I must briefly mention a phenomenon which is said to occur in the last stages before samadhi: the appearance of an 'inner light', and of various 'inner sounds' or nadas. Regarding the latter, the *Siva Samhita* says: 'The first sound is like the hum of the honey-intoxicated bee, next that of a flute, then of a harp; after this, by the gradual practice of Yoga, the destroyer of the darkness of the world, he hears the sounds of ringing bells; then sounds like roar of thunder. When one fixes his full attention on this sound, being free from fear he gets samadhi.'[1] On the other hand, the *Pradipika* gives a different order of nadas progressing through four stages: first light sounds 'like the tinkling of ornaments'; next 'the beating of a kettle drum'; thirdly, the sound of a different drum; lastly, 'the perfect sound like that of a flute'.

More interesting are the lights, because their descriptions have a certain resemblance to the 'white light' reported by Christian mystics – a dazzling, almost blinding radiance which blots out everything else. Bernard records:

[1] *Siva Samhita*, v. 22-30.

'In the second month the lights made their appearance. In the beginning it was not unlike looking into a kaleido-scope; but this condition soon passed, and single colours, brilliant and radiant, remained. Then came the "white light" that is referred to so frequently. This was an inter-esting phenomenon. At times it became almost blinding; however, it never lasted long . . . I was eventually able to see this white light with my eyes wide open in the daylight. The mind seemed to be wiped out completely and nothing existed but this brilliant light.'[1]

However, in view of the air-locking and eye-rolling tech-niques of Yoga, the lights and sounds may have a simple physiological explanation. Thus at the age of nine I had a curious experience: the dazzling white light appeared the moment before going under anaesthesia induced by ether, for a minor operation, and simultaneously with the appear-ance of the light the sensation of choking and fear stopped. Similarly, in the gruesome reports of delinquents who sur-vived a miscarried execution by hanging either because the rope broke or because they were cut down while still alive, colour hallucinations are mentioned, though the dominant colour is green.

I do not mean, of course, that accounts of mystical experi-ences should always be explained away by this kind of argu-ment. But I do believe that such experiences must be sought along a road other than that of Hatha Yoga. Kundalini's journey past the lotus-flowers from the base of the spine to the head, her transformation from a biological into a spiritual force, is a beautiful parable; but there is a tendency in the human mind never to leave a symbol alone, an itch to debase it by pseudo-rationalizations; and thus the Indian mystic is taught to force his tongue into the cranial cavity, to drink his bindu and to blink with his anus, to achieve union with Brahma.

[1] *Op. cit.*, pp. 89-90.

Yoga Research

ALL teachers of Hatha Yoga, from ancient masters to modern practitioners, have advanced three main claims: firstly, that it cures disorders of mind and body, and produces heightened physical and mental well-being; secondly, that it procures supernatural powers, siddhis, through control of the body's latent forces; thirdly, that it leads to the mystic Union. Thus there are, broadly speaking, three aspects to Yoga: the medical, the miraculous and the mystical.

Although a certain amount of overlapping is unavoidable, I shall discuss each aspect separately.

Medical Aspects

There exist, as far as I was able to discover, three centres in contemporary India where more or less serious Yoga research is being carried out. They are: the All India Institute of Mental Health in Bangalore, which works under the Union Government; the Kaivalyadhama Ishwardas Chunilal Yogic Health Centre, headed by Swami Kuvalayananda, recognized as a Research Institute by the Government and the Bombay State; and the Academy of Yoga under the auspices of the Yoga Institute, Bombay, Santa Cruz, headed by Shri Yogendra, and recognized by the Bombay State Government.

The Bangalore Institute has no clinic, and is not concerned with the medical aspect. The other two are not on friendly terms and are inclined to deny the validity of each other's methods.

The Kaivalyadhama maintains a Health Centre in Bombay's West End, the Marine Drive, and a Research Institute at Lonavla, on the road to Poonah. They are very competently

directed by Swami Kuvalayananda, a charming old gentleman who looks like a Brahmin edition of Albert Einstein,
with a bushy white moustache, a domed forehead, wispy hair
and white corkscrew sidelocks hanging down to his shoulders
like tresses. He reminded me of Einstein because he had the
same peculiar look in his large brown eyes: speculative,
puzzled and naïve at the same time. His manner was modest
and unassuming, yet impressive in its gentle authority – a
particular mixture shared by so many Indians, from Gandhi
downward. When I complimented him on his erudition in
modern physics and biochemistry, he said with evident
sincerity: 'I know a little about everything and nothing.'
The Health Centre, housed in a villa in the Indo-Victorian
style, with the usual rusty iron-lattice verandas, is dingy by
European, but fairly well appointed by Indian standards. It
employed four instructors, three male, one female, and had at
the time about one hundred and fifty male and twenty female
pupils or patients – the term is employed almost synony-
mously. They would come in for an hour or more a day,
during a course lasting, on the average, three months.

I watched a group of four or five middle-aged men doing
exercises in simple asanas; it looked like a slightly eccentric
version of the kind of thing taught in a Western gymnasium
to get some pep into tired office workers. It was a small and
modest institute which did its best according to its modest
means, under an evidently honest swami. It did not go in for
the 'advanced' practices described in the previous chapter.
As for clinical diseases, the Swami explained that these were
all treated individually, according to the principles of Yogic
medicine. The statistical results were printed in the Health
Centre's medical report for the years 1954–5, which he gave
me. Later reports were either not published or not available.
He then invited me to visit the other branch of the establishment, the Research Institute in the hills at Lonavla – about
which later on.

On my way back, the friendly Indian gentleman who had
accompanied me to the Centre, and who was a devotee of
the Swami's, told me his personal story. He had suffered from

chronic asthma, and the Swami had cured him – mainly by exercises of standing on the head in various postures, with appropriate breathing practices. What type of asthma he had suffered from, and how complete the cure had been, I was unable to ascertain, but no doubt there had been an ameliora- tion. Then my informant had gone on a visit to Italy 'where I foolishly acquired the habit of drinking wine', and this caused a relapse. On his return he was told – either by the Swami or by a physician, the point was not clear – that his liver, damaged by having drunk wine in Italy, would no longer stand the strain of the Yogic exercises. Shortly after- wards, he developed status asthmaticus and had to spend several days under oxygen in a hospital. 'Now it is too late,' he said resignedly; Yoga could no longer help him. We had two wineless meals together in dry Bombay, and I am fairly sure that he had never been a heavy drinker.

The report[1] which I took home said on the cover that the Centre 'teaches Yogic exercises for the promotion of Health and the Cure of chronic diseases, without distinction of caste or creed, under Yogic and medical supervision'. The list of disorders treated was impressive:

'Constipation, dyspepsia, piles, nerve-exhaustion, seminal weakness, impotency (other than congenital), general debility, chronic functional headaches, insomnia, heart disease (functional), chronic cold, chronic bronchitis, asthma (certain types), lumbago, sciatica and other rheu- matic pains, diabetes, obesity, high blood pressure, diseases of women including sterility (particular types), leucor- rhoea, disturbances of menstruation, flexions and displace- ments of the uterus, repeated abortion, ovarian insuffi- ciency, etc., etc.'

The cures listed were equally impressive: 84.65 per cent of the male patients treated were reported to be 'relieved or improving', and the corresponding proportion of female

[1] *The Kaivalyadhama Ishwardas Chunilal Yogic Health Centre – Medical Report for the Year* 1954-5, published by Kaivalyadhama, Bombay 2.

patients was 89·2 per cent. Considering that about 12½ per cent of the patients had been suffering from chronic asthma, about 13 per cent from 'neurasthenia', and nearly 10 per cent from psycho-neurosis, the results claimed were more impressive than any Western clinic could boast of. At closer inspection of the tables, however, I saw that out of the total of 1,024 patients of both sexes, 470, that is, nearly 50 per cent, had been written off under the heading 'results unknown due to short attendance'; and the percentage of those 'relieved or improving' had been computed on the basis of the remaining 50 per cent. The meaning of the term 'relieved or improving' was not further defined, nor was there a mention of follow-up. I had an uneasy feeling that by the time my unhappy asthmatic friend got under the oxygen tent, his case would have been included among those 'relieved or improving'.

I do not doubt the Swami's entire sincerity or belief in his own method, and merely wish to say that statistics of this kind do not carry much conviction. Since the Kaivalyadhama Health Centre is, to my knowledge, the only Institute of Yogic medicine in India with a claim to be taken seriously, one must conclude that the claims for the medical achievements of Yoga are not based on empirical evidence.

The rival establishment is in the Bombay suburb Santa Cruz. It is a small, modern building in a moderately well-kept garden, but inside it is much dingier than the Marine Drive place. The prospectus announces proudly that the 'Academy of Yoga' has a 'Practice Hall' and a 'Lecture Hall'; but in small print it explains further down that the Practice Hall accommodates 'a batch of eight persons' and the Lecture Hall 'has accommodation for sixteen persons'. They are, in fact, each about the size of a bed-sitter around Bayswater Road, and about as cheerful. The modest clinic, however, was clean.

The Founder-President of the Academy, Shri Yogendra, studied under the same guru as his rival, but in every other respect he is his exact opposite. Swami Kuvalayananda is gentle, meek and white-haired; Shri Yogendra is over six feet tall, black-bearded, beak-nosed and fierce-looking like a Patan tribesman. In a word, Yogendra to Kuvalayananda is as Esau to Jacob.

The biography of Shri Yogendra has been written by his wife (who is the Secretary of the Academy) and is worth briefly recording.[1] He was born in 1897 in Surat, Bombay State, as Manibhai Haribhai Desai, the son of a poor schoolteacher. At the age of eighteen, he was sent to St. Xavier's College at Bombay. A year later, a famous guru[2] visited Bombay. Young Manibhai and his room-mate Ambalal went to see him:

'In the big hall of the first floor, nearly 200 devotees had gathered to receive blessings from His Holiness. Manibhai, for no apparent cause, was thrilled when he stepped on the staircase. Ambalal was following him. Immediately Manibhai's head became visible to the audience, the holy man caught sight of him, and before the former could climb up the stairs, the latter rushed in to greet him with the words, "So you have come. I have been anxiously awaiting you for years. Seeing you, I get strength. Come!" It may be mentioned here that neither of them had ever met each other before. The devotees were taken by surprise, seeing the venerable teacher pull Manibhai up and embrace him ... His Holiness asked a very simple question in a low but firm tone "Now what?" Manibhai instinctively understood what was meant, and he replied with all the emphasis at his command, "I will go with you." They looked understandingly at each other; there was supreme silence and both seemed lost in a reverie.'

So Manibhai, after obtaining his father's consent, followed the guru to his hermitage and received the name of Mastamani, the Yoga-intoxicated. He remained two years and became the holy man's favourite pupil:

[1] *International Journal on the Science of Yoga*, April-September 1936, published by the Yoga Institute, Bombay.
[2] Paramahamsa Madhavadasagi of Malsar.

'When Paramahamsaji took Mani and another devoted student to Matheran hills for training in basti and vajroli [drawing up liquids through anus and penis], the unadorned beauty of Nature inspired the young author to poetic musings.'

The next year, he wrote several volumes of poetry, and translated Tagore's *Gitanjali* into the Gujurati language. He then 'experienced an inner awakening of a very complex but superior order which lasted a week and from which he emerged with the conviction that he must go to America to spread the message of Yoga'. The guru gladly agreed, as we gather from a letter which he subsequently wrote to his disciple in New York: 'I am proud of your work in America. You are doing the same thing for me what Swami Vivekananda had done for his guru, Paramahamsa Ramakrishna . . . I knew that you would follow his example in memorializing his guru'.

Swami Vivekananda, the favourite disciple of the founder of the Ramakrishna Order, had been the first swami who, at the turn of the century, popularized Yoga on lecture tours in the United States.

Before he set out for America, however, Mani found a wealthy patron, Mr. Dadena, in whose villa near Bombay he established his first 'Yoga Institute'. Here the twenty-two-year-old guru undertook to cure such varied afflictions as 'heart troubles, obesity, asthma, general debility, prostate enlargement, gout, hemicrania, and other diseases'.

In 1919, Mani and Mr. Dadena landed in America and established themselves at 125 Riverside Drive, New York:

'The early cases were for reduction of weight . . . Things moved smoothly so long as the money lasted, but about the middle of January, 1920, there was a day when Mr. Dadena, who was looking after the financial end, had only five cents with him . . . Mr. Dadena felt quite upset about the future. The Founder was unmoved when the gravity of the situation was explained to him. And what should happen but an urgent telephone call to rouse Mr. Dadena from his thoughts.'

The call was from an engineer employed in the South African diamond mines, whose wife was laid up with a headache. The Swami and Mr. Dadena rushed to the rescue, and the result is described in the simple words: 'A blank cheque was passed'. The next year another Yoga Institute was opened near Tuxedo Park in the Bear Mountains. The list of diseases treated now embraced every known ailment, and we are informed that 'the results were all that could be desired'. After two years, however, the Institute closed down, and Mani returned to India, where he changed his name to Shri Yogendra. The next few years were spent in fruitless attempts to raise money for starting a new Institute. When they all failed, Shri Yogendra 'invented a novel chemical product known as Yoco book polish – a preservative for books against dry rot, mould, moths, white ants, and other destructive agents . . . Its international reputation may be gauged from the fact that the Oxford University Press of London accepted the international sole agency for Yoco book polish on guaranteed basis'.

In 1927, he married Miss Sita Devi, who bore him two sons. Various Journals, Institutes and Academies, with branches 'in Latvia and Arabia' were founded, and prospectuses were sent out promising to students diplomas of 'B.Y.' (Bachelor of Yoga) in three months, or a 'Y.D.' in four years. 'Thanks, however, to the prejudice of the Provincial Government inspirited by the efforts of a contemporary, this pioneer scheme did not materialize.' The contemporary referred to was Swami Kuvalayananda. In 1958, after a lifelong struggle, Shri Yogendra's present Institute was recognized and endowed with a small subsidy by the Bombay Government.

This, briefly, is the story of the second of the two Indian Yoga Centres. Since it was recognized, the Institute has received, according to Shri Yogendra, fifty applications from candidates for the training course; of these twenty-six were accepted, but only seven have received their Teacher's Certificate after a nine-months course. Whether the others failed to pass, or gave up, I was unable to ascertain from the Founder. The number of medical patients, he claimed, was twelve – which is surprisingly small, and perhaps rather reassuring.

One interesting fact emerged from talking with the Founder and with a highly-strung young man working as his assistant: that they had abandoned the orthodox Hatha Yoga postures as impracticable. The classical asanas, Yogendra explained, were 'too hard and painful', and he had modified them according to his own ideas. This was a significant admission in view of the assurances of Yogic literature that the asanas are not meant to be a strain on the body. Equally interesting was Shri Yogendra's opinion, expressed with great force, that the various headstand postures 'do more harm than good'. The headstand asanas are basic to Hatha Yoga, and are much practised in Swami Kuvalayananda's rival Institute – which partly explains perhaps why Yogendra opposed them. He has also modified the classic breathing rhythms, such as the $1:4:2$ cycle, and replaced them by the 'Yogendra rhythm'. The prana, he holds, is not air, but 'biophysical energy generated by the rhythm' – and so forth.

Such disagreements about the therapeutic value of various postures and exercises need not be treated too seriously; after all, there exist conflicting schools in Western medicine too. But Western medicine, with all its inadequacies, prejudices and frustrations, has been constantly evolving since the days of Avicenna, who lived during the same period as the author of the *Hatha Yoga Pradipika*. Its achievements are based on the broadening empirical and theoretical insights of half a dozen interacting sciences: and it has developed methods of controlled experiment on a statistically relevant scale. On the other hand, Yoga therapy and ayurvedic medicine have remained unchanged for over a thousand years. Faith can move mountains and perhaps even kidney stones; but it would be sacrilegious to advise ordinary people to rely on it. Gandhi refused to have penicillin administered to his wife dying from bronchial infection because of the Hindu taboo on injections; Vinoba Bhave very nearly died for similar reasons, and the peaceful massacre by omission is continuing in India.

If it were difficult to prove that the simpler Yoga exercises are dangerous to health, it would be even more difficult to prove that they are beneficial in preference to Western methods of physical training. The breathing techniques, aimed at over-ventilation and auto-intoxication, are problematical to say the least of it; and the belief that training under an 'experienced teacher' guarantees against risks is another act of faith. As for the postures designed for meditation, different races have traditionally different ways of relaxing the body, from squatting on one's heels to sitting cross-legged; from reclining on one elbow to sitting with one's feet up on a table. The lotus posture, and its variants, seem to fit the Indian body-build and temperament; there is no reason to assume that they would make meditative repose easier for a Western monk than gently pacing in his cloistered garden.

Supernatural Claims

While in India, I talked to more than forty people who, at one time or another, had practised Hatha Yoga. They included elderly men, highly placed in the administrative hierarchy, young journalists and office workers, Yoga researchers and their professional subjects, religious believers and agnostics, Gandhians, Marxists, and one ex-Communist – but, to my regret, no woman. Leaving professionals aside, their records of sustained practice ranged from three weeks to twelve years; and the time spent on practising from half an hour to several hours a day. The only common element shared by these people of diverse age, profession and social background was the belief that, pursued with sufficient will-power and persistence, Yoga conferred siddhis, supernatural powers, on the practitioner. Only a few averred having actually exercised such powers at some stage; but all without exception believed that only slackness and incontinence were preventing them from attaining to that stage. This belief was also shared – though only reluctantly admitted – by the research workers concerned with the scientific investigation of Yoga phenomena.

In Patanjali's classic treatise, which consists of four chapters, most of the third[1] is devoted to these occult powers; they range from remembering past incarnations to prophecy, clairvoyance, levitation, entering into other bodies, the transmutation of elements, and omniscience. In the later Yoga literature, eight basic siddhis are mentioned[2]: (1) anima: to shrink to the size of an atom; (2) mahima: to expand in space; (3) laghima: lightness, levitation; (4) prapti: the power to reach anywhere, 'even to the moon'; (5) prakamya: omnipotence of will; (6) ishatwa: the power to create; (7) vashitwa: control over the self, and its immunity to outside influences; (8) kamayasayita: the suppression of all desires and bodily needs. The *Siva Samhita* adds to this list the power to become invisible, and to transport the body to any place at will.

In books on Yoga written by, or for Westerners, it is usually asserted that miracles are not the aim of Yogic training, but merely a by-product, and that every good guru would discourage his pupil from pursuing them. This would be in line with the attitude of Christian mystics who regarded such phenomena as acute embarrassments which are to be avoided. Thus St. Theresa of Avila says in her Life that the experience of being suddenly lifted into the air was 'a very sore distress to me'; she prayed to the Lord 'that He would be pleased to give me no more of those graces'; and when a nun surprised her suspended in the air and 'trembling all over', Theresa ordered her 'under obeisance to say nothing of what I had seen'.[3]

To prove that Hindu mysticism has the same attitude, a famous passage in *Patanjali* is usually quoted. In Professor Raghavan's translation, that passage is paraphrased as follows: 'Aphorism 37 says that these occult powers as such are really impediments to the attainment and completion of the state

---

[1] iii 16-50.
[2] The eight siddhis are not related to the 'eight steps' (pp. 74-75).
[3] Herbert Thurston, S. J., *The Physical Phenomena of Mysticism* (London, 1952, pp. 10 and 12).

of perfection'. In Ernest Wood's translation the passage reads: 'These powers of the spreading (or outgoing) mind are injurious to contemplation (samadhi)'. In an earlier translation[1] the warning is given in a conditional form: 'the [occult] powers hereinbefore described are liable to become obstacles in the way of perfect concentration, because of the possibility of wonder and pleasure flowing from their exercise, but are not obstacles for the ascetic who is perfect in the practice enjoined'. I am unable to decide which of the three versions is closer to the original – particularly as Wood refers to the aphorism as No. 36, Raghavan as No. 37, and Judge and Connelly as No. 38. But one fact stands out: that this aphorism is the *only* warning in the entire text; and it only refers to certain psychic powers mentioned in the preceding paragraphs, whereas the powers which are listed after the warning, such as entering into another's body, omnipotence and levitation, are held out as legitimate rewards to those who master the higher forms of contemplation. As for the later sources, the *Hatha Yoga Pradipika* and its companion texts, the eight siddhis are promised on practically every page in remuneration for the more difficult mudras. All disclaimers notwithstanding, the siddhis are an integral part of Yoga.

Conversations with Yoga practitioners, whether professionals or amateurs, followed more or less the same pattern. At the beginning, my informant would indignantly deny that he was after siddhis – such silly ideas were only spread by charlatans and mendicant fakirs. The sole purpose of Yoga was to acquire a healthy body and peace of mind for meditation. But once I had explained that I believed the evidence in favour of telepathy to be quite convincing, and had an open mind about related Indian phenomena, the atmosphere would change and reserve would fade.

There was, for instance, B., a young physicist of twenty-six, engaged in post-graduate research. He was a typical young Indian intellectual, earnest, sober and a little pedantic. I was

[1] *The Yoga Aphorisms of Patanjali,* An interpretation by William Q. Judge Assisted by James Henderson Connelly, The Theosophical Publishing Co., of New York, 1912, p. 52.

surprised to discover that he had practised Yoga for three years fairly intensely, and given it up 'for lack of will power'. He had not himself experienced any siddhis, though once or twice he thought he was just on the threshold; but he had seen at the age of nine, in his native village near Mysore, an itinerant Yogi levitate three to four feet above ground level, then slowly float down. At the age of twenty, he also saw another Yogi floating naked on a well of six feet by eight 'either in a crouching position or standing on his head'. I was rather impressed by his matter-of-fact manner of relating these events, until he produced a small tin statuette of Durga and explained in the same matter-of-fact voice that a certain miracle-working woman had made it materialize out of the air in the palm of his hand. I had read about the woman, who was a professional performer and did not even pretend to be more. I mentioned to the young scientist that his Durga could be bought for a rupee at any bazaar. He knew that, of course, and all he said was,'That has nothing to do with it; you have missed the point'.

Another encounter is perhaps best told in condensed form by quoting from my diary:

'Called for the remarkable V.N. at the College (where he lectures on philosophy), took him for lunch at the Taj. Tall, gaunt, dark, in dark European clothes, with dark-glowing eyes, and with rich, black fur growing upward from his earlobes, like a faun's; he actually uses a pocket-comb on them (the ears). At first reticent and "scientific"; then, on the long car journey to the hotel and during lunch he unbent. Aged thirty-three, unmarried ("it's easier that way"), has been practising for eleven or twelve years; changes diet, experimentally, every three months ("even Gandhi did that though he was only a Karma Yogi'). Has achieved various siddhis: e.g., he locked himself into a hermetically sealed room and by sheer will-power raised the temperature of the room by two to three degrees centigrade twice during one session ("but afterwards I was so exhausted, had to stay in bed for 2–3 weeks"). Repeatedly, when in deep trance, a snake appeared and moved through the room ("it was *not* a hallucination"). Once he stopped a monkey eating nuts next door by a mental command. One day, standing in front of his guru's house, he saw three stark naked tribesmen appear from nowhere at the door, talk to the guru and vanish again unexpectedly ("they had come to invite my guru to their 'club' "). In Europe I would have thought him a schizo, but here it's all in a day's work . . .'

This kind of story is indeed typical, and not merely of Yoga practitioners. India has never severed its ties with the magic world. The editorial columns of the great Indian dailies bear the imprint of the twentieth century, but the back of the page, except for the Linotype, could have been printed in the sixteenth. There, in the marriage advertisements, parents specify their sons' and daughters' religion, caste, colour, height, education, and 'powerful' or 'excellent' mahamsa. One or the other specification might be missing, but never the mahamsa, the horoscope. It is a decisive factor in the choice not only of the candidate, but also of the auspicious day and hour for consummating the marriage. In half a million villages, where eighty per cent of the population lives, every important activity and decision is still regulated by consulting the stars.

The reason is, simply, that although India is going through an Industrial Revolution of sorts, it has never gone through a Scientific Revolution of the kind which changed the structure of European thought in the seventeenth century, supplanting magical causation by physical causation. Before that turning point, Europe was almost as deeply immersed in astrology and other forms of magic thought as India still is. But in Europe, that transformation of thought preceded the transformation of society; in India it is the other way round. Underneath the power dams and steel works of the Second Five Year plan lies the ancient soil; one only has to scratch it and the black magic comes oozing out with its slightly rancid smell.

Levitation

I had to digress for a moment to explain how difficult it is, under these circumstances, to obtain any reliable evidence for or against the occurrence of the para-normal phenomena described in Yogic literature. Even otherwise shrewd European witnesses who have lived steeped in this atmosphere for some time cannot be relied on. Thus Ernest Wood writes in his Penguin book on Yoga: 'Levitation, or the rising of the body from the ground and its suspension a few feet up in the air above the seat or couch, is a universally accepted fact in India. I remember one occasion when an old yogi was levitated in a recumbent posture about six feet above the ground in an open field, for about half an hour, while the visitors were permitted to pass sticks to and fro in the space between'.[1]

One would expect a serious scholar to quote immediately the exact date and location of such an extraordinary event, accompanied by the testimonials of all the witnesses he could lay hands on. But all we get here by way of evidence are the words, 'I remember one occasion' – and this, alas, is typical of most writers on the subject. Equally characteristic is the fact that the only other piece of evidence which Wood adduces for the occurrence of levitation is a quotation from Fosco Maraini's charming book *Secret Tibet,* where the author tells us, that the Maharajah of Sikkim's daughter told him, that when she was a little girl her uncle 'did what you would call exercises in levitation. I used to take him a little rice. He would be motionless in mid-air. Every day he rose a little higher . . . There are certain things you don't forget'.

I am not arguing for or against the possibility of levitation, only about the quality of the evidence. Ernest Wood is right when he says that levitation is 'universally accepted as a fact' in India. Moreover, it is considered as one of the easier siddhis, generally attained by way of khecari mudra. Alain Danielou, for instance, another European convert who is held in high esteem as a student of mysticism in India, writes: 'This is considered to be fairly easy to do and is used for the

[1] *Op. cit.,* p. 104.

frequently performed act of levitation'.[1] But again no chapter, no verse.

One may argue that a popular belief which has survived for centuries must contain some truth, but this is not always the case; witches riding on broomsticks may be archetypal symbols, they are not racial memories. Two facts, I believe, ought to be taken into consideration. Firstly, most alleged eye-witness reports, whether first-, second-, or third-hand, seem to conform to a certain pattern. The witness always dates his or her experience 'when I was a small child', usually between the age of five and nine. Apart from my young physicist, I met two Indians (one a psychiatrist, the other a farmer) who also stated that they had seen levitation – both as children and both in a crowd on a village square. I know of no first-hand report (except Professor Wood's undated statement) in which the witness was an adult. In view of the impressionable nature of that age, even more pronounced in Indian children, the possibility of confusion between listening to a vividly visualized story and believing later to have actually experienced it, would be one possible explanation for its remarkable persistence.

Secondly, it seems to me odd that among the experimental work which has been done at various Yoga research institutes, no experiments on levitation were published or mentioned to me. Some of the experiments (to be presently described) require costly and complicated instruments. It would be a simple procedure to let the subject perform the appropriate mudras on his mat placed on the platform of a weighing machine, and see whether his body got any lighter. He would not have to levitate actually the loss of a few pounds would be decisive proof of the power of mind over gravity. At one research institute, where I made this obvious suggestion, I had the impression that it had been tried with negative results. But that is neither here nor there, and if the hoary subject of levitation is to be tackled seriously, some procedure on these lines would have to be patiently tried on any likely

[1] Quoted by K. Ratnam, 'Planning for Scientific Yoga,' *The Illustrated Weekly of India*, 28 December 1958.

subject; whatever the number of failures, a single positive result under suitable controls would mean a revolution in our outlook on the world.

The Pit Experiments

In view of the handicaps I mentioned, it is encouraging to know that serious experimental work is nevertheless being carried out. Foremost in this field are the All India Institute of Mental Health in Bangalore, and Swami Kuvalayananda's Research Centre at Lonavla.

If I was sceptical about the medical work carried out at the Swami's Health Centre on the Marine Drive in Bombay, this attitude does not apply to his research work. Lonavla lies on a high plateau in the Sahia mountains near Poonah, in a peaceful, rather Grecian landscape, blessed by a constant sea breeze. The Institute owns some fifty acres of land, which stretch over two hills, and include the Swami's private ashram. Its laboratory equipment is excellent, including a lie detector, breath analyser, X-ray department, electro-encephalograph, and so on. There is a spacious library, and a literary department where five scholars are engaged in preparing a ten-volume Yoga Encyclopaedia.

I was introduced to the present experimental subject – a middle-aged man of medium height and athletic build, with gentle manners and those curiously fierce eyes which I have come to associate with practising Yogis. He had been an itinerant showman at country fairs, until the Swami, in his search for likely subjects, discovered him and made him into his guinea-pig. He now regards the Swami with the white corkscrew tresses as his guru. While we walked through the various laboratories, he trotted behind the Swami like a faithful dog, listening to every word with utmost devotion. 'Whatever strength I have,' he explained to me, 'comes from Swamiji.' The inspection completed, the Swami told him to give a demonstration. The Yogi disappeared delightedly, and came back a minute later, wearing a gaudy dressing-gown of the kind in which circus artistes enter the ring, and a chain of medals round his neck. Discarding the robe, he was seen to be wearing trunks of tiger-skin, and a collection of wrist-bangles; he looked superb, his black eyes now all aglow. He began with the classic exercises, such as uddiyama – drawing in the abdominal muscles, while forcing the viscerae and diaphragm upwards, until a large, hollow cavity appears under the ribs, a kind of incredible grotto in the flesh, and the *obliqui abdomini*, the two transversal muscles, stick out in a rather horrifying manner as on anatomical figures stripped of skin. Then came nauli, the isolation and separate manipulation of the abdominal straight muscles, making them bulge out in a whorl at the navel, and subsequently rolling them to the right and to the left as if a rolling pin were moving under the skin – while the remaining areas of the abdomen seem to be emptied of content, and the navel is sucked in to within a few inches of the spine. It was fascinating and faintly nauseating to watch, and so were the various headstands, with arms and limbs threaded through each other and tangled like a complicated mariner's knot. The Yogi then demonstrated the extraordinary power of his chest muscles – the result of pranayama – by winding a sturdy steel wire round his torso (cushioned by a leather belt), tightening the wire with a tourniquet, and then snapping it with a single inhalation. Next, he wound a three-eighth inch gauge iron-chain round his chest, and put his naked foot inside the chain and slowly broke it (I have kept both the wire and the chain; they are structurally faultless). It was as good a strong-man act as one can see in a first-rate variety show, but the last one was something more special: the Yogi took a fresh palm-leaf, folded it twice, and, using his index and middle finger like a pair of scissors, cut the leaf neatly into two. His fingers felt hard and bony, but there was no callosity on them. His explanation was 'that he concentrated all his life-forces between the two fingers.'

These were remarkable achievements of muscle control, including the involuntary muscles. I must mention in this context a report given to me by an eminent Bombay psychiatrist who had watched, and photographed, a Yogi showman attaching with a string a twenty-pound weight to the tip of his penis, and lifting it by producing an erection in front of the audience. The photographs show the usual tall and emaciated individual, smeared with ashes, matted hair and a wild stare; the doctor told me that the man had been under the influence of drugs, and had admitted to him that drugs had been an essential part of the training by his guru. Bhang, the hashish-like substance distilled from *Cannabis indica*, plays an important part in Hatha Yoga. Dr. Bernard, for instance, was given bhang by his guru before his final initiation.

All this, however, has nothing to do with the siddhis. Of these only one had been thoroughly investigated at Lonavla: the classic Yogic experiment of being buried alive in a pit. They showed me their experimental pit: it was approximately six feet by three feet by three feet, its bottom about six feet down under ground level. It was closed by a tight-fitting concrete lid, and this was then covered by three feet of earth. I shall not go into the details of the experiment because, as the Swami frankly told me, it had proved abortive. Though the pit seemed sufficiently air-tight to make any human being die of suffocation after a few minutes, and would certainly have convinced any village audience that it was so, it transpired that everybody had vastly underestimated the porosity of the surrounding earth. They discovered this when, after a series of experiments, they tried to pump the air out of the pit, yet the pressure inside only fell by 0.5. During the experiment itself, they had only measured the relative oxygen and carbondioxide content inside the pit; the leakage of fresh oxygen into the pit became apparent when they had the idea of pumping it out entirely.

The thoroughness of the experiment, and the frank admission of its failure, were entirely to the Swami's credit. Though he himself evidently believed in siddhis, he was equally candid in admitting that all his experiments in this direction had given negative results. It seems that the only significant finding they had produced so far was that the EEG curves[1] of subjects in trance remained normal, whereas the

[1] The electroencephalogram records the intensity and rhythm of electrical activities in the brain.

psycho-galvanic reflex remained consistently below normal.[1]

The pit experiment was also carried out at the Institute of Mental Health at Bangalore by a team of five research workers, including one European. I had an opportunity to talk to three of them, to inspect the pit and later on to read a paper which they had jointly published.[2]

The dimensions of this pit were four feet by three feet by two and a half feet, which makes a volume of approximately one cubic yard. Its bottom was covered with a rubber sheet, and its lid was a one-inch wooden plank covered with six inches of earth. The subject was buried in the pit on three different occasions, for two hours, for nine hours and for eight and a half hours respectively. The instruments in the pit conveyed information on electrical activity in the brain and heart, on the temperature, humidity and chemical composition of the air in the pit, and made mechanical recordings of breathing motions of the chest (with spirometers). The subject, a Yogi by name of Shri Krishna Iyengar, was dressed in a loin-cloth only. He lay down on the floor of the pit with the various instruments and electrodes attached to him, lit an incense stick, and went into samadhi. Then he was buried for the periods indicated, varying between two and nine hours. The interval between the first and second experiment was one month, between the second and third, a fortnight. The results of the experiment were as follows:

The electrical records of brain activity remained the same inside the pit as those taken under normal conditions outside. They indicate that the subject was both alert and relaxed, but not asleep. The conclusion is that he was either not in samadhi, or that samadhi does not affect the electrical activity of the brain.

The most interesting results concern breathing. Unfortunately, as the report says, in this case, too 'the possibility of

[1] The psycho-galvanic reflex (used in lie detectors) reflects changes in the electrical properties of the body surface in response to emotional stimuli. These changes, like sweating, goose-flesh, or 'bristling,' are controlled by the sympathetic nervous system, and thus indicate emotive reactions.
[2] *Some Experiments on a 'Yogi' in Controlled States*, by H. V. Gundu Rao, N. Krishnaswamy, R. L. Narasimhaiya, J. Hoenig, and M. V. Govindaswamy, *Journal of the All India Institute of Mental Health*, Bangalore, July 1958, p. 99.

leakage of gases through the porous walls of the pit, dug in raw earth, has not been investigated. This is a serious source of error.' But even so, one significant fact emerged. The heart-beat remained steady throughout, and showed a regular pattern with slow variations between 40 and 100 beats per minute, which is within normal limits. Breathing, however, slowed down from the normal rate of about 16 per minute. to a slow rate of about 1 breath per minute, and sometimes even to a rate of 1 respiration in two minutes. This was apparently compensated for by doubling the amount of ventilation (of the volume of air passed through the lungs) from 0·5 litre to 1 litre.[1] Even so, the basic metabolic rate had been considerably lowered. Thus the results indicate a kind of slow-pedalling of the organism, shown by the lowering of the rate of oxygen exchange. This is a remarkable but by no means a supernatural achievement, and does not bear out the claim that Yogis buried in the pit survive without breathing at all.

Stopping the Heart

Related to this is another claim, that Yogis can stop their heart-beats at will. This claim was thoroughly investigated at the Andhra Medical College at Visakhapatnam. The subject was a Yogi called Ramananda – a very advanced prac-titioner; he had not only mastered khecari mudra by severance of the tendon of the tongue, but had his tongue surgically split lengthwise into two, because previously he could only cover the opening of one nostril at a time.

The experiment was carried out in 1957, when Ramananda was thirty-four, and had practised Hatha Yoga for sixteen years. He demonstrated with ease all the advanced routines, including the aspiration of fluids through colon and urethra, and the ejection of liquids from the stomach through mouth or nose at will. He had spent various periods buried in

[1] The amount of ventilation could not be directly measured; it was com-puted from measurements of the carbondioxide content in the pit at the beginning and end of the period of burial. At the beginning it had been 0.04 per cent; at the end of the two-hour period 1.34 per cent; at the end of the nine-hour period 3.8 per cent.

a pit, and claimed that the longest period had been twenty-eight days; but, the report[1] says 'this has not been investigated'.

The point of the experiment was the voluntary suspension of heart-beat and pulse. The results showed that Ramananda was capable of reducing both to a considerable extent for a period of 20-30 seconds. During this time the pulse could not be felt at all by the usual method of placing a finger on the artery; but the sphygmograph (a mechanical apparatus for measuring blood pressure) continued to record feeble pulse waves of an irregular and attenuated nature. The weakening of the pulse was produced by two independent methods: firstly, by contraction of the biceps, pectoralis and other muscles, thus mechanically compressing the brachial artery; secondly, by diminishing the flow through holding of the breath. Both can be learnt by any normal person; comparison of the sphygmographic records of Ramananda with those of an ordinary subject during suspended breathing, show only a slight difference, explained by training.

Examination of the heart's activity during the period of suspension yielded more impressive results. By the normal method of auscultation, the heart-beats could not be heard; on the tape record they were 'sometimes faint and sometimes inaudible'. The EEG record showed completely normal electrical activity of the heart throughout the experiment; on the other hand, the fluoroscope showed, according to the radiologist's report, the following: 'After he inhaled slightly and stopped breathing the cardiac pulsation was found to be arrested except for a slight flicker along the left border below the pulmonary conus and in the apical segment of the left ventricle. There was no pulsation in any other segment. This status was maintained for about 30 seconds. After he commenced respiration, normal cardiac pulsation was observed.'

Thus Ramananda had demonstrated beyond doubt his

[1] *A Preliminary Scientific Investigation into some of the Unusual Physiological Manifestations Acquired as a Result of Yogic Practices in India*, by G. V. Satyanarayanamurthi, M.D., and P. Brahmayya Sastry, M.B.B.S., M.Sc., Ph.D. *Wiener Zeitschrift für Nervenheilkunde und die Grenzgebiete*, 15, 1958, pp. 239-49.

ability to diminish the activity of his heart through voluntary effort, using a certain breathing technique. However, most normal people can affect the function of their hearts, though to a less dramatic extent, by holding their breath and 'willing' the heart to beat more quietly. In clinical jargon this is called 'Valsalva manœuvring'.[1] The degree of voluntary control of the heart varies, of course, according to the individual; but at least one case of an even more dramatic nature than Ramananda's achievement has been reliably reported in America. The report, by Dr. Charles M. McClure, was published in *California Medicine*, the official Journal of the California Medical Association.[2]

It describes the case of a forty-four-year-old aircraft mechanic of Danish descent, Vernon W. Hansen, who had acquired the ability to slow down his heart-beat and to stop it completely at will – including its electrical activity – for five seconds. Hansen, at the age of seven, had suffered from rheumatic fever, and had overheard the family doctor saying that he would not live to be twenty. The illness left him with a slight heart condition, and with the constant fear that his heart might stop beating while he was asleep. To prevent this, he learnt to exercise voluntary control over its functions: 'By sitting quietly, relaxing completely and "allowing everything to stop", he could induce progressive slowing of the pulse until cessation of heart action would occur, then a feeling of impending loss of consciousness. After a few seconds of this sensation, he would take a deep breath and normal heart action would resume.' During the cardiac arrest, 'his colour would become the ashen grey of sudden circulatory failure'. The electrocardiogram, reproduced in the report, shows with uncontroversial clarity the process of slowing down, and the complete stoppage of five seconds. The process was 'induced through some mechanism which, although under voluntary control, is not known to the patient himself. Careful observation did not reveal any breath-holding or Valsalva manœuvre

---

[1] The sinuses of Valsalva are bulges in the aortic walls; these interact with the valves that regulate the flow through the pulmonary and coronary arteries.

[2] Vol. 90, No. 6, June 1959.

in connexion with the cessation of heart-beat.' So he did not even have to resort to pranayama. Aircraftsman Hansen has certainly beaten all Yogic records.

Dr. McClure had known him for five years. Hansen could produce the phenomenon at any time, without any effort. How he did it, he did not know himself, as the report says. Apparently the damage caused by the rheumatic fever and his constant worry were instrumental in enabling him to concentrate his attention on that critically sensitivised focus in his body, and to increase the normal degree of control over it to an abnormal extent. His case is a further illustration of the fact that there is no hard and fast boundary between the 'voluntary' and 'involuntary' functions of the body; and that the degree of control exercised over the latter is a question of training in focusing attention.

Concerning other siddhis, I have seen neither the rope trick nor the mango-tree wonder, and could find no reliable person who has seen either of them. 'Fire-walking' as an ordeal, or a magic stunt, is as old as civilization, and not confined to India. It depends, of course, on the type of combustible used, the duration of contact and other technical points which have not been experimentally investigated by any of the Yoga research institutes.

A final remark about walking or floating on water, which does belong to the traditional category of Yoga siddhis. I have mentioned that my young physicist, who asserted that as a child he had seen a Yogi levitate, had also seen, at the age of twenty, another Yogi floating on a well 'either in a crouching position or standing on his head'. In contrast to the levitation memory, which was hazy, the well memory was quite precise – except on the crucial question of the exact posture in which the Yogi was floating. Like most Indians, the young man could not swim, and to float on water in any posture seemed to him a miraculous achievement in itself. Now, to float 'upside down', while turning a somersault in the water, or by keeping the trunk immersed as long as one's breath will hold, is a trivial matter for anybody who can swim; and the acrobatically pliant body, plus the breath-holding technique of a trained Yogi could doubtless carry it to spectacular lengths. As for the 'crouching posture', the young man was positive that the Yogi kept his legs folded, but whether his body was upright, or lying flat on the water he could not say; after reflection, he thought the latter more likely 'because his eyes were fixed on the sky'. To float on one's back, whether with legs outstretched or folded, is again a miracle to non-swimmers only, whose aquatic experience, like that of the majority of pious Hindus, is confined to a ritual sprinkle and dip, eyes closed and fingers clamped over the nostrils, in a temple tank or river.

My suspicion that the floating Yogis were practising a simple leg-pull on a naïve audience was amusingly confirmed when, a little while later, I read an account of it in the *International Journal of the Science of Yoga*,[1] published by the Santa Cruz Institute. The author of the article relates how Shri Yogendra had searched for several months for a famous guru, hidden in the Kashmir mountains, until he finally tracked him down. That guru 'was gifted with the power of floating on water through mastery over plavini pranayana, and demonstrated the same before Shri Yogendra left him'. On the next page there is a photograph of a man, comfortably floating on his back in shallow water, with arms folded behind his head. The photograph bears the caption: 'Mastery over the plavini process of Yoga breathing enables the student to float on water as illustrated in this photo. The posture assumed is the traditional Fish-pose.'

I then looked up plavini pranayana. It consists in 'suspending the breath outside the lungs' – that is, swallowing quantities of air – 'while focusing the mind on the space between the eyebrows until it swoons'.[2] Dr. Bernard expressly warns: 'the beginner is advised not to work on this practice'. As a reward for this effort, the *Hatha Yoga Pradipika* holds out this promise: 'when the belly is filled with air freely circulating within the body, the body easily floats, even in

[1] April-September 1936.
[2] Bernard, *op. cit.*, p. 54.

the deepest water, like the leaf of a lotus'.[1] It could be had in a simpler way.

To sum up: the demonstrable phenomena produced by Hatha Yoga are neither more nor less miraculous than the blisters and stigmata, the anaesthesias, catatonias and hallucinations produced under hypnosis or in hysterical states. Hatha Yoga is a specific method of inducing such phenomena, mainly relying on techniques of self-hypnosis through respiratory, circulatory and other visceral manœuvres, repetitive invocations, and hashish-type drugs. Its impressiveness to the Western observer rests on the systematization of the techniques for producing such phenomena, and on the mystic value set on them. The former enables it to demonstrate the power of mind over the autonomous functions of the body more forcibly than any Western school, but at the price of far-fetched, devious and debasing techniques. This leaves the question of mystic value as the last and most important aspect of Yoga to be discussed.

The Mystic Aspect

The ultimate aim of Yoga is samadhi, the mystic union. 'As salt being dissolved in water becomes one with it, so when atma and mind become one, it is called samhadi'.[2] Yet the word seems to have different meanings in different contexts. The *Gheranda Samhita* gives six kinds of samadhis, attained by six different methods.[3] Some translators render it as 'meditation' or 'contemplation' or 'absorption'; others as 'trance' or 'ecstatic bliss'; still others as 'super-consciousness' – or 'deep, dreamless sleep'.

In spite of this, there is a large area of agreement between the various sources on certain basic features of samadhi. These are, from the *physiological* point of view, a lowering of all basic functions: heart-beat, pulse, breathing, nutrition – a kind of hibernation of the body. *Mentally*, samadhi is said to consist of 'pure' consciousness, that is, consciousness without object or content other than consciousness itself. Thus

[1] *Hatha Yoga Pradipika*, ii, 70.
[2] *Hatha Yoga Pradipika*, op. cit., iv, 5.
[3] *Gheranda Samhita*, op. cit., vii, 12.

turned upon itself, pure consciousness penetrates into the Real Self, the atma, which is behind and beyond the sentient ego. The ego is a transient phenomenon, the atma is unalterable, transcending the phenomenal world, part and parcel of Brahma, the Universal Spirit, which it contains and in which it is contained. Lastly, from the *emotional* point of view, samadhi is a state of bliss, its onset signalled by a shapeless radiance which blots out everything else.

Samadhi may last a few minutes, hours or days. But there is also 'final samadhi' into which a holy man enters at will; it entails death of the body and of the body-bound ego, whereas the Real Self, liberated from the wheel of rebirth, remains permanently united with the universal spirit. Except in final samadhi, the mind returns each time into the sentient ego, without retaining any positive memory of the Union which it has experienced.

The Real Self has thus nothing to do with the Unconscious in the Freudian sense or with Jung's Collective Unconscious. For the unconscious, as we understand it, manifests itself above all in the dream, whereas in Hindu philosophy, dreaming is a function of the ego, not of the Real Self. Only in 'deep sleep', which is by definition dreamless, can the Real Self be approached.

Is samadhi, then, to be identified with 'deep sleep'? And if so, how can it also be called a 'super-conscious' or 'contemplative' state? Is it not, rather, a state of comatose 'sub-' or 'un-'consciousness? The answer is that Indian philosophy either does not regard these terms as contradictory, or is indifferent to the contradiction between them. Brahma is the fullness and the void, everything and nothing, aloneness and all-oneness at the same time, at no time. A state of mind, which is withdrawn from all objects of consciousness, voided of any content, contemplating nothing, would be called in Western psychology a state of un- or non-consciousness. The Eastern philosopher would have no quarrel with this description, but he would remark that 'pure consciousness' is there nevertheless. The dialogue would then continue on more or less the following lines:

Q: When you speak of 'pure consciousness', you mean consciousness *of what?*

A: Of consciousness itself, and of nothing else.

Q: But *who* is conscious of being conscious: the person who entered samadhi?

A: No, in samadhi the self no longer exists. It is his ego-less Real Self being conscious of the Real Self.

Q: Then if the person's ordinary self has ceased to exist, that person can no longer be conscious, and you must agree that he has entered a state of un- or non-consciousness.

A: That is correct. He has entered the state of super-consciousness which we also call 'samadhi' or 'contemplation' or 'being one with reality'.

And so the merry-go-round would continue.

The equation of samadhi with 'deep sleep' begins with the Upanishads and can be followed all the way down, to the writings of modern mystics like Krishna Menon – although some contemporary Hindu academics have tried to explain it away. Since the point is of some importance in dispelling Western misconceptions about Indian philosophy and Indian mysticism, I shall quote a few characteristic passages from the major Upanishads.

Prasna Upanishad
'Question IV

Then Sauryayanin Garga asked him: "Worthy Sire! In a man, who are they [the faculties] that sleep, who that are awake, which is that perceiving power that sees the dream. To whom does the happiness which they enjoy belong? In whom is everything established?"

Pippalada replied: "Gargya! Just as the rays of the setting Sun are, all of them, gathered up in that orb of light and they issue forth again when he rises again, even so is all that gathered up in the mind that perceives every-thing; hence it is that the individual does not hear, see, smell, taste, touch, speak, take, enjoy, discharge or move, and they say, he sleeps. The fires of the vital breaths alone are awake in this body . . . Here, this perceiving mind

enjoys its greatness in dream. [But] when mind is dominated by the inner light, it dreams no dream; there in
this body, the happiness of deep sleep ensues. Just as, my
dear, birds retire into their nests, even so everything is
absorbed into the Supreme Self . . ." '[1]

Mandukya Upanishad

This basic text begins with a discussion of the incantation
Om which signifies the Real Self; it continues:

'This Self is Brahman; and this Self is of four grades . . .
The waking state with knowledge of external objects is the
first grade . . . The dream state perceiving within oneself
an enjoyment devoid of gross objects is the second grade.
That is deep sleep where the sleeping one does not fancy
any desire and sees no dream – a state of deep sleep, unified, one mass of pure knowledge, enjoying only bliss – this
is the third degree . . . Perceiving neither internally nor
externally, neither knowing nor non-knowing; the imper-
ceptible, indescribable, unnamable, of the sole form of the
consciousness of the one Self, the negation of the phenomenal world, the Peaceful, the Happy, the One without a
second, this they consider is the fourth grade; that is the
Self, that is the thing to be realized.[2]

Chandogya Upanishad

'VI. viii. 1-7. Uddalaka Aruni˙told his son Svetaketu:
"Know from me, my dear son, of the state of sleep. When
a man is said to sleep, he becomes united, my dear, with
Reality; he attains (apiti) to his own real Self (Svam);
hence they say that he is sleeping (svamapiti): he has really
been re-united with his own self . . ."[:]

'VIII. i. 4. Now this serenity (in deep sleep) which arises
above this physical state, reaches the Light Supreme,
attains its own innate form; this is the Self; that is the
immortal and fearless; this the Brahman . . .'[4]

---

[1] Tr. Raghavan, *op. cit.*, pp. 63-4.
[2] *Ibid*, p. 71 f.
[3] *Ibid*, p. 84.
[4] *Ibid*, p. 92.

'VII. xi. "Where one sleeps deeply, in full serenity, and dreamless, that is the Self; It is immortal and fearless; It is the Brahman . . ." [1]

Brihadaranyaka Upanishad

'14-20 . . . Ajatasatru took Gargya by the hand; they came to a sleeping man; him Ajatasatru called by name; "O mighty one in white dress, Soma, King!" . . . Ajatasatru asked: "When this man was asleep . . . where had he gone? From where did he come back now?" Gargya knew this not. Ajatasatru: "When he . . . was asleep, he gathered the knowledge of the senses through their faculties and slept in the ether that is within the heart; when he draws (into himself) all those faculties, then the person sleeps; then the sense of smell is withdrawn, speech is withdrawn, the eye is withdrawn, the ear is withdrawn, the mind is withdrawn. When he moves about in dream, all those worlds are his, he becomes a mighty king or an eminent Brahman or rises high and falls low; just as a great king, collecting his forces, moves about in his country as he pleases, even so this person gathers the senses and moves about as he pleases in his body. But when he is in deep sleep, he is not aware of anything; there are seventy-two thousand veins which issue from the heart all over the body; returning through them he stays in the body; just as a boy, a great king, or an eminent Brahman, having attained exceeding happiness, lies down, even so he sleeps . . . This is the secret description of it that takes one to it; the Truth of the Truth; the faculties are the truth; of them, he is the Truth." [2]

'IV iii. 2-7.". . .Falling asleep, he transcends this world and all forms of death, i.e., mundane activities . . . 9. . . . In that state the person is self-illumined . . . 21. That state of deep sleep is the form of Self in which there is no desire, no taint of virtue and of vice, no fear; just as one, embraced by his beloved one, is oblivious to anything, outside or inside, even so this person in the embrace of the Self . . . is uncon-

[1] *Ibid*, p. 94.
[2] *Ibid*, pp. 100-1.

scious of anything, outside or inside; that is his form in which all desires have been realized, in which the Self alone constitutes the desire, in which there is no desire or sorrow . . ."[1]

Lastly, Krishna Menon:

'In the deep-sleep state shines that principle to which the word "I" points. There the mind has dissolved and cannot therefore perceive it. When the mind is directed to it, it changes into that, losing the characteristics of mind. This is called samadhi.[2]

If all this sounds like a hymn to Tanatos – that I believe is indeed its deepest meaning. The dreamless, trance-sleep of samadhi is a homage to Tanatos: an exercise in death while preparing for the 'final samadhi' in which it is consumed.

Sleep cannot normally be produced by an act of will, and dreamless sleep even less. The distinguishing mark of samadhi is that it can be so produced. And since the first and last aim of Yoga, from its Vedic origins to this day, has always been the mystic union of samadhi, we are now in a better position to understand the ultimate meaning behind its apparently perverse techniques. It is a systematic conditioning of the body to conniving in its own destruction, at the command of the will, by a series of graduated stages – from the suspension of the vital breath, through the temporary suspension of consciousness, to the ultimate step.

This connivance of the body can only be obtained by gaining mastery over all its functions – and in the first place over the involuntary functions governed by the vegetative nervous system. All bodily reflexes devoted to survival must be wrenched from the service of Eros, and pressed into the service of Tanatos. If the function of an organ can be reversed, this will be done, whatever the effort. Thus the lower openings of the body, designed for elimination, must be trained

[1] *Ibid*, p. 112.
[2] *Atma-Nirviti, op. cit.*, p. 18.

for intake. The openings designed for intake must be blocked, locked, sealed to the world. If this cannot be done completely, the functions will at least be partially suspended: breath, heart-pulse, pulse. The eyeballs are turned inward and upward in a violent squint so that only the blind white substance is directed at the world.

The Yogi's attitude to the various organs of his body may be compared to that of an experienced officer, training his unit for a dangerous, and indeed suicidal mission. To obtain absolute obedience, the unit must be kept in a fit condition; order, efficiency, cleanliness, must be carried to perfection; to keep up morale, it must be treated sternly but with understanding. In other words, the body must be at the peak of its form to become capable of annihilating itself, partially or totally, at the will's command. That is why the serpent life-force, curled round the base of the spine, must be first awakened, then forced upward, towards the Centre of Command between the eyebrows – and from there into the embrace of Shiva, the Destroyer.

The Christian ascetic mortifies his body to hasten its return to dust. He proceeds by a direct way; the Yogi's life is spent on a prodigious detour. He must build up his body into a super-efficient, super-sentient instrument of self-annihilation. That act of annihilation is samadhi. Beyond it there is no Heavenly Father, no smiling Virgin or loving Bridegroom waiting. Only the Real Self is waiting, whose attributes are all negative – 'without shape, without horizon, without end'; who is indicated by 'neti, neti' – 'not this, not this'; the ultimate Void – compressed in the reverberations of the single syllable *Om̐*.

No wonder that the naked rocks of this terrifying ascent are overgrown with weeds – the miraculous siddhis. For does not he who has achieved mastery over death acquire miraculous powers? Having realized that the world of the senses is illusion, should he not be able to prove that space, time and gravity are also illusions?

As the centuries went by, the weeds multiplied on the once-naked rock, and the postures of the climbers assumed more and more grotesque contortions. They reflected the perennial tragedy of the human condition – that the means become an end in themselves.

Pantanjali's *Yoga Sutras* date, within a century or two, from the same period as Aristotle's *Logic*. The *Hatha Yoga Pradipika* and its companion treatises coincide, within the same generous limits, with the works of the Aristotelian Schoolmen. Both were sterile and pedantic derivations from a great and original adventure of the human mind. But while the Schoolmen confined themselves to verbal logic-chopping, the Swamis did it with their bowels; and while scholasticism is a distant memory, Yoga is not. One is reminded of Erasmus' epigram on the Schoolmen: 'They are looking in utter darkness for that which has no existence whatever' – but then, the Indian mystic would accept this as a statement of fact, without any derogatory intent, and a worthy programme to be pursued.

Among Westerners who have tried to enter the spirit of Yoga the hard way, Dr. Bernard was probably the most persistent, modest and sincere. He wrote his last work on Hatha Yoga after many years of devoted practice, and in the index to that short book there are two moving headings:

Miracles, none transpired.

Supernatural, not revealed.

The Pressure of the Past

I

The Perils of Sex

PSYCHOTHERAPY is still a novelty in India; its practitioners are few, and they are making but slow headway against the competition of astrologers, swamis, Ayurvedists, hakims and wonder-workers of every conceivable kind.

The dominant trend is an unorthodox and eclectic combination of Freud and Adler. Freud, as one of them explained, 'provides the answers to the Indian's daily agonized reappraisal of his sexual and digestive functions; and Adler provides the label for his cherished inferiority complex'.

Jung, surprisingly, has no following, and his books are hardly read either by the profession or by the educated public. He is disliked on the grounds that he misrepresented Indian philosophy and religion, and 'understood nothing of India'. The motive behind this is a kind of mythological parochialism: Europeans are welcome to talk about King Oedipus, but the Hindu Pantheon they should leave alone.

My hope in seeking out Indian psychiatrists was to catch some glimpses into the Indian mind on its less obvious levels; more particularly, into ways of reacting to the breakdown of social traditions and religious beliefs.

The majority of my informants denied that there was any significant difference in the basic psychic make-up of Westerners and Indians. The apparent differences, they maintained, were on the surface; in the realm of the unconscious all men were equal, regardless of race, creed, religious tradition. A compulsion neurosis or a depressive psychosis followed broadly the same course, and produced the same symptoms in India as in Europe or America. I should mention here that the majority of Japanese psychiatrists took just the opposite line: the structure of the Japanese Id was, they said, a thing apart, which no Westerner could understand.

I shall not try to decide which group is right, and whether the unconscious mind is essentially the same throughout the human race, or not. But the type of conflict to which it is exposed, and the symptoms by which it most commonly reacts, are certainly characteristic not only of the individual but of the culture in which he lives; and this became at once evident when concrete problems were discussed. Thus the most typical complaint of patients in psychiatric clinics and Yogic health centres alike turned out to be a highly unusual one by Western standards: male spermatorrhoea – seminal loss through nocturnal pollutions or pathological discharges. It may be real or imagined, and is usually accompanied by complaints about lack of concentration, weakening of memory and general physical debility. Among Carstairs's informants in a typical village in Rajasthan, out of forty-five patients, thirty-one believed that they suffered from spermatorrhoea 'or else described special measures which they adopted to counteract it'.[1] A similar picture emerged, though without precise statistics, from my talks wth psychiatrists and medical practitioners, with an educated, middle-class clientele in the large towns. In a standard list of drugs of ayurvedic therapy, out of a total of thirty-nine proprietary medicines advertised, fourteen were cures for spermatorrhoea. One thus gets the impression that a considerable number of Hindu males suffer from what one might call spermal anxiety.

The cause of this is evidently the traditional belief, which I mentioned before, in the vital fluid as a kind of attar distilled from the blood, every loss of which, even for the legitimate purpose of procreation, is an impoverishment of body and spirit. Hence the extreme value set on continence – brahmacharya. Gandhi, who had such a decisive influence on the nation's mind, was an ardent, almost fanatical propagandist of brahmacharya on both physical and religious grounds. He denied that sex, apart from its procreative function, was a

[1] G. Morris Carstairs. *The Twice-Born*, London, 1957, p. 85.

human necessity; and since India was already overcrowded, total continence – a kind of civil non-cooperation between the sexes – would not only be a social boon, but also benefit the people's health: 'Ability to retain and assimilate the vital liquid is a matter of long training. When properly conserved it is transmuted into matchless energy and strength.'[1]

When Gandhi took the vow of continence, he realized that 'control of the palate is the first essential in the observance of the vow'.[1] Experimenting with various diets remained one of his lifelong preoccupations: 'I saw that the brahmachari's food should be limited, simple, spiceless and, if possible, uncooked . . . Six years of experiment have showed me that the brahmachari's ideal food is fresh fruit and nuts.' Even milk is dangerous, as we saw: 'I have not the least doubt that milk diet makes the brahmacharya vow difficult to observe.' By the Mahatma's standards, Mr. Milktoast was a wolf.

Gandhi was an extreme case; but the Hindu preoccupation with diet, the necessity to restrict it to 'cool' foods which nourish the vital fluid without arousing the passions, and to avoid 'hot', spicy food, which has the opposite effect, is nationwide. It has various causes, but sex is prominent among them.

The axiomatic belief that sex is both physically and spiritually debilitating must of course create open or unconscious resentment against woman, the temptress, who causes this deplorable expenditure of vital forces. It is reflected in the classic Hindu precept for the four stages, or seasons, of life: the Student living in continence; the Householder founding a family; the Detached Person who has stopped having sexual relations with his wife, though he still lives in the household; lastly, the Sanyasi, who has severed all social and family ties and become a wandering holy man. Thus three out of the four seasons stand in the sign of celibacy, and the second appears as merely a transitory station in the pilgrim's progress from one form of brahmacharya to the next.

The traditional form of marriage by arrangement, and the

[1] Gandhi, quoted by Louis Fischer, *The Life of Mahatma Gandhi*, London, 1951, p. 263.
[2] *Gandhi – An Autobiography – The Story of my Experiments with Truth*, London, 1949, p. 175.

absence of privacy in the joint household, prevent the
emergence of a genuine human relationship between husband
and wife – until middle-age, when the education of the children and other shared worries provide a belated and
unromantic tie. The young people meet as strangers, and for
a long time the shared bed, or mat, remains the only common
ground between them. During the day, they are hardly ever
alone and have practically no opportunity to talk to each
other, for such intimacy in the presence of the elders is considered offensive. Intellectual companionship, human understanding, shared interests, are absent to a degree which seems
almost inhuman to the European. When I mentioned this to
an Indian friend, he answered: 'What will you? Marriage is a
carnal and social arrangement.' By 'social' he meant the contract entered into by the two families. Even such exceptional
figures as Gandhi and Nehru discovered the capacity for understanding partnership in their wives only in their late years.
Gandhi writes in his autobiography: 'I have already said that
Kasturbai was illiterate. I was very anxious to teach her, but
lustful love left me no time. For one thing the teaching had to
be done against her will, and that, too, at night. I dared not
meet her in the presence of the elders, much less talk to her.'[1]

The Hindu Pantheon knows no Eros; his place is occupied
by Kama, the prime force of Desire. Sex is the only means by
which the young husband can assert himself in the eyes of his
stranger-bride, and the only token of affection that he can
offer her. At the same time, sex is a source of anxious worry, a
depletion of the vital forces of body and mind. As a result,
the Indian attitude to sex is perhaps more ambivalent and
paradoxical than any other nation's. On the one hand, the
rigid separation of the sexes, prudishness, praise of the
spiritual and physical value of continence, fussiness about
'cool' foods, thrifty hoarding of the precious fluid. On the
other hand, the cult of the lingam, a sex-charged mythology,
erotic sculptures in the temples displaying the most astonishing features of copulative acrobacy, the *ars amandi* of the
Kama sutras, the hottest curries, shops with the alluring sign

[1] *Op. cit.,* p. 11.

'Sex Pharmacy', an unrivalled trade in aphrodisiac prepara-
tions and spices. By comparison, though Victorian behaviour
was hypocritical, Victorian ideology was single-minded: it put
draperies on marble statues and attempted to bowdlerize the
universe. Even the Middle Ages had, in theory, a fairly consistent attitude to sex, recognizing the conflict between the
life of the spirit and the weakness of the flesh.

In India, the contradiction goes much deeper. The most
familiar, and yet the most striking example of it, is the cult
of the lingam. Millions carry it on a chain round their necks.
There is hardly a village without a shrine dedicated to Shiva,
with its cylindrical column of stone, standing erect on a slab
with a round hole. At all times of day, women and girls
can be seen making their offerings, usually by rubbing butter
and honey on the phallic column, without the slightest sign of
self-consciousness. In the bazaars, lingams are on sale everywhere; in holy Benares especially, whole streets look like
forests grown over with lingams of every size and quality. Yet
the symbol is to some extent dissociated from its origin, and
its meaning banned from the conscious mind. I say 'to some
extent'; but to what extent is impossible to know. One of the
psychiatrists I visited in Calcutta, assured me: 'If you
ventured to suggest in a Benares bazaar what a lingam really
represents, you would not get away unhurt.' This may be so
– I did not try the experiment – but it would only illustrate
the intensity of the defence reaction. Similarly, I find it hard
to believe that women ministering to the lingam in the shrine
are completely unaware – on every level of instinctual knowledge – of what they are doing. The more so, as the origin of
the lingam cult is explained in great wealth of detail in
several of the Puranas, and is therefore an essential part of
Indian folk-lore. In the version of the *Linga Purana*, for
instance, Brahma, Vishnu and their suite, while paying a visit
to Shiva, surprised him in the act of sex with Durga, his wife.
Shiva, in his drunken passion, took no notice of them and persisted in his activity; but when afterwards told what
happened, both he and Durga died of shame in the very position in which they had been discovered. Shiva then decreed

that the faithful should worship him in the symoblic form of his lingam, in which he was to gain perpetual life.

The simultaneous shameful denial and triumphant affirmation of sex in the legend is an indication of the deep and ancient roots of Hindu ambivalence. The erotic temple carvings, in which a luxuriant and feverish imagination overflows in endless and tireless variations in hundreds of scenes along the walls, make the visitor feel that he has stumbled into a sacred bordello of the gods; and the temple dancers of a still recent past must have been a tangible confirmation of it. The ubiquitous colour reproductions of Shiva and his beguiling Parvati, of Krishna's dalliance with the Gopis, the worship of the lingam, are perpetual reminders of the procreative force, and create an atmosphere saturated with insidious symbolism; yet at the same time, sex is to be feared and avoided, and the symbol denied its meaning. It is another example of the indifference to contradiction, of the peaceful co-existence of logical opposites in the emotional sphere. Indians hate what they love, and love what they hate – but more so than other people.[1]

The Perils of Pollution

The formula applies to almost everything that is important – women, parents, food, gods, Englishmen. It is, for instance, conspicuous in the attitude to bodily cleanliness. On the one

[1] I have nowhere else seen a country where young people of opposite sex are so helpless and paralysed in each other's presence, and so intensely aware of each other's sex. The following letter, which I cannot resist quoting, was addressed to an Indian psychiatrist who kindly allowed me to copy it from his files. The writer of the letter gave his profession as a lecturer at a State College.

Respected Sir,
From the last three years my brain is seriously working to celebrate my marriage with a particular girl.
I have seen her for the first time when she was ten years of age.
And, from that moment onwards she approached me many a time, but if I happen to see her, my body shivers, my heart-beat rises and I feel a sort of bodily weakness also.
Recently I came to know that she is also suffering with the same defect. Please suggest us the remedy for that.

Thanking you,
Yours sincerely,
(signature)

hand, there is an elaborate ritual of purification practices, on the other, a notable indifference to dirty surroundings. In fact, the ablution rites are governed by religious rather than by hygienic considerations, and the orthodox Hindu method of bathing is hardly what the word indicates, but a series of more or less symbolic sprinklings of the body in a prescribed order. At the other end of the scale is the deliberate neglect of the body practised by some holy men: the traditional long, 'matted' hair, grown into a solid tangle of dust and dirt, the texture of a doormat; nails grown several inches long, the body covered by a scaly crust. The Maharishi, one of the last great gurus, had such a period in his life. It is meant to express contempt for the material body, but is often indistinguishable from morbid infatuation with filth.

This leads again to a subject briefly mentioned before – the orthodox Hindu's preoccupation with the digestive functions. Out of the thirty-seven informants whom Carstairs asked to describe the happenings of a day in his life, every single one 'began by mentioning his going to stool and then his bathing, as being two of the most significant events of the day'.[1] Indian villages have, as a rule, no privies, and the day starts with going out to the fields – one side reserved for men, the other for women – armed with the lotha, a metal vessel filled with water. In primitive villages, the size of the lotha is considered a measure of a person's piety. The procedure to be observed while following the calls of nature, and the order of ablutions with earth and water are laid down in elaborate detail. Thus the Brahmin manual, *Nitya Karma,* devotes twenty-three paragraphs of its first section to the subject.[2] By way of comparison, the Old Testament scriptures dispose of it in two simple sentences,[3] and to my knowledge no other great religion treats it with such detailed, indeed obsessional, insistence. One of its conspicuous symptoms is the taboo on the left hand: since this hand alone is used for toilet ablutions, it is considered permanently unclean and unfit to touch food.

[1] *Op. cit.*, p. 81.
[2] Quoted by the Abbé J. A. Dubois, *Hindu Manners, Customs and Ceremonies* (Oxford, 1928, Third Edition), p. 237 *seq.*
[3] Deuteronomy xxiii, 12, 13.

Accordingly, the left hand is kept as far as possible out of sight during meals; on formal occasions, particularly when Europeans are present, the more self-conscious members of the gathering hold the offensive arm pressed to the body, as if it were carried in an invisible sling or shrivelled by disease.

The taboo on the left hand is rationalized as a necessity to avoid the danger of defilement; and this obsessive fear is closely related to the concept of untouchability. The outcasts were the only section of the population whose professional duties brought them into contact with slaughtered cows, dirty linen, and, above all, excrement; hence any direct or indirect contact – the use of the same well, in some regions the mere sight of the outcast – was a source of pollution. When Gandhi started his crusade against untouchability, he demonstratively took to cleaning the latrines in the ashram and sang the beauties of the bowel functions as one of the divine wonders. He gave the collective latrine-consciousness a twist in the opposite direction.

Thus the whole complex hangs together – compulsive ritual, pollution-phobia, taboos on commensality, rigid social segregation. The indignity inflicted on the outcast reflects the obsessive preoccupation with the indignity of one's own bodily functions. This is one instance of petrified religion exerting an evil influence on Hindu society.

The Perils of Distraction

I must return once more to the noisy profanity of the temples.

The absence of privacy, which characterizes life in the family, makes itself even more strongly felt in the attitude to religion. In the joint household, a man is rarely alone with his wife; in the temple he is never alone with his god. If he wants to be alone with his god, he must become a hermit and retire to the Himalayas. Hence the prominent part the cave-dwelling hermits play in Indian lore. The West, however, misunderstood their significance by regarding them as typical representatives of a nation that values quiet meditation above everything else. In reality, they are the exceptions, the rebels against the debasement of religion, who take to the wilderness because the nature of Indian society is inimical to the contemplative life.

It is interesting to note what Gandhi had to say on the subject. In 1924, after one of the periodic outbursts of religious hostilities, he wrote in an article:

> 'Hindus and Muslims prate about no compulsion in religion. What is it but compulsion if Hindus will kill a Muslim for slaughtering a cow? . . . Similarly, what is it but compulsion if Muslims seek to prevent by force Hindus from playing music before mosques? Virtue lies in being absorbed in one's prayers in the presence of din and noise.'[1]

It is a revealing passage. Logically, Gandhi ought to have admonished his Hindu brethren to asbstain from making 'a din and noise' in front of Moslem places of worship; instead, he admonished the Moslems to tolerate what they must regard not only as a nuisance, but a desecration. The justification for this curious attitude is found in his next sentence: as a Hindu the notion of hushed silence in the House of God, common to Christian and Moslem, was alien to him: 'Virtue consists in being absorbed in one's prayers in the presence of din and noise.'

Gandhi was expressing a basic principle of Hindu education, its emphasis on concentration, on the quasi-Yogic power of shutting oneself off from any outside distraction. By an effort of concentration, everybody ought to be able to live in his own Himalayan cave in the midst of the turbulent household. It looks as if these extraordinary powers had been ascribed to the individual as a compensation for the denial of privacy. It was all right for Gandhi, who could withdraw into himself in the midst of a crowd; and it was probably all right in a traditionalist society which discouraged individualistic tendencies. But to the young University student, the person with artistic or intellectual or religious aspirations, the denial

[1] Quoted by Frank Moraes, *Jawaharlal Nehru*, New York, 1956, p. 103.

of the right to privacy, and the concomitant demand that he should make up for its lack 'by concentration' means a frightful mental strain. Hence the recurrent complaint in out-patients' departments and consulting rooms about 'inability to concentrate' and 'weakening of memory' – usually combined with seminal anxiety. This is another major problem which waits to be solved in the process of transforming India.

II

Father and Son

The problem which overshadows all others is that of family relations.

Mr. X., an Executive, past forty, the father of four children, asked me for lunch. When I offered him a cigarette, he refused, and watched me light mine with a rather wistful look. I asked him why he did not smoke, and he explained, as if it were the most natural thing in the world: 'Up to the age of thirty-two I studied in England and smoked quite a lot. I also liked an occasional glass of beer. When I came back, I had to hide these habits from my father who disapproved of them; but I do not enjoy doing things in secret, so I gave them up.' I asked, half jokingly, whether he would start smoking again when his father passed away. He answered seriously: 'I might.'

I told this story to another acquaintance, the elderly Director of a social research institute. He did not think there was anything odd about it. 'Why,' he said, 'my father died when I was forty-five, and until his death I spent all my evenings with him. A few years earlier I used to go occasionally to a lecture, or a debating society to which I belonged, but one evening my father told me that he always felt lonely on the evenings when I went out, so from then onwards I did not go out any more but would talk or read to him instead.'

I told both stories to a psychiatrist in Bombay. His only reaction was: 'Why yes, the father-to-son relationship among Brahmins is a particularly happy one. My father also lives in

my house with my family. I am now over fifty, but it would
never occur to me to sit down in his presence until invited by
him to do so, although it is my own house. Nor would I consider making any major decision without his advice and
consent.' 'And as a student of the human psyche, you consider
this a desirable state of affairs?' 'Entirely desirable.'

Only one Indian psychiatrist dissented, and he came from
southern, Christian stock. He said with an engagingly cynical
smile: 'Among Hindus it is the oldest son's privilege to set
light to his father's funeral pyre; but he has a long time to
wait.' As an afterthought he added: 'You are naïve if you
expect a straight answer from a Brahmin on any question concerning one of our collective phobias and compulsions.' 'Even
if the Brahmin is a psychiatrist?' 'Even more so.'

A Sidelight on Gandhi

One of Gandhi's favourite Hindu myths has a bearing on
the subject. The Demon King Hiranyakasipu was plotting
against the Lord Vishnu. But the King's son, Prahlada, was
devoted to the Lord; and when his father took him on his
knee, Prahlada professed his faith. Some time later, the King
asked the same question, and his son gave the same answer.
'Hiranyakasipu flung his son from his knee. With burning
eyes he ordered Prahlada to be forthwith put to death by
poison or any other means. Elephants, serpents, black rites,
poisoning, starvation, wind, fire, water, throwing down from
precipices – nothing could kill Prahlada who had fixed his
mind on the Lord.'[1]

The King then instructed the boy's tutors to convince him
that he must obey his father, who was more powerful than
God. When this, too, was of no avail, the King proceeded to
cut his son's head off with his own sword (in another version,
the boy had to embrace a red-hot metal column). But out of
a pillar suddenly leapt the Lord Hari, half lion, half man,
'threw the King across his knees and with his sharp nails tore
him open'. Prahlada then asked that his father be purified
from his sins, and sang a hymn: 'Parents are no refuge

[1] Bhagavata vii, tr. Raghavan, op. cit., p. 369.

for the boy, nor a boat for one sinking in mid-ocean; the remedy becomes fruitless if you, O Lord, have neglected them.'[1]

The story is one of the well-known episodes from the Bhagavata; it is often sung and acted, and the lesson it contains seems to be an obvious one. But it was not at all obvious even to Gandhi. Although all India called him Bapu, which means father, and although he was the epitome of kindness, he treated his two oldest sons abominably. To start with, he refused to send them to school, and denied them a professional education, because he wanted to keep them close to himself to mould them in his image. When, at the age of forty, he decided to renounce sex for ever, he expected the two boys to do the same. When, at twenty-three, the younger one, Manilal, let himself be seduced by a married Hindu woman, 'Bapu made a public scandal, fasted, persuaded the woman to shave her hair, and said he would never allow Manilal to marry.'[2] He only gave in twelve years later. By that time, however, Manilal had been banished from Gandhi's ashram because he had helped his struggling older brother, who was also in disgrace, with a sum of money. 'Father did not send me away completely empty-handed. He gave me just sufficient money for my train fare and a little extra . . . During his lifetime, I was able to spend a very few years actually with my father . . . I had to live away from him in exile, in South Africa.'[3]

Manilal survived all this; his older brother, Harilal, did not. He, too, had the temerity of wishing to marry at eighteen (Gandhi had been married at thirteen). Bapu refused permission and disowned him. Harilal had the guts to marry nevertheless; but when his wife died, and he wished to re-marry at the age of thirty, the same story was repeated again. After that Harilal went to pieces. He took to women, was arrested for public drunkenness, embraced the Moslem faith, and attacked his father in print under the pseudonym Abdulla. When he became involved in a business scandal,

[1] *Ibid*, p. 371.
[2] Fischer, *op. cit.*, p. 229.
[3] *Ibid*, p. 230.

the Mahatma pilloried him in an unctious open letter in *Young India*:[1]

> 'I do indeed happen to be the father of Harilal M. Gandhi . . . Could I have influenced him he would have been associated with me in my several public activities and earning at the same time a decent livelihood. But he chose, as he had every right to do, a different and independent path. He was and still is ambitious. He wants to become rich, and that too, easily . . . Men may be good, not necessarily their children . . . *Caveat emptor.*'[2]

Harilal, an alcoholic wreck, died in 1948 in a Bombay hospital.

Gandhi was as near a saint as anybody can be in the twentieth century; as a father he came as near to the Demon King of the Bhagavata as any Western-educated Hindu could. His inhumanity to his sons may be written off as exceptional, but it nevertheless conforms to the specific pattern of tyranny exerted by Hindu Bapus. This we can glean from Gandhi's relations with his own father, and his comments – or rationalizations – on the way he treated his sons.

When Gandhi was sixteen, and already married, his father was 'bed-ridden, suffering from a fistula . . . I had the duties of a nurse . . . Every night I massaged his legs and retired only when he asked me to do so or after he had fallen asleep. I loved to do this service. I do not remember ever having neglected it . . . I would only go out for an evening walk either when he permitted me or when he was feeling well.'[3]

This was in 1885; but we find exactly the same pattern as in the stories of my Indian friends seventy-five years later – the nursing of the sick father, the evenings spent with him, the sacrifice of the son's private life. However, since Gandhi's autobiography is called *Experiments with Truth,* he proceeds, in the next paragraph, with this confession:

[1] 18 June 1925.
[2] Fischer, *op. cit.*, pp. 231-2.
[3] Gandhi, *op. cit.*, p. 24.

'This was also the time when my wife was expecting a baby – a circumstance which, as I can see today, meant a double shame for me. For one thing I did not restrain myself, as I should have done, whilst I was yet a student. And secondly, this carnal lust got the better of . . . my devotion to my parents . . . Every night whilst my hands were busy massaging my father's legs, my mind was hovering about the bed-room – and that too at a time when religion, medical science and common sense alike forbade sexual intercourse. I was always glad to be relieved from my duty, and went straight to the bed-room after doing obeisance to my father.'[1]

Thus in one breath he says that he 'loved to do this service'; in the next, that he was 'glad to be relieved from that duty'. About the education of his own children he had this to say:

'My inability to give them enough attention and other unavoidable causes prevented me from providing them with the literary education I had desired, and all my sons have had complaints to make against me in this matter. Whenever they come across an M.A. or a B.A., or even a matriculate, they seem to feel the handicap of a want of school education.

'Nevertheless I am of opinion that, if I had insisted on their being educated somehow at schools, they would have been deprived of the training that can be had only at the school of experience, or from constant contact with the parents . . . Often have I been confronted with various posers from friends: What harm had there been, if I had given my boys an academical education? What right had I thus to clip their wings? Why should I have come in the way of their taking degrees and choosing their own careers?

'I do not think that there is much point in these questions . . . There are within my knowledge a number of

[1] *Ibid*, pp. 24-5.

young men today contemporaneous with my sons. I do not think that man to man they are any better than my sons or that my sons have much to learn from them . . .'[1]

This was sent to the printers at about the time when the loving Bapu had banished Manilal from his presence and pilloried Harilal in public.

Gandhi was an extremist in every respect. The secret of his genius, of his power over the nation's imagination, lies perhaps in his unique gift to exaggerate (sometimes to grotesque proportions) and to dramatize (sometimes to the degree of showmanship) precisely those elements in Hindu tradition which had the deepest emotional appeal.[2] This is true for the whole range of his activities: his vegetarian and fruitarian apostolate; his (sometimes fatal) activities as a nature-healer; the loin-clothed appearance of the 'naked fakir' in Buckingham Palace; the Stakhanovite cult of home-spun *khadi*; the principles of tolerance and non-violence carried to Jacobin extremes; the martyrdom of the fasts; the prayer meetings in the patriarchal ashram; the rejection of sex, even among married couples, as a source of spiritual and physical debility; the inhuman 'detachment' from his family in the interest of public service; and the belief in the life-long absolute right of the father to rule over his sons.

When Gandhi forbade his sons to marry, he seemed to be going against Hindu tradition; in reality he was carrying the repressive authority of the Hindu father to its extreme limit. To quote Carstairs again:

'A man, so long as he remains under his own father's roof, must keep up the fiction of denying that he leads an active sexual life of his own. Not to do so is to be disrespectful. Consequently, a man and his wife can never talk to each other naturally, in his parents' presence; nor is it

[1] *Ibid*, pp. 167-8.
[2] Even in the one domain where he opposed tradition, he owed his success to the explosive, ambivalent power of a national complex. He transformed the concept of Untouchability into its opposite extreme: from a source of faecal defilement into an object of worship; the outcasts became 'harijans', the children of God.

proper for either of them to show affection for their own children in front of their elders . . .

'The very marked insistence upon the need to submit oneself reservedly to one's father's authority, to treat him as a god, suggested that the relationship was not an effortless one: but . . . the alternative of defying one's father's command was generally regarded as unthinkable . . . a man must always defer unhesitatingly to his father's word.[1] . . . He stands for self-control, disciplining of the passions and the emotions; for everything that is formal, restrained and correct. In the measure to which one can adhere to his austere standard of behaviour, one has the assurance of one's father's acceptance and support. On the other hand, to yield to spontaneous emotion or to sensual appetite is felt to be both wrong and dangerous: this is especially the case with sexual satisfaction, which is always felt to be illicit and somehow impious.[2]

All this is designed to keep the young man in a position of dependence – 'to clip his wings', as Gandhi puts it – and to deny him a fully adult status till middle-age. The symbol of adult manhood is sexual maturity, and since this cannot be prevented, it must be camouflaged and denied by convention. Once again, Gandhi's life demonstrates the conflict between sex and filial loyalty in a highly dramatic form. At sixteen, he had a ghastly experience which influenced his whole later attitude to sex, and to his sons, born 'of carnal lust'. He was, as usual, massaging his sick father's feet, when his uncle offered to relieve him. He accepted with alacrity, made straight for his pregnant wife's bedroom, and had intercourse with her. 'In five or six minutes, however, the servant knocked at the door' – and informed him: 'Father is no more.'

'I ran to my father's room. I saw that, if animal passion had not blinded me, I should have been spared the torture of separation from my father during his last moments. I

[1] Carstairs, op. cit., pp. 67-9.
[2] Ibid, pp. 71-2.

should have been massaging him, and he would have died in my arms . . .

'This shame of my carnal desire even at the critical hour of my father's death . . . was a blot I have never been able to efface or forget . . . It took me long to get free from the shackles of lust, and I had to pass through many ordeals before I could overcome it.

'Before I close this chapter of my double shame, I may mention that the poor mite that was born to my wife scarcely breathed for more than three or four days . . . Let all those who are married be warned by my example.'[1]

Larger than life in all he undertook, Gandhi did indeed give a warning example to a Bapu-ridden nation. He not only sat on his sons' shoulders like the djini of the Arabian Nights, doing his best to deprive them of their manhood, but tried to do the same to his collaborators. 'I presented to my co-workers brahmacharya as a rule of life, even for married men in search of Truth.'[2] Continence was absolute law for couples living in the ashram, and when a young couple was caught in the act, he went on a public fast to cleanse the ashram of its pollution. He was a tireless preacher of brahmacharya both in public and in private, and young women who came under his spell were particularly prone to become victims of his persuasion. He broke up several marriages in this way – in one case by persuading a young woman to take the vow while her husband was away on a mission. His obsession took even odder forms: from time to time, right to the end of his life, he insisted that young girls share his bed or mat in order to prove to himself that he was immune against the temptations of carnal lust.[3] It was a sad travesty of Krishna's dalliance with the shepherdesses. The effect of such experiences on the girls concerned did not appear to worry him. On one of these occasions, when British police came to arrest him at night, they found the Mahatma in bed with a

[1] Gandhi, *op. cit.*, p. 26.
[2] Fischer, *op. cit.*, p. 229.
[3] More precisely, the temptress would sometimes have to share his bed or mat, sometimes sleep in a bed next to his, and sometimes two girls would sleep in beds adjoining his.

girl of eighteen. Unaware of the purely spiritual nature of the experiment, they made an indignant report, which the British authorities wisely kept secret.[1]

Tolerance was Gandhi's guiding star and the main source of his magic charm. He was tolerant of every human failing, but not of the love between man and woman. That love he hated. He could never forgive God for his mistake that 'male and female He created them'.

That resentment smoulders in Hinduism throughout its history. It is immortalized in the carved and hewn images of the ruling goddesses. Their number is legion, but the most popular ones are black-faced, four-armed Kali, dancing on the breast of her prostrate consort, tongue protruding, mouth agape, with a garland of skulls around her neck; Durga 'the unapproachable', cutting off her opponent's head to drink his blood; and beguiling Parvati, the decoy, to whom Shiva likes to make love while standing on his head.

[1] This significant chapter in Gandhi's life is common knowledge among those who were close to him, but has been carefully hushed up in India. It was described in *My Days with Gandhi*, by Nirmal Kumar Bose (Nirvana Publishers, Calcutta 1953). Bose, an anthropologist, was one of the most distinguished scholars of India, who for a while acted as Gandhi's secretary as a kind of public service, and resigned this post on the grounds that he disapproved of Gandhi's experiments with young girls. The Gandhians were so thorough in effacing every trace of the scandal that Bose's book is unobtainable not only in India, but also at the British Museum.

The Crossroads

The Guru

THE Hindu Pantheon suffers from overcrowding. But none of its countless deities[1] represents a heavenly father. None of them wields the paternal authority vested in the Godhead of the great monotheistic religions, or even in Zeus and Jupiter. Brahma is the de-personalized universal spirit without anthropomorphic features; the others, from Vishnu, Shiva, Kali, Durga downward to the bloodthirsty, hybrid monsters, are anything but paternal. My knowledge of the Hindu scriptures is sketchy, but as far as it goes I have nowhere seen a paternal attitude attributed to any of the gods. In one of the popular prayers, 'The Vishnu-Sahasra-Nama (The Thousand Names of Lord Vishnu)', the God has every conceivable epithet, from Chief Serpent to Golden Navel, from Boar Incarnator to Destroyer of Lust, in a chain of incantations which extends over fifteen closely printed pages; but the word 'father' occurs only twice, both times as the progenitor, but not as the paternal protector of man.

In the absence of a Father who art in Heaven, the father in the flesh, Bapu, and the father in the spirit, Guru, are worshipped in a manner barely distinguishable from divine worship. It is reflected in the characteristic prayer to the Guru, usually recited at the beginning of prayer meetings:

'The Guru is Brahma, the Guru is Vishnu, the Guru is Shiva; the Guru is the supreme Godhead itself in the visible form; Obeisance to that Guru.

To him who has the highest devotion to God and has

---

[1] All the counts seem to differ, since most gods have several names which may either be synonymous or refer to manifestations in different shapes. *The Brihadaranyaka Upanishad*, one of the basic texts, gives '3 and 300, 3 and 3,000,' but says that these are merely manifestations of the one Brahma.

to his Guru the same devotion that he has to God, to that great soul these things which have been taught, and indeed those too *which had not been taught expressly*, reveal themselves.

Obeisance to that blessed Guru, who, with the balmy ointment of knowledge, opened my eyes blinded with the darkness of ignorance.[1]

The words that I have italicized refer to the belief that to be in the mere presence of the guru conveys darshan, a spiritual enrichment and an intellectual lesson which need not be conveyed in words. This belief plays an important part not only in the religious, but also in the cultural and political life of India.

It seems to me – though this is rather speculative – that the quasi-deification of the father and guru is closely related to the belief in reincarnation. The father's seed – the mother's function is reduced to that of a biological incubator – provides the body which the migrating soul will occupy. But that soul did not descend along the family lineage; it followed the course of its own independent karma. Since nothing happens by chance, there must be a metaphysical design behind the choice of that particular body, engendered by that particular father. It must be the one and only which corresponds to the specific needs of the migrating spirit, according to the balance of merit and de-merit acquired in previous incarnations. In other words: everybody gets the father whom he deserves, assigned to him by an infallible, transcendental justice. The father-son relationship is not one of biological causation, but a meeting of two souls pursuing their independent courses, an interlocking of two wheels by divine design. It is therefore unimaginable to question the father's character or to disobey his whims, since destiny ordained that a father with just that character and those whims should be assigned to the soul at the present stage of its progress. He represents the will of God and God himself.

This reasoning seems to be supported by the traditional

[1] Tr. Raghavan, *op. cit.*, p. 445.

manner in which the young aspirant is supposed to meet his spiritual father, the guru. He must set out in search of his guru and must, if necessary, continue his search for years until he finds the guru destined to him – like a soul in search of his assigned body. Once they meet, the pupil will instantaneously recognize his appointed master. The guru may respond in the same manner – as Shri Yogendra's guru did; but he may also put the disciple on trial by telling him harshly to go away, and refusing to speak to him for months or even for years. The disciple has to lump it without a murmur, and derive darshan from his mere nearness to the guru since it is due, like the choice of his father, to an appointment by destiny.

The De-boning Process

The Hindu ideal of society was stable and static, immune against change; an ideal shared with several Asiatic and with Christian mediaeval societies. It had its rigid caste hierarchy, each horizontal layer of which was divided and sub-divided into sub-castes, the extended family, and the joint-family-household, comprising several interlocked nuclear family units. Each of the sub-groups of Hindu society was a self-contained unit; and the life of successive generations seemed to unfold inside a closed, slowly revolving centrifuge, designed to sort out its elements and keep them permanently separated – the mechanical opposite, in terms of social engineering, of the American cement-mixer.

Within the microcosm of the joint household, the oldest male, and within the nuclear family the father, commanded absolute obeisance; in the lower branches of the hierarchy, the older brother held sway over the younger, the mother over the daughter-in-law, and so forth. The system varied, of course, according to region and caste, and it is difficult to say to what extent real life conformed to the theory; but this at any rate was the ideal schema. And, notwithstanding all racial and cultural differences, the absence of a common language and even of a common alphabet, this religious-social ideal did produce something like a Hindu national character with certain recognizable, specific traits and behaviour patterns. For this, after all, was the purpose of the system: to breed conformity and submission to the metaphysical and social order, and to preserve it by preventing individual deviations from the traditional norms of behaviour.

The young male's unconditional submission to the will of his father, and the hierarchic structure of the family, were designed to mould him into the stable, traditional cast, to undermine his initiative and independence; the family household was a school of conformity, obedience, resignation. All decisions were made for him by his elders: they chose his bride for him while he was a child or before he was even born; his education, vocational choice and later career would be decided for him, after more or less liberal discussions, yet ultimately nevertheless by others. The result was an ingrained reluctance to make decisions, a lack of self-reliance and independence, a tendency to evade responsibilities. As long as he lived in the joint household, his behaviour must be a symbolic denial of the fact that he had a wife, children, a life and a will and opinions of his own; respect for the parents implied denial of his own manhood. Strictly speaking, no Hindu could consider himself fully grown up as long as his father was alive. All this was often no more than polite pretence; yet to this day a large number of Indians give that curious impression of never having quite grown up, of a rather moving, child-like quality, an arrested development not of the intellect but of the character, which seems somehow blurred, soft, undecided and vague, without proper contour and individuality. In extreme cases, they indeed seem to have no will and no personality of their own – eager for praise, over-sensitive to criticism, smilingly irresponsible, always ready to oblige, yet stubborn in an infantile way, shy, prim, prudish, and sexless. This impression is, of course, more often than not completely misleading, for underneath the meek and gentle manner there may be a furnace of repressed passions, leading to unexpected outbursts, or to the chronic, nagging conflicts which plague the undecided.

The pressures in the family work in the service of the same

idea of perfection which is proclaimed as the ultimate goal in Hindu religious philosophy: the shedding of the ego, its passions, appetites, ambitions, idiosyncrasies – the elimination of individuality. The process of character formation in the family was a kind of de-boning process, inspired by the model of shapeless, spineless non-individuals, drifting through the world of illusions towards the ultimate deep sleep of Nirvana. The result of this ideal is still much in evidence on the contemporary scene. It is at the root of the spiritual and social crisis, the tragic predicament of India.

In the past, and in the vast rural areas where the past still survives, the system served to preserve the continuity of tradition and the stability of the social structure. It offered the individual spiritual certitudes and emotional stability within the womb of the family and the web of his social group. He knew that in every material difficulty and moral crisis they would stand by him. Throughout his life he remained surrounded by the protective affection of his kin.

Whether these benefits were worth the sacrifice of individuality and independence which it entailed, is a question of metaphysical values, and for a member of an alien culture it would be both arrogant and foolish to try to answer it. Besides, even in our own culture, a price on a comparable scale was exacted from the individual in exchange for such spiritual consolation and social security as the Christian feudal society had to offer.

Thus the problem is not one of value judgements; it arises out of the historical fact that the old social, economic and religious structure of India is in the process of collapsing; and that the traditional values and methods of character formation are incompatible with the requirements of the new structure, based on alien blueprints, which a Westernized minority is imposing on the nation.

Twenty per cent of its population is now living in the towns, yet it has never become urbanized. Apart from the millions who sleep in the streets, the average town-dweller either continues within the joint-family-household on a restricted scale but in much the same hierarchic tradition, or leads the existence of a Displaced Person, uprooted in oppressive loneliness, pining after brothers, sisters and mama, the uncles and aunts, in-laws and grandparents, who constituted his closed, crowded, secure universe. As a young psychiatrist remarked to me about his contemporaries: 'They either go to the temple to offer coconuts and flowers, or to the out-patients' department.' Indian towns have no compensations to offer for this cruel loss of security, because their life is patterned by an anachronistic tradition, including the continued taboo on commensality, conviviality, contact between the sexes. Except among Parsees, and a very small, Europeanized upper-class élite, boy will never meet girl, typist will never meet clerk outside the office; couples will not visit, young people have nowhere to go, social life does not exist, even the concept of relaxation after work is absent. Indian towns are sprawling agglomerations, as de-personalized, amorphous and featureless as the Hindu character-ideal.

The process of industrialization and urbanization has been accelerated since the start of the first Five Year Plan; but an urban society cannot in the long run exist without some form of social life, coherence, communal interests, human interlocking. The large towns of India are crowded deserts visited by periodic sandstorms: the Hindu-Moslem massacres right after Independence, the Gujurati-Marathi language riots, the hysterical outbreaks among students which occur on the flimsiest pretexts. Yet they were merely the symptoms of the silent drift towards a spiritual no-man's land.

'Nipped in the bud'

Gandhi was the father of the nation; and though Pandit Nehru is a different type of person, he had to step into the same role; whether he liked it or not, he became the new father figure. India is a democracy in name only; it would be more correct to call it a Bapucracy.

This is the inevitable consequence of a tradition which set a premium on uncritical obedience, penalized the expression of independent opinion and proclaimed, in lieu of the survival of the fittest, the non-survival of the meekest – through entry into Nirvana. How could a citizen be expected to elect a government when he was not allowed to elect his own bride? How could he be expected to decide what is best for the nation's future when he was not allowed to decide his own future? Out of the sacred womb of the Indian family only political yes-men could emerge. Their compliance to the will of the leader was not due to opportunism or cowardice, but to an implanted reflex. In this atmosphere was the Congress Party born, and it is still governed by the same traditions. As long as Gandhi remained the Bapu, the men around him, including Nehru, were virtually incapable of going against his decisions, even when these struck them as illogical and dangerous – as they quite often did.[1] Nehru gives several astonishing examples of this in his autobiography.

When Nehru's turn came, the same pattern was repeated with a vengeance: for now India had become an independent State, and the decisions of its first Government were bound to influence the whole sub-continent's future. Yet the Congress politicians seemed to be unaware of this; and those who did realize what was at stake were unwilling or unable to make themselves heard. Nehru's social outlook and political programme were formed during his European visit in the late 1920s, at the dawn of the 'Pink Decade', by the then fashionable brand of British left-wing Socialism. Its Swamis were the Webbs, Harold Laski, the *New Statesman and Nation* group – with their enthusiastic beliefs in Nationalization, the Soviet Five Year Plans, a centralized, blue-printed State Economy, and their almost mystic horror of Capitalism and Private Enterprise. In 1929, Nehru submitted to the All India Congress Committee a resolution which committed the future State to be built on these principles. By this time, he was already the Bapu-apparent.

[1] On most occasions when the Congress Executive Committee took a line apparently different from Gandhi's, this happened because the Mahatma encouraged, almost ordered them to do so – see, for instance, Fischer, *op. cit.*, pp. 370, 382, 388, 461, 464.

'As with many Nehru-inspired proposals at this period, the All-India Congress Committee merely passed the resolution, "not realizing", in Jawaharlal's words, "what they were doing" . . . "Another of Jawaharlal's whims" was the general verdict. "Let's humour him and pass it." '[1]

They regarded it as a paper-resolution without bearing on reality, like so many others which Congress had passed – a habit which once made Gandhi exclaim: 'We have almost sunk to the level of a schoolboys' debating society.'

Yet this innocuous paper-resolution, passed in 1929, was to determine the future State's policy. It had been reaffirmed from time to time 'to humour Jawaharlal', as home-spun clothes and slit latrines had been adopted to humour Gandhi; until, in 1955, the Avadi session of Congress finally adopted the pink Utopia of the 1920s as the blue-print for the social and economic development of India. The result is, as one of Nehru's ardent admirers has put it,[2] 'that India is the only country to develop on Fabian lines in the atomic age'. In the intervening years, Nehru had been much too busy to realize that Professor Harold Laski and Beatrice Webb were not the last word in Social Science. To quote another of Nehru's admirers, his biographer, Frank Moraes: 'What many people do not realize is that Nehru's ideas on most political, economic and social matters have been fixed and consistent for at least a generation.'[3] The same remark could of course be made of other great statesmen; but in a working democracy they are forced to make concessions to changing circumstances, or else to yield their place. In India no such safeguards existed, nor can they exist as long as the Prime Minister is not regarded as a politician, but as a father figure.

This role entails duties and privileges of a quite different order from those in a Western-type democracy. As I write this, Pandit Nehru has been in office as Prime Minister uninterruptedly for thirteen years. During the first twelve years he took no holiday, and he works on an average seventeen

[1] Frank Moraes, *Jawaharlal Nehru* (New York, 1956), pp. 137 and 185.
[2] Taya Zinkin, *The Guardian*, 15.8.1959.
[3] *Op. cit.*, p. 136.

hours a day. During the first week of my stay in India, he made five public speeches in five different towns, at distances varying from three hundred to a thousand miles, on subjects ranging from the manufacture of cast-iron to 'Literature and Realism' and 'The Duties of Girl Guides'. As Gandhi before him, as Vinoba Bhave or Jayaprakash Narayan, he was on the move most of the time, touring the country, making speeches, opening conferences and horticultural shows. He seemed to be combining the functions of British royalty with the whistle-stop campaigns of American presidential candidates; in fact, he was merely living up to the idea of the nation's father, omnipresent, accessible to all, conveying darshan by his presence. Gandhi in his ashram never refused a visitor; the airplane enabled Nehru to do the visiting himself, and all India had become his ashram.

Gandhi had genuine humility and respect for other opinions; Nehru had a self-confessed contempt for the 'weak and inefficient'. As he wrote in an anonymous pen-portrait of himself, he was 'the darling of the crowds . . . From the Far North to Cape Comorin he has gone like some triumphant Caesar, leaving a trail of glory and legend behind him . . .'[1] Leading this kind of existence left Nehru, who was not given to the contemplative life, little time for reflection on the momentous decisions confronting him all the time; for all the levers and controls were concentrated in his hands. He had absolute dominion over Congress, and Congress controlled the State by an overwhelming Parliamentary majority. Constantly rushed, always on the move, refusing to delegate power to his collaborators, Nehru's régime could be described as Rule by Improvisation. Its methods were, in 1960, still much the same as in 1929 when he made the innocent Congress Committee swallow the Socialist medicine 'to humour Jawaharlal's whims'.

And yet, Pandit Nehru is no doubt a bona fide believer in democracy. He had no dictatorial ambitions; circumstances left him no choice but to accept the mantle of the dictator handed to him by politicians reared in the Hindu tradition.

[1] Quoted by Guy Wint, 'The Age of Nehru,' *The Observer*, 28.6.1959.

There is no lack in India of constructive thinkers; many among the younger generation have their own ideas about India's future; there are even opposition parties. But they are powerless against the vast traditional forces of Bapuism. One of Carstairs's informants told him that when he was at the university, he and his friends started a debating society and some other activities – 'but my father nipped them all in the bud with a lion's roar'.[1] That about sums up the political scene in a nation of recent origin, which was made into a nation by a revered father – and would perhaps cease to be a nation without one.

Conclusion

Except for Japan – which is an island in more than one respect – India is the only great Asiatic country between Cairo, Jakarta and Peking under democratic rule; at least in theory. It could only become a working democracy in the Western sense after a revolution which strikes at the very roots of Hindu society and Hindu tradition. The great question facing India is whether such a radical operation is possible, or even desirable.

Ten years ago, Nehru and his planning staff believed that the answer was an almost unqualified yes. The Constitution of 1949 which they gave the country was patterned on Western models; it was a complete break with Hindu tradition and contained no breath of the Gandhian spirit which had awakened and inspired the nation. The social and economic policies they pursued during those first ten years disrupted the traditional structure of society and undermined its values, but failed to provide convincing alternatives. They did not succeed in stirring India's three hundred million peasants out of their 'protoplasmic apathy'; the short-lived euphoria after Independence yielded to disillusionment, frustration, and cynicism. The New Delhi of Le Corbusier, of Government Offices and Planning Departments, has an air of unreality about it, as if its legislators, politicians and five-year-planners lived in another air-conditioned bathyscope, a

[1] *Op. cit.*, p. 268.

hermetic world of abstractions, blue-prints and paper-resolutions inspired by wishful thinking. The result is a pseudo-democracy in a political vacuum. It looks as if India had telescoped the history of the French Parliamentary régime, from the storming of the Bastille to the Fifth Republic, into a single decade.

Wherever we look on the map, from the Arab countries to Indonesia, the experience of that decade has shown that Western-style Parliamentary party-democracy is not for export to Asia. It was an illusion to regard it as a universal panacea. Even in some major countries of the Continent of Europe it has not worked very successfully; rammed down the throat of an alien culture it produces convulsions. If the administration persists in its ramming methods, the system will collapse, and India will follow the example of the other Asiatic countries: at best it will settle down under a benevolent dictator in the Kemal-Sukarno-Ayub tradition; at worst become a totalitarian state after the Chinese model – see the warning signs in Kerala, West Bengal, or Andhra.

An alternative solution can only emerge on specifically Indian lines. The enterprise of Vinoba Bhave may end in failure; it has nevertheless revealed the untapped resources of the nation, its responsiveness to an inspired appeal, its potential of generosity, enthusiasm and self-sacrifice. It has also shown that this response came from all strata of the population, from Rajahs to Harijans, and that it cut across all party-divisions, which are to a large extent fictitious. Concurrent with the Bhoodan movement, new trends of thought have emerged whose spokesmen[1] propose to replace the Western-style democracy, mechanically copied from highly industrialized, urban societies, by a 'grass-root democracy', based on the traditional nuclei of Indian self-government, the village councils, together with the fostering of native crafts and regional industries. I believe that the salvation of India lies in a gradual transformation, on some such lines, discarding the petrified elements in past tradition and harnessing

[1] cf. Jayaprakash Narayan's *A Plea for the Reconstruction of Indian Polity*, published for private circulation by Sarva Sangh, Benares, 1959.

those spiritual resources which Gandhi and Vinoba revealed, to create, not an artificial pseudo-democracy, but – to coin a word – a home-grown 'Indiocracy'.

This may be a wish-dream, and at any rate it lies outside the scope of this book. Reverting to its proper subject, one conclusion seems to emerge: if the copying of Western blueprints has lead India into a *cul-de-sac* out of which it must find its own way, it appears equally clear that India, with all its saintly longings for samadhi, has no spiritual cure to offer for the evils of Western civilization.

PART TWO

Japan

If East is East and West is West
Where will Japan come to rest?

The Lotus and the Robot

D URING my stay in Japan I went through three emotional phases. The first few days I lived in a colourful haze of euphoria. This was followed by a period of mounting exasperation, occasionally verging on hatred. In the third phase, some bits of the puzzle began to fall into their places with a succession of almost audible clicks, and progress in understanding led to the acceptance of what Zen-inclined Japanese call 'the such-ness of things'.

The three phases were not neatly separated in time; towards the end of my stay they would alternate in quick succession within a single day or hour – a rather unsettling experience. The old hands whom I met seemed to live permanently in this unstable equilibrium and were showing the strain, regardless of how many years they had spent on the islands. Life in Japan may be compared to a scented bath which gives you electric shocks at unexpected moments. At least, I think that is as good a metaphor as any – for it is a country that compels one to think in images and to write with a brush.

Lotusland

The first phase of sensuous and sensual delight is the tourist's inevitable reaction to a culture with a surface polish of utterly refined pretty-prettiness, smiling ceremonial, kneeling waitresses, paper-screen houses, dolls, kimonos, and, above all, an atmosphere with an erotic flicker like the crisp sparks from a comb drawn through a woman's hair – a guilt-free eroticism which Europe has not known since antiquity. I responded to all this the more readily as, coming from India, I felt as if I were suddenly emerging in my bathyscope from the pressure of the black deep, with its tangles of ghostly seaweed and primeval monsters, into a brilliant, sunlit world.

In India I had almost forgotten that you could walk on a pavement without fear of stepping on a huddled figure; that cafés, bars and theatres existed; accustomed to the sight of females swaddled in shapeless cotton sheets, I was thrilled to re-discover that women have curves – not to mention their disconcerting habit of glancing straight, if slantingly, into your eyes, from iris to iris, instead of pretending to be struck blind, deaf and dumb by the shameful secret of the Lord's Creation. In a word, it was a relief to live through Augustine's *Confessions* in reverse gear, as it were.

Strolling through the Ginza in the spring sunshine was like being taken to a toyshop in one's childhood: huge, gaudy balloons, hung with streamers, were floating in the sky; helicopters were humming like dragonflies; uniformed chauffeurs were dancing around their parked shiny cars with feather-dusters, like chambermaids in the first scene of a French comedy; girl guides, waving yellow flags, were leading an Indian-file of cow-eyed rustics through the roaring traffic of their capital; two elderly gentlemen in black morning-coats were bowing and bowing and bowing each other through the revolving doors of a bank; earnest infants with running noses, strapped to their mothers' backs, were riding through the world as if in kangaroo pouches put on the wrong side; everybody seemed to be taking snapshots of everybody else, and buying little bunches of scented violets from dignified urchins, and giggling at their narrow escapes from kamikaze taxi-drivers with music streaming from their transistor radios.

Later on, during the rush-hour, when the whole town seems to thrash out in a kind of frenzied fit, charging into the electric trains with no holds barred, smiles effaced and courtesies suspended, the shy young men are transformed into vicious brutes, and the frail Misses Butterfly into all-in wrestlers. Then the lights go up, the town changes into a bubble-bath of coloured neon, and the bars, night clubs, restaurants and geisha houses provide pleasures for all incomes and tastes, enjoyed with equal decorum and in the same spirit of innocence.

This phase lasted for about a week. With some visitors it

lasts throughout their whole stay, and half the literature on Japan from Lafcadio Hearn to contemporary travelogues, reflects the euphoric stage, with Kabuki, Nō, Zen, Tea Ceremony and Flower Arrangement brought in under the same romantic angle. The majority of Westerners who become involved with the country one way or another, tend to become either Japan-addicts or Japan-haters. The Japanese way of life contains a challenge to Western man which provokes extreme responses.

Robotland

During the first phase, one looks as if through the wrong end of the telescope at a distant and idealized scene, free from the blemishes of close involvement; and one feels envious of a spirit of graceful hedonism which the Westerner lost a long time ago. During the second phase, other aspects of Japanese life come to the fore, and these are no longer seen through the lenses, but as reflections in a distorting mirror, caricatures of our Western civilization held uncomfortably close to one's face.

Many Japanese, for instance, walk through life wearing anaesthetists' masks, which cover their mouth and nostrils. These masks, or pads, of cotton are worn by men and women of all ages in the streets, in buses and trains, in cinemas, schools and at home. On the day of my arrival, when I saw the first muzzled couple walk past, I thought they were victims of leprosy or some other frightful disease. Then I learnt that the masks were meant as a protection against inhaling germs from the air and exhaling germs on others – a triumph of *modan* – modern – ideas of hygiene. Yet a great number of them suffer from chronic catarrh and most children have running noses, owing to the notorious absence of heating in Japanese houses. I was irresistibly reminded of Gulliver's voyage to Laputa, where some people carried huge bundles on their backs, filled with models of all things they could think of, and conversed by pointing at the appropriate models because they held the effort of speaking to be unhealthy for the lungs.

If the masks are a harmless travesty of Western 'scientific living', the nation-wide addiction to tranki – tranquillizers – can hardly be called that. It struck Japan with 'typhoon force' – as *Time* magazine had it – in the autumn of 1956; three years later, there were about fifty different brands on the market, all sold without prescription, praised on huge billboards by unscrupulous advertisers who invite their customers to take a couple of tablets three or four times a day, or even to 'take as many as you want any time you have worries'. Drugs with the opposite effect are used with equal readiness; the trainer of the Olympic team of swimmers admitted in 1958 in a statement to the Press that his athletes had been pumped full of vitamin injections before the Japan-U.S.A. swimming contest, and that they intended to continue this practice on similar occasions.

An even more depressing aspect of 'scientific living' is reflected in the Japanese ways of family planning. According to Dr. Margaret Sanger, the birth-control expert, 'in no nation in the world has the birth-rate been cut so drastically in such a short time'.[1] The Japanese have indeed succeeded in halving their birth-rate – but at the price of one and a half million abortions per year. A law, passed a few years ago, makes abortions legal for a fee of £1 if the expectant mother can prove economic hardship or impairment of health – which is a pure formality. Contraceptives are also legal but unpopular, except among the upper classes and in extra-marital relations; the result is the slaughter of the unborn with its concomitant ill-effects on the women.[2]

Another major curse of a different kind is miniature electronics. Transistor radios have spread in Japan like myxomatosis, and though its effects are not as deadly, in the long run they must affect the nervous system of the millions who carry the insidious gadgets all day in their handbags or trouser-pockets. Sometimes in a bus, when the announcer's voice seemed to pipe out from inside the body of my impas-

[1] *Time,* June 29 1959.
[2] Abortion was the traditional method of keeping the population of the overcrowded islands stable – but that was in an age before contraceptives came into use.

sive neighbour, I took him for a ventriloquist. On a train journey from Fukuoka to Nagasaki, which takes about three and a half hours, three pocket-transistor sets were loudly and simultaneously transmitting three different programmes from three different window-ledges in the carriage. Nobody seemed to mind.

This train journey was part of a trip, in the company of English friends, to a popular hot-spring resort, which gave us an idea of the terrors of modern Japanese holidays. The Unzen Amakusa National Park on Kyushu, the southern-most island of Japan, is dominated by an extinct volcano; it is surrounded by the sea, has splendid scenery with steaming geysers and fumaroles, in addition to hot-water swimming-pools for mixed nude bathing, archery grounds, tennis courts, bars and Pachinko Parlours. The latter resemble recreation rooms for the Other Ranks in the Pioneer Corps, with rows of pin-tables, all of uniform type, standing in uniform lines, worked by addicts with grimly set jaws who, deafened by the monotonous burr-zurr of thousands of tiny metal balls, hypnotized by their incessant dancing and spinning, imper-sonate the damned in a Sartresque limbo.

At Obama, a seaside resort, we boarded a huge and shiny motor-bus to the dead volcano, Mount Unzen. It was crowded with excursionists; the moment we started, a pretty hostess in a blue airline uniform appeared with a portable micro-phone to explain to us everything we saw. It took the bus about an hour and a half to climb the three thousand feet to Unzen, and during that time her soft patter, hoarsened by the loudspeaker, never let up for a minute. When in danger of drying up, she would point at a shop above the last hair-pin bend and inform us that it used to be a millinery shop but now it was a confectionery shop. At this all the heads in the bus would turn in the indicated direction, and all eyes would assume that glazed stare which indicates the process of digesting information; for the Japanese believe in the nutritive value of information regardless of the subject – they ingest knowledge wholesale, as a boa swallows a rabbit.

When she ran out of confectionery shops, our hostess burst

into unaccompanied song. First she sang a song in praise of the village of Obama; it ran something like this:

> 'Obama is a beautiful village on the sea,
> As with your delighted eyes you all may now see.'

Then we had one about Shimabara; apparently the bus companies employ poets to write these boating songs about the villages on their route.

The distance from the bus terminal to the entrance of the cable-car which takes you to the peak was about a hundred yards. Since this would have meant a dull walk of nearly a minute with nothing but the mountains to look at, a new thrill was thoughtfully provided. A line of horses, meek and saddled, was queuing up at the terminal, and the passengers were queuing up to mount them and be led on reins over the hundred yards to the cable-car entrance where, earnest and unsmiling, they dismounted and filed into the car.

On the top of the mountain there was, as yet, no loud-speaker. But there were arrows directing us to 'View Point No. 1' and on to No. 2 and No. 3. Each viewpoint consisted of a small wooden platform, and each platform in its turn was occupied by all members of the excursion simultaneously, blocking out each other's view. By walking first to View Point No. 3 and then anti-clockwise to No. 1, we three foreigners had each platform to ourselves. But we could feel the Japanese blushing for us.

I spent my last fortnight in Japan at the tip of the Miura Peninsula, about eighty miles south of Tokyo. Friends of mine owned a small Japanese house at the very tip of the Peninsula, and lent it to me as a retreat to do some work. The house stood quite isolated on a small tongue of land; on three sides the cliffs fell straight into the ocean. It seemed an ideal place for work – except that I had hardly a quiet moment from morning till nightfall. About ten miles to the south lies the great fishing port, Misaki – the home port of the 'Lucky Dragon'. Ten miles seemed a safe distance, but I had reckoned without the excursion boats. The excursion boats plied the sea at intervals of half an hour between Misaki and Kamakura, with loudspeakers blaring over the waves. As one began to fade out of hearing, another approached from the opposite direction. As a matter of principle, apparently, they were always tuned in to different stations. The intervals were filled in by a third radio source from the direction of the mainland, too faint to be heard when the boats were passing. It was a lonely loudspeaker mounted on a pole in a cabbage field, because the labourers had insisted that the farmer provide them with music while they work. This, apparently, is becoming a general custom in the countryside. A mud-tide of musical slush is engulfing the crowded islands, and soon there will not be a dry spot of silence left. Tranquillity can be obtained in pill-shape only.

The best customers of tranki are the university students. On my second day in Tokyo, driving towards Yokohama, I saw a large, silent, anxious crowd in front of an imposing public edifice. I stopped the taxi, expecting to see a funeral cortège emerge from the building, and learnt that it was Tokyo University,[1] and that the mournful crowd consisted of the parents, brothers and sisters of the candidates who, behind the barred gates, were undergoing the ordeal of the entrance examinations. I further learnt that there were 38,000 candidates for the 6,000 available vacancies, in other words, that over six out of seven candidates would fail. Among the 33,000 failures, over 13,000 will more or less seriously contemplate suicide – according to the statistics of a prominent Tokyo psychiatrist, Professor Takeyama; but only eighteen will actually kill themselves.

Since the new education law was passed in 1947 by the American occupation authorities, universities have been shooting up like mushrooms, the annual number of enrolments is approaching the one-million mark, and a university degree has become a *conditio sine qua non* for obtaining a

---

[1] Formerly Tokyo Imperial University, the most distinguished in the country.

clerical job. If the candidate fails at one of the select universities, such as Tokyo or Waseda, he can still try his luck
at a minor one, and the dates of the entrance examinations
are conveniently staggered for this purpose. But the examination fees are high, and the nervous strain is dreadful, both
on the candidate and his family. For the fortunate ones who
pass, the strain of the coming years will remain considerable:
about half of them will have to work their way through the
university, and, according to a 1953 poll, more than half of
the students at Kyoto University who filled in questionnaires
were suffering from tuberculosis.

The faces in the waiting crowd were tense and blandly
non-committal at the same time. There were practically no
conversations and no relieving jokes. Near the entrance gate
there was a stand at which printed sheets were sold, giving the
correct answers to the examination questions.

At last a bell sounded, and the students, boys and girls in
their late teens, came tripping out. They greeted their
relatives, sporting nonchalant airs, but talked very little. I
had expected a rush at the printed sheets to find out how they
had done in the examination. The sheets were priced at 10
yen ($2\frac{1}{2}$d.), but none of the relatives, and hardly any
candidate, bought one.

The next day I had a discussion meeting with a group of
students, and asked them for an explanation of the puzzle.
But they did not think it was a puzzle, and found it quite
natural not to inquire into the outcome of single examinations in the series which lasts several days; for to know that
one has given the wrong answers would have a demoralizing
effect. It was better to wait stoically for the final result on
which the family's economic and social future might depend.

To a middle-class family the money spent on the candidate's education meant a considerable sacrifice. To the candidate himself it meant being burdened with a heavy *on* –
an obligation that must be repaid under penalty of disgrace
before the world and oneself. That is one reason why they
take it so hard. Another is, that their whole future is at stake.
The rush at the universities indicates the advent of a new

type of competitive society, for which they still lack the mental equipment.

All my remarks in the preceding section refer to elements in Japanese life which were either directly copied from the West or developed on imitative lines. These elements added together constitute one aspect of modern Japan. But is it a reflection of the West in a distorting mirror – or in a true mirror, which magnifies blemishes not otherwise noticed?

The mirror in ancient Japanese tradition was a symbol that meant almost the opposite of what it means to us. It was not an instrument of vanity, but of contemplation, and is often seen in Shinto shrines. The person gazing into the mirror does not do so to examine his appearance, but to gaze through the 'door of the soul', his eyes reflected in the glass, into his innermost self. It is a method of short-circuiting his self-conscious, 'observing self'; what he sees reflected in his eyes in the glass is the original purity and calm of his spiritual being.

Western man, on the other hand, either gazes at himself in the looking-glass in the attitude of Narcissus – or the shaving mirror turns into a picture of Dorian Gray. When we see ourselves reflected in the most westernized nation in Asia, it is that ghastly experience that comes to the mind; the mirror reveals the image of a robot with built-in duodenal ulcers. Hence our violent reactions: the lotusland seen through the reversed telescope evokes our nostalgia for the golden age before the Fall; the robotland reflected in the mirror makes us shudder. This is, of course, an exaggerated reaction, for the reflection in the mirror is only half the truth about Japan, and half the truth about the West. But this is the only half common to both, and there's the rub.

However, the contrast between lotusland and robotland exists not only in the beholder's eye. The Japanese themselves have failed to reconcile the two planes of existence, and two half-truths together do not make an integrated whole. India is a welter of paradoxes and ambivalent attitudes, but the vast majority of the people still leads a tradition-bound existence; and even the westernized minority is Western in thought more than in its way of life. All nations are bundles of contradictions, but nowhere except in Japan are the conflicting strands so neatly sorted out, and arranged on two mutually exclusive levels which alternate in taking control, and produce dual personalities in a dual culture as sharply defined as a Japanese colour print.

The Trojan Horse

This unique quality of contemporary Japan derives from the uniqueness of Japanese history. No nation has suffered such earthquakes both in the literal and the figurative sense as the Japanese have in the course of the last century. When, after two hundred and fifty years of hermetic isolation and mental inbreeding, the Meiji Restoration of 1868 suddenly threw the islands open to the world, the results were as explosive as if the windows of a pressurized cabin had been broken. Nothing similar had in fact happened to any race in recorded history.[1] Within a single generation, the pent-up energies of the nation exploded in a frantic effort to catch up with everything that the West had accomplished in half a millennium. They succeeded to a spectacular degree; at the beginning of the twentieth century, Japan had become one of the leading military and industrial powers of the world.

By the force of circumstances, this result could only be achieved through learning-by-imitation. The Industrial Revolution of the eighteenth and nineteenth centuries in the West had grown organically out of the Scientific Revolution of the seventeenth century, whose roots reach back to the revival of Greek learning between the twelfth and sixteenth centuries. The Japanese could not be expected to duplicate the whole process, to produce their own Roger Bacons, Isaac Newtons and James Watts'. They had to proceed in reverse; starting with the mechanical copying of the end-products of the applied sciences, they had to work their way back to the theoretical foundations – from Edison to Galileo.

[1] China, too, pursued, in theory, a policy of seclusion from the beginning of the Ming dynasty for about three hundred years, but it was never strictly enforced. Cf. G. B. Sansom *The Western World and Japan*, London, 1950, p. 148 *seq.*

The starting point of this evolution in reverse gear is a bronze howitzer which Commodore Perry, after forcing his entry into Tokyo Bay, had presented as a gift to the Japanese authorities. A year or two later, they fired a salute to the American fleet from a battery of 'handsome bronze howitzers, exactly copied in every respect from the one Commodore Perry gave them; every appointment about the gun, down to the smallest particular, was exactly copied: percussion locks, drag ropes, powder or cartridge holder and all'.[1] They had to begin by copying mechanically, since they were not yet able to understand the exact purpose of the various parts of the gun; their eagerness to copy was not due to any inherent imitative tendency in the Japanese character, but to the hunger for knowledge of a people just emerging from two hundred and fifty years of solitary confinement.

Before that long period of segregation imposed by the Tokugawa Shogunate, whatever the Japanese imported from abroad – Chinese philosophy and art, Indian Yoga, Mongolian cooking – they transformed and adapted to their special needs and tastes, until only a remote resemblance to the original remained. They even created a specific Japanese way of using, or abusing, the English language. But the spectacular success of that first experiment in imitating the West was a dangerous precedent. It created a breach in their intellectual and spiritual defences, in their loyalty to a great and singular tradition. Western science and technology acted as a Trojan Horse; out of its belly poured alien philosophies, fashions, political concepts, attitudes to life. They could not be copied like Perry's bronze howitzers, and they did not blend with the traditional culture.

Perhaps Japan would have been able either to assimilate, or to discard these alien imports, had it not suffered a series of further shocks, which shattered its social structure. The Meiji Restoration of 1868, which opened up the country to the world, had started as a *coup d'état* with exactly the opposite programme; its slogans had been: 'Honour the Emperor – expel the Barbarians'. Yet within a few years, the Barbarian

[1] *The Complete Journal of Townsend Harris*, New York, 1930, p. 309 f.

influence was victorious all along the line, and the country had caught the 'European fever'. It was one of the symptoms brought on by the Government's radical reforms, which were like a surgical operation on the body social. Within a span of five years, the feudal system had ceased to exist. The legal inequality between the four traditional castes – warriors, peasants, artisans and merchants – was abolished. The daimyos, great feudal lords, lost their fiefs and privileges; the samurai lost their two swords, were paid off with a pension, and replaced by a people's army. Nobody was allowed to wear the dress and insignia of his former caste, and the eta – the sweepers, scavengers and tanners – ceased to be untouchables. A nation-wide network of schools was set up; a minimum of six years of schooling became compulsory for all boys and girls in the land, and generous provisions were made for Secondary schools and Universities. A Code of Laws was drawn up, following partly the French, partly the English example; for that purpose a new word had to be coined, for 'civic rights', which previously had not existed in the Japanese language. To put it briefly: 'Japan, just emerging from mediaevalism in the last half of the nineteenth century and as weak then as Siam is today, produced leaders able to conceive and carry out one of the most statesmanlike and successful jobs ever attempted in any nation.'[1]

But – and this is a decisive but – these pressure-cooker reforms failed to create a socially and ideologically stable society. The upheavals continued. A Japanese who lived for four score years, from 1865 to 1945, would have witnessed developments which, in European history, occupy several centuries: Absolute Monarchy, Constitutional Monarchy, Liberalism, Imperialist Expansion, Military Dictatorship, Totalitarian Fascism, Foreign Occupation. He would also have witnessed the disestablishment of Buddhism, the proclamation of Shinto as the State Religion, and the subsequent disestablishment of Shinto – changes which struck at the very root of ethical beliefs. Furthermore, he would have watched

[1] Ruth Benedict, *The Chrysanthemum and the Sword*, Tokyo-Vermont, third printing, 1958, p. 79.

a remarkable transformation in the physique of his younger compatriots, from the average height of five feet one inch of conscripts at the turn of the century to five feet two inches in 1914 and five feet four inches in 1952 – an increase of three inches in fifty years.[1]

As if to dramatize these developments, Nature contributed tremors and flames. There were disastrous earthquakes in 1892 and 1894, the Imperial Palace burnt down in 1873, most of the Capital was destroyed by the Great Earthquake and Fire of 1923, which claimed 150,000 victims. The 700,000 houses which had gone up in flames were re-built in a hurry – and destroyed again twenty years later, in 1945. That was the year in which the two man-made suns descended on Hiroshima and Nagasaki – but the two conventional fire-raids on Tokyo, earlier in the same year, had claimed another 100,000 victims, and reduced the Capital to charred rubble, for the second time within a generation.

In the course of the next five years, the first conquering invader whom the Japanese had known in history, imposed a revolution which transformed the nation even more radically than the Meiji reform. That had come from within; the new régime was enforced by the Occupation Authority. The State religion was abolished, the school textbooks of history and geography were burnt, the Prime Minister was hanged. The Emperor was no longer a god, the Army and Navy no longer existed. Forty per cent of the total area under cultivation was confiscated from the absentee landlords and distributed among the tenants; a new constitution established Western-style Parliamentary rule; women were given the vote and legal status equal to men; compulsory education was extended to nine years, and the number of universities mushroomed from forty-odd to nearly five hundred.

The Japanese, dazed by fire and brimstone, by the wholesale collapse of their houses, leaders, gods and values, did not

[1] *Encyclopædia Britannica* 12/900. The average stature of women is nearly two inches less, but the difference is rapidly decreasing. The change in physique is attributed to dietary reasons, medical care, sports, etc. The only comparable phenomenon was the increase in average height in the offspring of Eastern European immigrants to the United States. But the Japanese keep getting taller at home.

resist. Quite the contrary. Their attitude varied from enthusiastic collaboration with the foreign reformer – and this was the attitude of the overwhelming majority – to passive and polite acquiescence. If a small minority was cynically amused, they did not show it. The undefeated armies overseas, whose standing orders had been death before surrender, peacefully yielded up their arms at the Emperor's radioed order; there was no fighting on the beaches and no fighting in the streets, and no attempt to 'repel the Barbarian invader with bamboo spears'. The most ferociously warlike foe turned overnight into the most peaceful and affable population which an occupation army ever had to deal with.

The key to this almost unbelievable event is contained in a single syllable: chu – the absolute and unquestionable duty to obey the Emperor's command. The Emperor had spoken, and the war was over. That some were relieved and others would have preferred death; that they were disillusioned with their political leaders and that their towns were in shambles, was beside the point. Nor did it matter much whether a person believed that the Emperor was really a god and a descendant of the Sun, or whether he regarded these as symbolic statements. Chu was much older than State Shinto; it meant unconditional loyalty to the head of the social hierarchy, whether he was called Emperor or Shogun, whether of divine origin or not. Chu was the First Commandment of Japanese ethics; ko, the loyalty due to parents and ancestors, was the Second; all other rules of conduct came lower down in the list. The dramatic change which, on 14 August 1945, transformed the nation overnight from a tiger into a lamb was thus, paradoxically, a proof of its basically unchanged character; it showed that, in spite of revolutions and reforms, the traditional code of feudal ethics had never lost its hold; that the ancient pattern had survived underneath the imported, prefabricated superstructure.

The Graft that Never Took

To change the metaphor: Japan absorbed Western science and technology like a sponge; but Western culture and the

Western way of life were skin-grafts from an alien donor which, though eagerly accepted, never took.

With its population of nine million citizens, Tokyo-Yokohama is, according to Japanese statistics, the largest city in the world; yet its streets have no names and the houses have no serial numbers.[1] During the Occupation, the Americans tried to introduce some rudimentary order into that colossal labyrinth by naming the most important thoroughfares A Avenue to Z Avenue, and 1st Street to 60th Street. But when the Occupation ended, the municipal authorities refused to renew even the few decaying street-signs which the Americans had put up at the main junctions; and no Japanese will ever refer to N Avenue or X Street. He will name the district and sub-district in which he lives, and then draw an artistic map. The more important shops, restaurants, hospitals, offices, have cards with printed maps; and the maps, as often as not, are incomplete or misleading.

When I questioned Japanese acquaintances on the subject, the usual answer was: 'The streets in your towns are laid out in geometrical order, but ours are winding and tortuous, so it would be impossible to number them.' When informed that the streets of Paris and London were equally crooked, he would express his delighted surprise, and change the subject. He would, for instance, point out that Tokyo Tower is twenty feet higher than the Eiffel Tower, and would perhaps add with a chuckle that this fact was never mentioned during the recent visit of the French Trade Delegation, lest they should lose face.

Other answers were more direct: 'Street names are all right for Westerners, but we find our way without them.' The truth is, they do not. Among the anonymous millions who inhabit the capital, the large majority lead a life which is confined to their immediate neighbourhood; they shop along their street and have few friends or outside contacts, whose

---

[1] To be exact: a very few main streets do have names – e.g., the Ginza – but these names are applied to the whole neighbourhood. And most houses do have numbers of a sort, but these indicate the order in which they were built and have no relation whatsoever to their position in the street. Thus number 3561 in a nameless street, where a friend of mine lived, had number 1810 as its neighbour.

houses they locate by memory. The higher strata of the population attach private maps to invitations or business appointments, or send their cars. Postmen must know their clients in the district by name, or locate the addresses by house-to-house inquiry. Taxi-drivers follow a similar procedure; the extra time one must usually allow them for finding an address is about half an hour. The same applies to Ambulances and the Fire Brigade, when called in an emergency.

My last memory of Japan sums up a number of previous experiences. The head of a cultural organization and his secretary, both natives of Tokyo, promised to drive me to the airport. I waited at my hotel for twenty minutes after the appointed time; then I left a message with the hall-porter, and took a taxi to the Town Office of the Scandinavian Airlines, to have my luggage weighed in. When this was done, and there was still no sign of my friends, I took an airline bus to the airport. They turned up, in near-hysterics, at the moment when my flight was called up, and had just sufficient time to explain that they had been driving round and round the town, but were unable to find the Scandinavian Airlines' office. This was actually three blocks away from my hotel, but all they had to go by were, of course, the hotel porter's directions (left, then right along the tramline, then right and left again, etc.), to find an office in an un-numbered house in a nameless street.

An American editor[1] has described his incredulous astonishment when he visited the building of one of Japan's mammoth daily newspapers, with a circulation of four to five million. He saw its scientific wonders, from the rotation presses in the basement, through the telephotographic and speed-graphic equipment, to the helicopter park and the carrier-pigeons on the roof; he saw every trick and gadget of mass-communication, except – typewriters. To our minds, a journalist without a typewriter is like a samurai without a sword; in Japan not only newspaper offices, but business offices and government departments must do without them.

[1] Melvin F. Lasky, Der Monat, Berlin, No. 57-58, 1953.

Fantastic as it seems, business in one of the great commercial empires of our time is almost universally transacted by handwriting – and without keeping carbons for the record.

The reason is that a Japanese typewriter must have 2,000 to 3,000 keys to provide even the limited vocabulary of the popular Press; for higher literary purposes, it would have to possess 3,000 to 4,000 signs. That is the number of Chinese ideograms which the average educated Japanese is supposed to be able to read and write correctly; and each of these is an abstract design in miniature, requiring up to twenty-five strokes of the brush or pen. As if this were not enough, the Japanese script has been further complicated by past attempts to simplify it. The Chinese ideograms were introduced in the early centuries of our era; before that, the Japanese had no written language. From the eight century onward, a movement developed to use ideograms, drawn in a simplified form, for denoting sounds instead of ideas. Thus a phonetic script developed, whose signs, however, expressed not single letters but syllables; it was not quite a phonetic alphabet, but a syllabary; and instead of one system, there were two. One is called *kata-kana,* the other *hira-gana;* each has fifty signs. This was still a far cry from the simplicity of, say, the Hebrew or Greek alphabets with their twenty-odd signs; but it was nevertheless a great step forward, and led to the first flowering of Japanese literature in the eleventh and twelfth centuries. Its pioneers, oddly enough, were the ladies at the Emperor's Court; they were sophisticated and bored, and took to writing languid diaries in the phonetic script. The great classic novel of Japan – the *Tales of Genji* – dates from that period; its author was the Lady Murasaki. One wonders what would have happened to Japanese literature if it had been left to the use of the phonetic script – and preferably to the women who, burdened by fewer social responsibilities than the men, preserved, throughout the ages, a more spontaneous approach to life. That was perhaps the reason why the *sensei,* the learned, pedantic scholars who are the bane of Japanese culture, would not acquiesce in a phonetic script that made writing an altogether too simple and spontaneous

affair; they persisted in writing in Chinese – the equivalent
of the mediaeval Latin used by European scholars – whereas
the ladies wrote in Japanese, using *kana*; and when, in the
end, the national language carried the day, the scholars still
stuck to the Chinese ideograms. Thus arose, in the course of
the centuries, the Sino-Japanese hybrid script, which survives
to this day, and is the most cumbersome written language in
existence. It is a combination of Chinese ideograms, which
denote concepts, and various forms of *kana*, which denote
sounds. To complicate matters a little further, *kana* is not
only used to fill in the grammatical gaps between the unin-
flected ideograms, but also as a kind of parallel comment, to
indicate the pronunciation or to clarify the meaning of the
former.[1] This is necessary because many Chinese ideograms
have several different meanings in Japanese; and *vice versa*,
the mere sound of a Japanese word rendered in phonetic
kana, may mean a dozen and more different things. The
result is a script which combines, as it were, Egyptian hiero-
glyphs with Pitman's shorthand signs and musical notations
for several instruments. If one glances at a printed page, the
Chinese ideograms stick out like massive scars among the
graceful crow-feet of *kana* and *hira-gana* – the result of
another, much earlier, cultural skin-graft.

That is why the Japanese have transistor-radios but have to
do without typewriters. Only the big banks and business
trusts possess huge machines which are a luxury, like elec-
tronic computors.[2] The typical modern Japanese business
firm, with its high-pressure sales methods, transacting its
business through a host of calligraphers, is once again
Gulliver in Laputa.

A reform of the written language would not only do away
with a major hindrance which clogs the wheels of the nation's

[1] In fact, both the history and present forms of the written language are
considerably more complicated. The above is meant to convey no more than
a rough idea of the problems involved. Japanese guidebooks do not even do
that, and merely confuse the reader – see, for instance, the quite incompre-
hensible explanation in *Japan – The Official Guide*, Tokyo, 1958, p. 123 *seq.*
The most scholarly and lucid treatment of the subject is G. B. Sansom's
An Historical Grammar of Japanese, London, 1928.

[2] After writing this, I have been told that a revolutionary kind of typewriter
will shortly appear on the market, using a mere 900 keys.

affairs; it would also save years of heavy intellectual grind in the life of every successive generation. It would have even more far-reaching consequences, because the confusions and ambiguities of the Japanese script are reflected in the structure of Japanese thinking. And that, perhaps, is the cause of their instinctive resistance against reform of the script. They refuse to part with the comforts of ambiguity, and prefer the printed page, like the streets of the capital, to remain a labyrinth, where only the initiate, guided by his intuition, can find his way – or lose it in agreeable detours.

I remarked to an elderly professor about the contrast between the courtesy of the Japanese at home, and the brutality of their behaviour on public transport. 'But is that not natural?' he answered in a tone of surprise. 'Railways are new.'

The first railway, between Tokyo and Yokohama, was opened in 1872, but railways are 'new' in the sense in which everything that came since the opening of the country is 'new'. It means that tradition provides no precedent and no guidance for the proper way of behaviour in the situation in question. Trains and buses exist, but they exist outside the traditional pattern, in a cultural no-man's-land where no rules of etiquette apply.

Similarly, electric lighting, European clothes and Western water-closets are situated in an aesthetic no-man's-land. In the austere surroundings of square boxes with sliding paper-panels which make a Japanese house, every object, down to the smallest, is chosen with meticulous care, as if it were to be part of a museum – except for the naked electric bulb hanging from the ceiling, or the Woolworth standard lamp. They are useful but not part of the landscape, and aesthetic considerations such as are given to a saké cup or a flower vase do not apply to them. Nor to European-style clothes and shoes, still regarded by the majority as civilian uniforms for office wear which offer no scope for the expression of one's taste and personality, in contrast to Japanese clothes – into which they like to change as soon as they get home. The classic footwear are slippers in the house and geta – wooden clogs – outdoors; and the traditional Japanese housewife's attitude to European foot-gear is best described in that hilarious classic *The Honourable Picnic*.[1] The lady is talking about her husband's shoes, which he has to wear at his office:

'. . . They are so inconvenient to take care of. A year or two ago I put them to wash with the geta in a basin of warm water. They sank to the bottom and the water soaked them through all the better. But then, impossible to get them dry. In vain I put them on the very embers in the stove, they scorched and smelled and that was all. And by reason of going out with wet shoes, my husband caught bronchitis. It even seems that they shrank and gave him pain, as well. So this winter, in spite of the bad weather we had, I prohibited the maid to touch them, and in spring they had the mud on them still of New Year's. It was very ugly to see.'

That lady was evidently a member of Japan's psychological maquis, the unconscious resisters, the smiling saboteurs of Western-style clothes, road signs, plumbing, manners, customs and languages. On the plumbing front the maquis operates with particular success. The interior of the house is kept scrupulously clean, as it always has been – except for the W.C., which is a post-Meiji import. It is either permanently blocked, or installed without the odour-insulating syphon; while outside the house the open sewer runs, as often as not, along the front wall, with a plank serving as a bridge to the entrance door. The Japanese have a most delicate sense of scent, but they become smell-blind when it suits them.

The least successful grafts were those in art and philosophy. They imported, together with machine tools and railway engines, German metaphysics, French scepticism and Russian nihilism; a Bismarkian form of government, with the French system of prefectures; Darwin and Beethoven, Chekhov and

Rodin, K. Marx and H. Spencer, with polite impartiality; but somehow these component parts proved more difficult to assemble than cameras and motor-cars. At Waseda University in Tokyo, they built a faithful replica of a Shakespearean theatre, which houses a Kabuki Museum; and one professor is reported to have spent his life in writing footnotes to *Beowulf* without knowing modern English.

On the printed sheet for the Tokyo University entrance examination which I have mentioned, the first 'correct answer' in the translation test was given as follows: 'She should have told it to him when she found his failure'. It was not a misprint, but a fair sample of how English is taught at Japanese universities. The first invitation I received from a Professor of English at one of the leading colleges, began with: 'Sir, I esteem it a high honour to write you this letter'; it ended with, 'Of course, I have no intention of interfering in your private concerns or matters, or hurting you, except full of good-will. From the bottom of my heart I hope your good health'. When we met, the Professor turned out to be a delightful person, who never realized how deeply involved he was with the maquis.

Japan is the most Westernized among the great Asiatic nations, with the highest standard of literacy and living, the highest achievements in the Sciences and Arts – yet the most drastically cut off from verbal commerce with the West. Even the surprisingly small number of Japanese intellectuals who profess to have studied English, twist and torture the language out of all recognition to fit their own way of thinking.[1] Time and again the discussions and round-table talks in which I took part, or whose minutes I read, got bogged down in nerve-racking semantic confusion. Even where relatively simple questions of science are concerned, the difficulties are considerable. To quote a single example: I

[1] D. J. Enright has given a series of delightful examples of 'English as she is japped' (quoting a classic quip by J. H. Chamberlain): from 'Extract of Fowl', meaning eggs, to 'Stand Bare', meaning a small bar without seats, to the 'Bar Ber', formerly called the 'Head Cutter'. (*The World of Dew*, Tokyo-Vermont, 1959). I would like to add to his list the compliment paid to me after a lecture, that it left the audience 'sprinkled with delight'; and the apologetic remark of a young lady who did not have time to change before dinner: 'I am very sorry I cannot be gorgeous tonight.'

came to be on friendly terms with a Japanese psychiatrist of outstanding gifts, who had studied for a while in the United States. At that time, a medical congress in Tokyo was discussing a problem in which I was particularly interested, and Dr. X. very kindly offered to send me a translation of a newspaper report on the proceedings. It ran as follows:

'*A Report From the General Medical Congress in Tokyo*
    The 3rd day; Topics in Mental Hygiene
        from the Asahi Newspaper, the April 5th edition.
1. Prof. and Dr. Akira Kasamatsu, the Tokyo University, published his result in his study of the celebroencephalography when the monk in his Zen concentration.
Due to his observance of the graph the monk in the Zen concentration looks like quite relaxed like the one's state in sleep. And it seems impossible for an amateur to pretend in relaxation in the Zen concentration . . .
Dr. Kasahara got successful to get the grph of 14 monks and 8 amateurs in the Zen Concentration of the orthodox temple of Buddhism from summer till winter last year. It should be the first event in this field.
The graph on the paper shows relaxed when the number of breating grows less with strange increase of pulses. It seems showing this state is not at all dull like as the sleeping state but one soon before the coming action.
"In the thinking in the Western style both of mind and body seem in tension like as the sculpture of Rodin's thinker. That of the East looks like the opposite one. The sculpture of Buddha give no impression of stress. She is always relaxed in his thinking," said he.
2. Many other physicians of psychiatry stated that we find now the original pattern of neurosis even in childhood. And all seems growing serious with us in present Japan through baby age through the continuous increase of suicide of the teenagers, and due to the vicious practices of the youngsters under the social stress of our state.
And it might be the other difficult to find the increasing worried aged.'

As I happened to be familiar with the subject, I got the gist of it. Besides, the report dealt with tangible matters like pulse, EEG and breathing; but when it comes to abstract ideas or shades of meaning, the dialogue breaks down.

It would be absurd to assume that the Japanese suffer from some inherent racial handicap which makes them unable to master a foreign language. If, in spite of their imitative genius, they are such awkward linguists, the explanation must rather be sought in certain idiosyncrasies rooted in the collective psyche – a term that sounds less abstract in Japan than elsewhere. Isolation both in the historical and geographical sense may be one factor; the absence of a phonetic alphabet another – a language whose elements are not single sounds but syllables moves, as it were, in fixed phonetic grooves.[1] But the main reason is perhaps the same unconscious resistance which makes them cling to their cumbersome and anachronistic script. They could no doubt master the vocabulary, syntax and grammar of a Western language – if they were willing to adopt the matter-of-fact type of thinking and the logical categories which the structure of that language implies. But this, it seems, is what they are unwilling or unable to do. To ask a Japanese to *think* in English terms amounts to asking an Impressionistic landscape painter to adopt the methods of a land surveyor.

The Diver and the Bends

Though the graft never took, it prevented the growth of natural tissue. Tradition survived – stubbornly rather than triumphantly – but it ceased to develop. The Meiji era was one of rapid material progress and spiritual stagnation. The evolution of poetry and drama, of painting and music, architecture and interior decoration, came by and large to a standstill. Haiku and Nō, flower arrangement and tea ceremony, became more and more self-conscious rituals – fossil pleasures embedded in petrified aestheticism.

To the young they have little to offer. The mobo and

---

[1] Thus, for instance, the name Koestler is spelt and pronounced in Japanese Ke-su-to-ra.

apuregeru – modern boy and *après guerre* girl – live in a spiritual desert more scorching than that of their coevals in the West. They call themselves neither angry nor beat, but 'the generation which lost its identity'. For the simple-minded there is the Pachinko Parlour, American flicks and sutorippu – striptease. For the highbrow, the dark cafeterias, beatnik affectations, and existential angst. They admire T. S. Eliot, not because they read him, but because *The Waste Land* has become their slogan; and with an unerring instinct they extract from Western art and philosophy those elements only which nourish the traditional Japanese melancholia and self-pity, their feeling of 'the Ah-ness of things'. They are like an imaginary species of bees which, mutated by irradiation, are only attracted by bitter flowers, yielding a bitter honey.

They hate the robotland in which they live, and they hate themselves for succumbing to its temptations. They yearn for a lotusland which they know to have become an anachronism, yet they are unable to struggle free from its ancestral grip. At middle-age, the majority revert, as previous generations did, to the ancient pattern – the frigid joys of moon-viewing in the abstract rock-garden, and the stilted repartees of an equally middle-aged geisha concubine. But in each generation there was also a small minority searching for a new way of reconciling the two patterns. One day, no doubt, they will succeed, but that day is not yet.

The opening up of the country after a quarter-millennium of segregation made the nation resemble a diver suddenly breaking surface. The brutal change of pressure causes bubbles to form in his veins, and he suffers the agony known as the bends. In contrast to the small élite of westernized leaders in India, whom I compared to travellers in a bathyscope isolated from their surroundings, the Japanese are a nation of skin-divers. Unfortunately, they cannot go back into the pressure chamber to dissolve the bubbles by getting gradually de-pressurized. They must find some original cure for a malaise without precedent.

The Unstable Crust

I MUST return to the question of earthquakes, which play such a conspicuous part in the nation's life. The term 'crustal instability', which is used to describe the country's geophysical condition, has a curious applicability to the Japanese character – it conveys the idea of a rigid surface, unyielding to pressure from inside, until it suddenly cracks up. The zone of 'crustal instability' extends in an arc from south-east Asia across the Japanese isles northward to the Aleutians, then curves down to the southern tip of South America. 'This zone,' says the *Encyclopædia Britannica*, 'is noted for its numerous earthquakes and intensive volcanoes, which give rise to its popular name, the "Circum-Pacific Ring of Fire" '. About eighty per cent of the seismic energy of the earth is released within that belt.

The Japanese islands are traversed by seven chains of volcanoes, many of which were active in historical times, and some of which still are. 'Seismic disturbances', that is, slight tremors, occur on an average four times a day in one part or another of the islands. Many of them are detected by instruments only, but the average tremor is noticed by a brief rattling and shaking of the house. Severe earthquakes, which are invariably followed by destructive conflagrations, occur on an average once every six years.

I had my first experience of an earthquake during my stay on the Miura Peninsula. I was alone in the house, engaged in writing, when the floor under me suddenly lurched a couple of times. It was rather like bumping into an unseen pothole while one is driving on a smooth road. The whole wooden house rattled briefly, but alarmingly, twice in succession. By pure reflex I dashed out into the garden, feeling thrilled rather than frightened; but an hour later I found to my surprise that my hands were still shaky, as if I had a hangover. I have lived through the London blitz and was bombed out by a V2, but this quite insignificant tremor was something different. It gave a new meaning to the cliché about 'the bottom falling out of the world'.

No doubt one gets used to it. The old hands will tell you that they can detect even very faint tremors, for instance, by the swinging of a chandelier, and that this happens about once a week. Yet it does not seem too wildly speculative to assume that the frequent tremors and the six-year cycle of major catastrophes must have influenced the Japanese attitude to nature. Mount Fuji is worshipped as a sacred mountain and the national symbol of Japan. According to tradition, this twelve-thousand-foot volcano, with its two-thousand-foot crater, emerged suddenly in a single night, together with the two hundred and twenty-five square miles of Lake Biwa, during the great earthquake of 286 B.C. A cataclysm on this scale would have destroyed all Japan; but the legend is typical of the Japanese catastrophic view of the working of nature. Since most houses are built of wood – sixty per cent of the country is still woodland, and it used to be eighty per cent – even a minor earthquake can start a major conflagration; and, as if this were not enough, there are the frequent and devastating typhoons. One of their popular proverbs lists as the 'five main terrors of Japan': 'earthquakes, fires, thunder, floods and fathers'. About the surprising inclusion of fathers, later; the other four are the terrors of crustal instability. They are, I believe, a relevant factor in that peculiar approach to nature which pervades Japanese art, and their concept of a cultured life. Nature is too hostile and frightening to be approached 'in the raw'. To be aesthetically acceptable, it must be stylized, formalized, miniaturized. Uncouth reality must be transformed into civilized artefact.[1]

---

[1] This does not exclude, of course, sporting activities such as skiing or alpinism, which are of recent origin, nor a certain romantic admiration for landscapes of desolate grandeur. I am speaking of the traditional Japanese attitude to nature in general.

The Horrors of Flower Arrangement

Trees growing straight towards the sky are rarely encountered nowadays in a Japanese park or garden. Their branches must be twisted and tortured into artistic and symbolic shapes. As a popular guide-book puts it, 'the real beauty of the pine-tree can be seen only in Japan. A very special art is required in shaping those trees. While still very young, the tree is formed into desired shape by means of a system of strings and wires'.[1] In addition to strings and wires, wooden stakes are used to force one branch upward and to pull another down; a row of trees in a park looks like a procession of invalids walking on crutches.

Even so, real trees are aesthetically never quite satisfying, except on occasions like the cherry-blossom viewing ceremony. Much preferred is the cultivation of bon-sai, that is, trees planted in pots – from pine to cypress to Mongolian oak – and made to grow into genuine dwarfs by constant root-surgery. The aim is to produce a faithful imitation of a majestic old tree; weights hung on the growing branches, plus strings and wires, twist the dwarf into picturesque shapes. Some have two trunks, some a single trunk, and sometimes a different species of tree is grafted on the trunk. Some bon-sai are said to be more than a hundred years old, and fetch fabulous prices from connoisseurs.

A development of bon-sai is bon-seki the miniature representation of a mountainous landscape by stones, pebbles and sand on a tray. When living plants and models of houses and people are added, it is called hako-niwa. As a Lilliput craft it has its charm; and so has ikebana, the Art of Flower Arrangement; elevated into an esoteric cult, with all the mystical, symbolic claptrap attached to it, it becomes rather depressing. There exist at present three hundred different schools, or sects, of Flower Arrangement in Japan,[2] and there are special magazines devoted to it. The one I have before me contains mostly photographs of arrangements, and critical Comments on each arrangement by well-known experts. The

[1] *We Japanese*, Miyanoshita, Hakone, 1950, p. 91.
[2] *Japan, The Official Guide*, Tokyo, 1958, p. 241.

first photograph – I shall not try to describe it – is accompanied by the following specification:

'Materials: Burnt wood, pink tulip
Subject: "Whispering"
By Kohfu Sera (Shin Nippon Kado School)
Arranger's Note: Springtime in the Valley of City Buildings'

The first Comment is by Shoyo Miyama:

'An arrangement that presents much food for thought . . . The tulip well expresses "whispering". But to place only one tulip in the centre. Does it not seem rather weak to express the "whispering" of "spring in the city"? What about adding more burnt wood and add another spot of "whispering" effect?'

The second Comment on the same arrangement is by Keiji Yoshida, who occupies a position of authority among ikebana reviewers comparable to Mr. Raymond Mortimer's in the *Sunday Times*:

'In any case, although elegant and graceful, we cannot but notice a certain mannerism. Is he approaching that dangerous stage? I wonder.
I can note the touch of the well-experienced hand, and this somehow makes the arrangement easy-going. Could it be so?'

A few more samples of Comments on other arrangements:

'The use of a container in black and white with dark brown lines makes us think of carefree youth.
A seemingly realistic impression is given, but I think that actually we should not form such an opinion too soon. This is because this arrangement is such that it is easy to overlook its true worth . . .
There is something here that seems strange. The bold use of the palm may be very well, but why did it have to be used in this particular manner? Most likely it was not an

automatic expression of the picture the arranger had in mind but only an idea on the spur of the moment.

Though this arrangement does not claim to have anything of a deep meaning, the effect is that of endless vigor and strength. A truly interesting work.

Green, of course, it goes without saying, is the most important colour in Ikebana, because it means "life" and "energy". Of recent years there has been a tendency to overlook and ignore the use of green, which I greatly deplore, because "green" is of the most vital importance to those who practice Ikebana.'[1]

The first thing one learns from the Beginners' Section in the magazine is that 'in using narcissi for ikebana it is impossible to utilize them in their natural state . . . First remove the flower, then the leaves, one by one from the centre, which will leave the empty white sheath'. When this is done, the stem and the leaves are stuck together again in a more pleasing shape. Chrysanthemums are made to display their petals to better advantage by the insertion of a small wire rack into the living flower. If I lived in Japan, I would start an I.S.P.C.F.T. (Imperial Society for the Prevention of Cruelty to Flowers and Trees). But then – I shall come to that later – every Japanese child also has a kind of invisible wire rack inserted into its body and mind.

The Japanese garden is built on similar principles. The following is from an illustrated guide-book, *Gardens of Kyoto*.

'*Garden of Tofuku-Ji*. Tofuku-Ji was built about seven hundred years ago by Michiie Kujo as a cathedral of the Zen Sect of Buddhism. The projector of this garden is Mirei Shigamori, a well-known garden expert of Kyoto. The peculiarity of this garden is that it is consisting of nothing but rocks and stones.'

This sounds like a joke, but is not meant to be one. Of the two main categories of Japanese gardens (there are endless sub-categories), the so-called 'flat garden' is a rectangular, walled-in arrangement of stones, sand, stone lanterns, and small basins or wells, all of which have elaborate symbolical meanings. The description of the most famous of all, the Ryôanji Garden in Kyoto – quoted from the guide-booklet sold in the Temple – will make this clearer:

'Not a tree nor a blade of grass is used. It only consists of 15 stones and sand and in addition some cryptomeria moss, depicting the islands in the Ocean and pine-plantation on the sea-shore, is the finest of renowned gardens by "Karesansui". The sand signify the water and the stones give one a feeling of a weight of an iceberg. Listen carefully to the sound of the waves. If you are able to hear the sounds then you are able to understand the fine points and appreciate this garden. It is the finest of stone-setting art in Japan. Note the contrast of tone color of the mud wall and the garden. Standing from where you are and without moving, can you count the 15 stones? "Crossing the tiger with her child" is named from the middle stone which seems to be a tiger swimming, head above the water and carrying its young on the back.'

According to another guide-book,[1] the fifteen stones represent 'a tiger fleeing from one island to another with its cubs against the attack of a leopard'. I stood in that famous garden, but could neither hear the sound of the waves nor feel the weight of the iceberg against the escaping tiger – only the sad, heart-sinking sensation of watching Anandamayee Ma rubbing her toes.

The 'hill gardens' as distinct from the 'flat gardens' feature on a miniature scale artificial hills, ponds, winding streams, islands and waterfalls, curving bridges and warped trees – sometimes with real water, but sometimes the water is symbolically represented by raked gravel and specially shaped rocks. (To understand the symbolic meaning of the rocks, an elaborate system of classification must be studied.) The effect of the hill garden is at first rather charming, although it could

[1] *Japan, The Official Guide*, p. 247.

be more precisely described by the American word 'cute'.
But soon one begins to feel the same kind of embarrassment as a passenger travelling on a toy-train. I watched
Japanese excursion parties obediently trotting through the
miniature landscape behind their guide; they looked like
rugged giants and seemed to be pleasantly aware of it; they
crowded round the guide to listen to his explanations and
took snapshots all the time – unseeing, using their cameras
for eyes. But that was perhaps the subtle purpose of this
trompe-l'oeil scenery: to represent Nature at a safe distance,
seen through the reversed lenses.

The Golden Temple

A similar trend seems to run through all traditional forms
of Japanese culture. I felt, for instance, a curious affinity
between the stone gardens and that most esoteric of Japanese
arts, the Nō opera. In the garden, a rock symbolizes a mountain, or a cataract, or a tiger; in the Nō dance (which is rather
a succession of still poses than a dance), the slow lifting or
lowering of the paper fan in the dancer's hand symbolically
indicates extremes of happiness or despair, of bereavement
or loving surrender. All violent emotions, like uncouth
nature, have become stylized, symbolized, daintified. Even
the *aficionados* of Nō are obliged to read their textbooks to
understand what is going on on the stage – just as the flat-
garden viewer must learn which stone symbolizes what. One
of the acknowledged experts on Nō, Mr. Yone Noguchi, has
summed up the matter in an admirably concise way: 'When
we must spend two or three years in realizing how many
others fail in becoming Nō appreciators, it means that those
elected in this particular art, where appreciation is not less,
perhaps is greater, than the acting itself, will find their own
lives vitalized with the sense of power in Japanese weariness.'[1]
To be vitalized by weariness may seem an odd notion to an
Occidental, to the Japanese it means what it reads – romantic
melancholia as the main source of poetry, the woeful expression of the Nō dancer as a symbol of man's dignity, a *mal de*

[1] Quoted by Enright, *op. cit.*, p. 71.

siècle which dates from the beginning of time. But the relevant words are 'appreciation greater than the acting itself'. This means that the onus of providing the emotional experience is not on the actor but on the spectator. One is reminded of Liechtenberg's aphorism on a German mystic: 'His writings are a picnic where the host provides the words and the guests the meaning.' In the West, the costs of the picnic are about equally divided: a work of art is judged by certain objective criteria, the rest is up to the spectator's power of imagination. In Japan, the emphasis lies much heavier on the latter: it is shifted from the object of contemplation, which can be a mere symbol or hint – a finger pointing at the moon – to the act of contemplation itself. 'A jest's prosperity lies in the ear/Of him that hears it, never in the tongue/Of him that makes it.' In the West, this is taken for a half-truth, in Japan, as very nearly the whole truth. This conviction is derived from that familiar tenet of Eastern philosophy that the perceiving subject and the object perceived, the seer and the seen, form an indivisible unity. We have repeatedly met with it in discussing Indian philosophy, and we shall be constantly reminded of it in the sequel.

The following quotations from Yukio Mishima's *The Temple of the Golden Pavilion*[1] will illustrate the point. Mishima is the most successful author of the post-war generation. The narrator of the story is a young Buddhist priest:

'It is no exaggeration to say that the first problem I faced in my life was that of beauty. My father was only a simple country priest, deficient in vocabulary, and he taught me that "there is nothing on this earth so beautiful as the Golden Temple" . . . As the time approached for me to come face to face with the Golden Temple which I had never yet seen, a certain hesitation grew within me. Whatever happened, it was essential that the Golden Temple be beautiful. I therefore staked everything not so much on the objective beauty of the Temple itself as on my own power to imagine its beauty.'

[1] Tr. Ivan Morris, New York, 1959.

At last the great day came when his father took Mizoguchi to Kyoto, and he stood, for the first time, face to face with the Golden Temple:

'I changed my angle of vision a few times and bent my head in various directions. But the temple aroused no emotion within me. It was merely a small, dark, old, three-storied building. The phoenix on top of the roof looked like a crow that had alighted there for a rest. Not only did the building fail to strike me as beautiful, but I even had a sense of disharmony and restlessness. Could beauty, I wondered, be as unbeautiful a thing as this?

If I had been a modest, studious boy, I should have regretted my own deficiency in aesthetic appreciation before becoming so quickly discouraged as I did . . . Inasmuch as I believed only in the beauty that one can see with one's eyes, my attitude at the time was quite natural.

With a respectful air Father now led me up to the open corridor of the Hosui-in. First I looked at the skilfully executed model of the Golden Temple that rested in a glass case. This model pleased me. It was closer to the Golden Temple of my dreams. Observing this perfect little image of the Golden Temple within the great temple itself, I was reminded of the endless series of correspondences that arise when a small universe is placed in a large universe and a smaller one in turn placed inside the small universe. For the first time I could dream.'

The episode is a perfect expression of the Japanese aesthete's approach to reality: his preference for the golden miniature model to the indifferent object, blackened by time and disasters; his enamouredness with the symbolic world-within-the-world; his deliberate self-hypnosis as an escape from and substitute for direct experience – 'for the first time I could dream'.[1]

---

[1] In the end, the young priest burns down the Golden Temple – Mishima's novel is based on a true episode.

Character-Gardening

JAPANESE aesthetics and ethics are intimately related. The invisible wire rack planted into the nervous system twists the child's behaviour into a stylized pattern, like the shape of the bon-sai tree, until it has become 'second nature'. Its purpose is to conquer uncouth 'first' nature – the unpredictable erruptions of the subterranean passions[1] – and to create human artefacts whose conduct is mapped out in minute detail to eliminate as far as possible the dangers of the unforeseen.

Without unduly stretching the parallel, traditional Japanese education may be called character-landscape gardening. Its aim is the creation of a perfect work of art. The element of daintiness in the garden is reflected in the mincing ceremonials of etiquette. The cascades and toy waterfalls, suggesting *joie de vivre,* represent the permitted, and therefore guilt-free, pleasure of saké and concubinage. For these, a special corner is set aside – the geisha districts are called 'the flowery-willowy world' – but the remainder of the character-landscape belongs to the flat-garden type. Its guiding principles are rigid perfectionism on the one hand, and elusive symbolism on the other.

The rigidity – rock, sand and pebbles in the walled-in garden – is indispensable in a Spartan education aimed at

[1] Its archetypes are the Ainu – the aborigines of Japan with their stone-age culture. They are said to be the hairiest race on earth, while the Japanese are among the most hairless. They worship bears, which they capture as cubs and allow to suckle at their women's tits; and they go into religious ecstasies known as 'Arctic hysteria'. Although there are only a few thousand of them left, and they have become quite tame huddled together in the northern island Hokaido, the Japanese still have an irrational horror of the 'Hairy Ones'; a Japanese psychiatrist has even suggested to me that their reluctance to live in near-empty Hokaido, despite the overcrowding of the main islands, is partly due to its association with the Ainus. They are, he suggested, a symbol of the conquered Id – of human nature in the raw, before it was displayed by the civilized artefact. A simpler explanation of the Japanese dislike of Hokaido is its cold climate.

hardening the character against its innate crustal instability. In her autobiography,[1] Mrs. Sugimoto relates a typical lesson in classics with her private teacher:

'Throughout my two-hour lesson he never moved the slightest fraction of an inch except for his hands and his lips. And I sat before him on the matting in an equally correct and unchanging position. Once I moved. It was in the midst of a lesson. For some reason I was restless and swayed my body slightly, allowing my folded knee to slip a trifle from the proper angle. The faintest shade of surprise crossed my instructor's face; then very quietly he closed his book, saying gently but with a stern air: "Little Miss, it is evident that your mental attitude today is not suited for study. You should retire to your room and meditate." My little heart was almost killed with shame. There was nothing I could do. I humbly bowed to the picture of Confucius and then to my teacher, and, backing respectfully from the room, I slowly went to my father to report as I always did, at the close of my lesson. Father was surprised, as the time was not yet up, and his unconscious remark, "How quickly you have done your work!" was like a death knell. The memory of that moment hurts like a bruise to this very day.'

To what extremes the ideal of self-discipline can be carried is illustrated by the classic story about Count Katsu, a nineteenth-century noble, who, when a boy, had his testicles bitten by a dog. While the surgeon operated on him, his father held a sword before the child's face and told him that if he uttered a single cry he would 'die in a way which at least is not shameful'. The remarkable thing is not so much the story itself, but the fact that it is still quoted as an admirable example of pedagogy.

Yet it would be quite wrong to read any deliberate cruelty into it. A traditional form of correction in Japanese education was moxa – the burning of a cone containing the leaves of a

[1] *A daughter of the Samurai*, London, 1933, p. 35 f.

special plant on the child's skin, where it often left a life-long scar. But this was considered as a cure rather than a punishment. Cauterization is widespread in Asia as a medicine against various ailments – so much so that even modern Japanese psychoanalysts revert to it. As one of them wrote: 'I use moxa therapy – a stimulus therapy. Moxa therapy is a classical Japanese medical method. I think it is a minor form of shock therapy.'[1]

Thus the apparent cruelty of Japanese education is really a form of conditioning, which does not exclude love and affection – on the contrary, it is based on the axiomatic conviction that the child in its innermost being *wants* to be properly reconditioned that way, as the flower welcomes the wire rack to display its petals to best advantage. But the methods and techniques of this conditioning are more radical, and reach into deeper strata of the subconscious than Western pedagogy would ever dream. They transform not only overt comportment, but also the autonomous responses and unconscious controls – as exemplified, for instance, by the peculiarities of Japanese behaviour in war, in sleep, and in mental homes.

On the first subject, more than enough is known; the Japanese soldier behaves as if his instinct of self-preservation had been switched off, and his nervous system brought under a kind of remote control which causes the laws of humanity and commonsense to be supplanted by utter ruthlessness towards himself, his comrades, enemies, and prisoners alike. Yet the moment the master-switch is thrown back into normal position, he instantly reverts to his kind and gentle self, without a twinge of remorse – precisely as the worthy businessman, after a night spent in his cups and his mistress' bed, returns in the morning to his smiling family, without embarrassment or guilt. He emerges from his debauches – physical or moral – fresh as a daisy, at a single turn of the switch which makes him change from one conditioned behaviour-circuit to another. The average German's attitude to the horrors of the Nazi period is to deny that they

[1] Kenji Ohtski, quoted by J. C. Moloney, *Understanding the Japanese Mind*, Tokyo-Vermont, 1954, p. 207.

happened, or to disclaim any personal share and responsibility in them. The Japanese attitude is entirely different. It is reflected in the following paragraph from the Preface of a popular guide-book, from which I have quoted before: 'We printed the third volume of *We Japanese* during the war, but bombing came to destroy it all while it was being bound. We were rather lucky, however, to have it destroyed by bombing because unawares we were influenced more or less by the current ideas of nationalism during the pre-war and war periods. We have re-written *We Japanese*, Volume III, since the close of the war.' There is no trace of hypocrisy in this statement; it has the innocence of the daisy with a drop of morning dew.

The early conditioning of the Japanese child penetrates even its sleeping habits: 'From the time I can remember I was always careful about lying quiet on my little wooden pillow at night . . . Samurai daughters were taught never to lose control of mind or body – even in sleep. Boys might stretch themselves into the character *dai*, carelessly outspread; but girls must curve into the modest, dignified character *kinoji*, which means 'spirit of control'.[1] On the other hand, Japanese men and women have an astonishing capacity to fall asleep in any posture and in any surroundings – once more as if turning off a switch. Soldiers, for instance, were reliably reported to be able to sleep while marching;[2] but they can also go without sleep for longer periods than Westerners.

One of the maddest things about Japan is that Japanese madmen do not get mad. This may be a poor pun, but it serves to demonstrate that insanity carries different associations in different cultures: 'mad' is used here first in the English sense of 'odd', 'incongruous', 'abnormal'; then in the clinical sense; and lastly in the American sense of 'angry' or 'violent'. The classic type of the 'mad' Englishman is the eccentric or infatuated person who is mad 'about' actresses or racehorses, while Americans are mad 'at' their wives or bosses. The prototype of the Japanese madman is the gentle, docile,

---

[1] Sugimoto, *op. cit.*, p. 39.
[2] Benedict, *op. cit.*, p. 181.

withdrawn, well-behaved mental patient. Violent emotional display is simply 'not done', even among lunatics.

I visited two Japanese mental hospitals – one specializing in a therapy derived from Zen (to be described later), the other in Western-type psychiatry; and in each case I was struck by the absence of safety precautions, and by the atmosphere of grave courtesy that prevailed. The recreation room, with its ping-pong tables, was hardly distinguishable from a Pachinko Parlour, and even patients with severe depression-psychosis, lying motionless on their mats, their empty stares fixed at the ceiling, turned their heads slowly and worked up a mask-like smile as the doctor entered their rooms. It was a weird experience, and one which commanded respect – though this be madness, yet there was decorum in it. Later on I discovered that most Western psychiatrists visiting Japan had remarked on the absence of violence and tension in the mental wards:

'Japanese males, even when insane, conform to authority. In March, 1949, I had an opportunity to observe the effect of the early infantile discipline of the Japanese male. During my visits to Japanese insane asylums, one at Kyoto and the other about thirty miles from Tokyo, I observed a situation that was almost unbelievable: there were no special facilities for confining the insane; the most violent lived together in rooms that were separated by unsecured rice-paper partitions opening into long corridors. The windows were unscreened glass of ordinary thickness, waist-high even for the Japanese. When I had first read reports of the Japanese insane, I was skeptical, and at the Ko-no-dai National Hospital I kept insisting that the institution must house more violently disturbed males. The Japanese psychiatrist, trained at our own Boston Psycho-pathic Hospital, understood my disbelief, because he was familiar with American insane. Yet, in his willingness to help me, he practically gave me the keys to the hospital; and like a man from Missouri, I saw every room through-out the institution. What I saw confirmed the reports I had read: the male Japanese did not become rabidly disturbed . . .

It is customary for occidental psychiatrists and psychoanalysts to expect unpredictable violent behaviour from some categories of insane . . . Yet . . . it is astonishing that violent categories of insane are not encountered in the Japanese asylums.'[1]

Moloney also quotes sample statistics which indicate the relative rarity of the paranoid type of schizophrenia. In Japan its frequency was about fifteen per cent among all forms of schizophrenia; in a typical U.S.A. hospital the corresponding figure was nearly sixty per cent – four times as high.[2]

This is an even more impressive achievement of Japanese education than bravery in war. It seems to be attributable to three related factors in early conditioning: the inhibition of emotion in overt behaviour; the unquestioning acceptance of one's proper station in the complex web of a hierarchic society; and the unconditional obedience to authority. As a result of this, if an unstable person has a grudge against the world, the chances are that his aggressive impulses, finding all outlets barred, will be internalized and deflected against the self. In pathological cases, this may lead to depressive psychosis, melancholia or suicide; in a diluted form, it leads to the traditional cult of the woeful Ah-ness of things, and the morbid flirtation with suicide. So solid and elastic is the web that it cannot be torn even in fantasy – in delusions of grandeur or of persecution. The flight into paranoia is barred as too obvious and direct. Aggression can only be vented in symbolic acts: mental patients are inclined to arson, or to tearing into small pieces, slowly, with rapt concentration, their tatami mat – the revered symbol of family life.[3]

---

[1] Moloney, *op. cit.*, pp. 36-7.
[2] *Ibid.*, p. 38 f.
[3] Mishima's neurotic young priest is an arsonist. Some of his pronouncements are: 'beauty is a decayed tooth', 'beautiful scenery is hell'; 'I wondered what it was that made Mother so particularly ugly. Then I understood. What made her ugly was – hope. Incurable hope, like an obstinate case of scabies, which lodges, damp and reddish, in the infected skin, producing a constant itching, and refusing to yield to any outer force' (*op. cit.*, p. 200).

Japanese psychiatrists know how to put the early conditioning of their patients to therapeutic use. In Japanese mental
hospitals—

> '. . . the social structure is tighter and control is more
> rigidly hierarchical than is generally true for hospitals in
> the United States. Moreover, the Japanese hospital is
> organized much more in terms of a "family model", as is
> also true for many other types of organizations in Japan.
> This firm control within a family model has many implica-
> tions for behaviour at each level of the hospital. For
> example, the relations between doctor and patient are
> clearly, if benevolently, authoritarian. There is no question
> who is the doctor and who is the patient. Perhaps because
> of this sharp status difference which provides a sense of
> security and inevitability, the casual relations between
> doctor and patient seemed to the writer to be more relaxed
> and friendly than in American psychiatric hospitals.'[1]

If the psychiatrist assumes the role of the father, it is that
of an authoritarian Japanese father, not of the Freudian
father-image – and even Freudians burn moxa. Whatever his
therapeutic merits and achievements, he certainly has remarkable control over the patient's overt behaviour.

But there is a brighter side to this picture. The traditional
organization of the mental hospital provides the patient not
only with an authoritarian father, but also with loving mother
substitutes. These are called tsukisoi; they are a special
category of nursing personnel, who act as personal attendants
to the patient, sleep in his room, and are meant to establish an
intimate contact with him. They are called 'women of love
and mercy'. One old tsukisoi told an American psychiatrist in
the course of an interview: 'We had to learn how to get a feeling of mothering others. It is still so at present. These young
tsukisoi have to learn what is the best way to think of the
patient as their own precious and beloved person. We have to

[1] William Caudhill, *The Psychiatric Hospital as a Small Society*, Cambridge,
Mass., 1958, p. 370.

keep our eyes on the patient twenty-four hours a day. If we don't they may start a fire or commit suicide. As you see, these young tsukisoi cannot possibly have a feeling of being a mother, so I teach them that they should face their patients with the feeling that they are brothers or sisters . . . We built a feeling of love and mercy toward the patient, knowing that they are entirely depending on us . . . (The writer asked about whether or not the tsukisoi took a day off occasionally.) To tell the truth people in the so-called modern world are quite useless. When I was young I did not lie down for twenty-one days while I was serving one patient.'[1]

Such personal care for the patient – not confined to psychiatric hospitals only – was, of course, only possible in an overpopulated country where a minimum level of employment was maintained by the paternalistic principle of over-staffing the establishment with underpaid employees. But running the country on the paternalistic model did provide emotional security as a compensation for the low living standard.

This emotional security is fostered with affectionate care; it softens and sweetens the Spartan rigours of education. The Japanese baby in its kangaroo-pouch on the mother's back is in more constant and intimate contact with her than occidental infants ever enjoy. Strapped to her by sashes under its arms and buttocks, inside the padded jacket that she wears in winter, the baby clings, spreadeagled, to the back of the mother who carries it around everywhere: shopping in the busy street, visiting neighbours, enjoying the comforts of the hot family bath. The older brothers and sisters also act as child-nurses and deputy riding horses, so that the baby lives a rich and exciting life, very soon takes an interest in everything that goes on around it, and starts to talk earlier than occidental babies, usually before it can walk. It is talked to and treated as if it were an adult; and if a boy, his mother and sisters show him the deference due to his sex. At the same time, it begins to learn etiquette literally in the cradle, or pouch, for each time the mother bows to an important person, she makes the baby bow too by pushing down its shoulders

[1] Caudhill, *op. cit.*, p. 372.

and head. Its toilet training also starts very early, at three or four months, by being held out of the door and over the gutter in the firm grip of its mother's hands, and it soon learns the purpose of this manoeuvre; some anthropologists regard this early training as an important preparation for all later forms of conditioning.[1]

But in other respects, the Japanese child enjoys much greater freedom than a Western child. The natural and uninhibited approach of the Japanese to sex starts in the cradle; the fond mother calls the male infant's attention to his virile member as an object of masculine superiority and pride; sexual play among children is regarded with amused indulgence, and masturbation is considered a normal and harmless phenomenon. Until a few years ago, gadgets for auto-erotic purposes were freely advertised, and they are still sold in certain shops. Equally popular were the 'bride books' and 'spring books' – artistic woodcuts, with or without text, descriptive of love-making, for the education and stimulation of young couples. Fathers make no secret of keeping mistresses; and it was not unusual for a boy to be initiated into the legitimate pleasures of sex, by being taken, as a kind of birthday treat, to a nice establishment in the flowery-willowy district by a benevolent uncle or friend of the family.

On the other hand, marriage is an important, quasi-political affair between the two contracting families, involving the ancestors on both sides and a careful mutual scrutiny of family records. Once they reach adolescence, social contact between young people of opposite sex in the same social class becomes rigidly formalized. Lotusland lies outside the family.

As a result of his conditioning, the average Japanese behaves in certain situations rather like an automaton with built-in controls, but regarding sex and bibulousness, he enjoys much greater freedom from inhabitants and guilt than his Western counterpart. Hence the occidental's fascinated bewilderment in this country of stoic hedonists, of Spartan sybarites.

[1] Cf. Geoffrey Gorer, *Themes in Japanese Culture*, Transactions of the New York Academy of Science, vol. 5, pp. 106-24, 1943, quoted by Benedict, *op. cit.*, p. 259. This, however, is a controversial subject among anthropologists.

The Fear of the Unexpected

With the approach of adolescence, the young boy (and, to a slightly lesser extent, the young girl) is gradually caught in a web of increasing complexity of *gimus* and *giris*, that is, obligations, to repay *ons*, that is, debts. Some of the *ons*, e.g., towards the Emperor and the ancestors, were incurred before he was born; some of them tend to conflict with each other, or with the giri he owes to his own name; and there are still other rules of conduct which cut across the web. It is actually a labyrinth rather than a web, because there is no universal guiding principle, no religious commandment and no transcendental idea of Good and Evil attached to it. Of the three religions of Japan, Shinto has no holy writ, Buddhism is ethically neutral, and Confucianism is not really a religion but a statute of social law. The concepts of Sin, Guilt and Divine Justice are virtually absent. It is a system of ethics confined to offences against the social code for which amends of a prescribed nature are extracted; and the individual has to account for his actions not before a divine judge, but before society with a small 's', that is, his superiors in the hierarchy, his family and friends. Accordingly, the urge to gain the approval of others is not considered as vanity, nor is anxiety to avoid disapproval considered a sign of weakness, as in the West, but as the very essence of ethical behaviour. To gain approval, and avoid censure, is all there is to ethics, because a transcendental system of values does not exist.

Even the respect and obedience due to one's parents is devoid of that religious quality which it has in India, or in the Fifth Commandment. The father repays his *on* to his ancestors by caring for his children, and the children owe *ko* to their father in repayment of the care he spent on them. The relationship is based on a kind of *quid pro quo*, the settling of a mutual obligation. It does not exclude love and tenderness – nor the opposite attitude, which regards the father as a curse next to earthquakes; but basically it is a pragmatic relationship. Similarly, the attitude of pupil to sensei – the Teacher, Master and Sage – is as fervent and devoted as the Indian disciples to the guru or swami, but without its mystical undertones. The sensei is respected, to the point of worship, because he imparts learning – but not any spiritual darshan.

In the absence of a metaphysical frame of values, the rules of behaviour governing any particular situation are often contradictory and full of pitfalls. The classic literature of Japan is a compendium of unresolvable conflicts between various types of obligations towards others and oneself, between *chu, ko, jicho* and *jin,* with loss of face threatening from all directions. The national epic of Japan, the *Forty-seven Ronin,* is by all Western standards a tale of sheer dementedness. A brief summary of it is indispensable in any discussion of the Japanese character.

It is based on a true episode in the year 1703. The Lord Asano was appointed as one of the Masters of Ceremony to the Shogun's court. Lord Kira was given the task of instructing him in etiquette. Since Asano omitted to make suitable gifts to his instructor, Kira gave him misleading instructions, and Asano appeared wrongly dressed at court. He was now bound by 'giri to his own name' to slay Kira, and bound by giri to the Shogun (chu) not to do so. The logical solution was to kill Kira first and then commit hara-kiri. He failed to kill Kira, but was successful with his hara-kiri. His three hundred samurai retainers, who now became masterless *ronin,* all decided to commit hara-kiri, in giri to the name of their departed lord. But the forty-seven most faithful among them went one better and decided to kill Kira first, although this was a breach of their chu. Since Kira lived in a fortified castle, the forty-seven conspirators had to use all sorts of ruses and dissimulations to carry out their plan. Some had to dishonour themselves in public, which is worse than death, another sold his wife to a brothel, another killed his father-in-law, another sent his sister as a concubine to Kira, to spy on him. At last they stormed the castle, slew Kira, and then all committed suicide, including, of course, Kira's concubine. 'Verily,' as the proverb says, 'etiquette is weightier than a mountain, while death is lighter than a feather.'

The graves of the forty-seven ronin are still preserved.

They have become a popular place of pilgrimage, and it is customary for the pilgrims to deposit their visiting cards on the graves.

The safest way to evade the pitfalls of the labyrinth was to draw up maps with explicit instructions where to turn right or left, and to avoid as far as possible situations fraught with the danger of the unexpected. The tragedy of the forty-seven ronin is the archetype of Japanese conflict. A nobleman is made to appear at court in the wrong costume; this creates an unforeseen situation, not covered by the map, and therefore pregnant with terror. The predicament evokes familiar echoes from European history: the rigidly hierarchic mediaeval universe suffered from a similar phobia of the un-precedented, of dread 'mutability', which always threatened to disrupt its crustal instability. Ulysses' famous monologue from *Troilus and Cressida* could almost have been written by a bard of the Tokugawa Shogunate:

> The heavens themselves, the planets, and this centre
> Observe degree, priority, and place,
> Insisture, course, proportion, season, form,
> Office, and custom, in all line of order . . .
>   . . . but when the planets,
> In evil mixture, to disorder wander,
> What plagues and what portents! what mutiny!
> What raging of the sea! shaking of earth!
> Commotion in the winds! frights, changes, horrors,
> Divert and crack, rend and deracinate
> The unity and married calm of states
> Quite from their fixture! O, when degree is shak'd,
> Which is the ladder to all high designs,
> The enterprise is sick! . . .
> Take but degree away, untune that string,
> And, hark, what discord follows! . . .
> Force should be right; or, rather, right and wrong, –
> Between whose endless jar justice resides, –
> Should lose their names, and so should justice too.[1]

Feudal Europe, like feudal Japan, designed a protective ritual against the terrors of the unexpected, a rigid etiquette which governed every detail of social conduct – from the

[1] Act I, scene III.

order of precedence when going through a door to bowing
and scraping, and down to the hierarchy of the kitchen,
where the spit-masters had precedence over the soup-masters,
and the bread-carriers and the cup-bearers over the carvers
and cooks. The *Niebelungen saga,* a tale of conflicting *giris,
ons,* and settlings of accounts, is not as far removed from
the *Forty-seven Ronin* as one might think. One could pursue
the parallel even further, and compare the influence of
Japan's three religions to the three dominant trends in
mediaeval Christianity: Buddhist contempt for the illusory
world of the senses to the Neoplatonic otherworldliness
of Augustine; the Confucian social hierarchy to the
Aristotelian-Thomist hierarchy of perfection; and ancient
Shinto to the pagan elements imported by the Germanic
tribes.

However, Europe broke out of that static, walled-in universe, by re-discovering its own Greek and Judaeo-Christian
heritage; about A.D. 1600, the break-away was nearly completed and from there onward the journey led, with increasing speed, to ever broader vistas in a transformed world. At
almost the same time, A.D. 1600, Japan chose exactly the
opposite road: it closed its frontiers like an oyster its shell,
and remained in that state for the next, decisive, two hundred
and fifty years. Its industrial revolution and social reforms
were bought second-hand, as it were, superimposed on a
fundamentally unchanged mental structure. They brought in
their wake an endless succession of unprecedented situations
– to a people trained for centuries to avoid such situations,
and to whom the deadliest comment on a man's conduct was:
'He behaved unexpectedly.'[1]

In the Meiji era, and again in the post-1945 world, the conflicts resulting from exposure to 'uncharted' situations were
of a less heroic, but no less obsessional, nature than in the days
of the samurai. The altered landscape of the Westernized,
industrialized, democratized country made the labyrinth
even more confusing, its rules more contradictory. The

[1] Feyashu, the first Shogun, authorized the Samurai to cut down on the
spot any commoner who behaved 'in a manner other than expected'. (Murdock
and Yamagata, *A History of Japan,* III. p. 802).

warriors became worriers, and the whole nation became 'tangled with giri'. This manifested itself in curious symptoms, such as the mania for exchanging gifts and favours. This nationwide passion – a symbolic survival of the feudal past – is governed by elaborate rules for the reciprocation of the gift, or the service rendered, by precisely the right gift or service after the right interval of time – neither too short, because it would betray keenness to get rid of the *on*, nor too long, lest the burden of the *on* become unbearable.'[1] In extreme cases, this constant checking of one's account of *ons* and *giris* resembles the nervous compulsion to count one's matches before going to sleep. In Politics and Business, there is a certain amount of scheming for opportunities to slip an *on* on another person, thus placing him under an obligation which is sometimes indistinguishable from moral blackmail. The reverse phenomenon is that odd delicacy which makes the Japanese reluctant to help the victim of an accident for fear of placing an *on* on his shoulders. And there is also that patient biding of one's time to avenge an assumed insult by a subtle twist – a miniaturization of the mediaeval vendetta. The *Forty-seven Ronin* is still the favourite epic of little boys and television producers, of Kabuki and comic-strip; and beneath the democratic superstructure the ancient code of behaviour still asserts its power – partly expressed in symbolic ways, but extracting real penalties, from nervous worry to suicide.

If Japanese society had been given the chance to evolve organically, its codes and customs would have gradually relaxed and adapted themselves to the changing conditions. As it happened, however, the breakdown of the hierarchic social structure led to an unconscious tendency to preserve the integrity of the national character by a rigid moral – and aesthetic – perfectionism with impossibly high standards. The main purpose of education was to lay down rules, learned by rote, in answer to any conceivable situation that might arise; to make conformity the supreme ideal, and approval by

---

[1] Even the choice of the wrapping paper and string for gifts, and the manner of folding the wrapping-paper for different occasions, are governed by complicated rules.

the world the ultimate value. This world, however, is no longer aristocratic and feudal, but commercial and competitive; the result is a society with a feudal super-ego entangled in plebeian surroundings; a nation of Don Quixotes jousting with the pigs. The student faces his university entrance examination as if it were an ordeal by fire. If he gains admission, he is still taught what to think, not how to think, and worships his teacher as an infallible sensei. Not only the sensei, but every professional man, from the physician to the plumber, has been brought up to apply the same standards of perfection to himself; in giri to his reputation he cannot admit mistakes, and any critical remark is still considered, if not a mortal offence, a wound to the ego.[1] The office-worker owes giri to the boss, but if reprimanded, he will wilt away like a flower, or plot subtle vengeance in giri to himself. This puts a considerable strain on professional and private relationships, and not only the foreigner walks constantly on thin ice over the unstable crust of brittle super-egos – the Japanese must use equal circumspection, but he has the advantage of having learnt to skate. To lose face – or to cause, inadvertently, loss of face to others by what seems an innocent remark – is a constant danger in everyday life.

An unsympathetic Western writer compared the Japanese ego to an inflated balloon which collapses when pricked; yet he could not be more wrong. It would be nearer the truth to speak of a people with moral haemophilia, mutually afraid of inflicting the slightest scratch on each other – and yet condemned to wrestle for their existence in a competitive society where the large majority still lives on the bare subsistence level. What makes them into bleeders is the pathogenic discrepancy between the conditions under which they live, and the unattainable standards of perfection which they have been taught to apply to themselves, almost from their first outing in the mother's pouch.

[1] One of the heroic tales of Japan concerns three samurai who were asked by their lord to identify the maker of a precious sword. Only one guessed correctly – and was in due time murdered by the others, because they had to avenge the insult of having been proved wrong.

A Plague of Blushing

One of the odd and relatively harmless consequences of this predicament is a specifically Japanese form of anxiety-neurosis called 'homophobia' (or anthropophobia). It is described by a leading Tokyo psychiatrist as follows:

'Of nervosity symptoms, homophobia appears most frequently. In this is included fear of blushing when appearing before a person, or erythrophobia, feeling of getting stiff or oppressed before an individual, worrying over oneself of being unable to see straight into the speaker's eyes, worrying that one's own facial expressions give displeasure to the other party, etc.'[1]

In other words, 'homophobia' is an extreme form of self-consciousness and timidity – combined, one supposes, with a good deal of repressed aggression. If one looks for a correspondingly common affliction in the West (or in India), one would have to coin the term feminophobia – the behaviour of shy young men in the presence of members of the opposite sex. But that is just the point: in Japan this kind of blushing, bashful behaviour is not caused by a sexual, but by a social complex – the constant, nagging anxiety of losing face or causing loss of face. Even more striking is the fact that blushing itself – the principal symptom – is in Japan mostly caused by, and attributed to social, not sexual, embarrassment. The Japanese are great blushers; when flustered they have a characteristic gesture of hiding their cheeks between the flat palms of their hands. We say that somebody 'blushes like a maiden'; the Japanese of both sexes get 'hot in the face' – the reaction, perhaps, of anticipating a symbolic slap.

In a psychiatric hospital that I visited, I saw a patient – gentle and docile like the rest, and only a little more timid – who had developed a tremor in his right hand which made him unable to work, simultaneously with 'homophobia'. He was a draughtsman in a building firm, and both complaints

[1] 'On the Principles and Practice of Morita Therapy,' by Prof. Takehisa Kora, Dept. of Psychiatry, Tokyo Jikei-Kai Medical College, stencilled, undated, p. 21.

had started the day after his boss had reprimanded him for a mistake. In the same hospital, a pretty, though somewhat sluttish girl was pointed out to me. She had worked in a factory, led a rather gay life and, with another girl, had invented a game of recognizing men by their trousers without looking into their faces. They spiced the game with appropriate jokes, so there was no question of being unaware of the motive behind it. One day, she tried to teach the game to a third girl, who pointed out to her that it was 'rude'. She thereupon developed 'homophobia'. The men's trousers had not made her blush, the loss of face did.

In 1957, twelve years after the collapse of the old order, an American psychologist interviewed a number of Japanese and asked for their comments on Ruth Benedict's famous book written during the war. The following are passages from the book which he read to his informants, and their comments:

> ' "All kinds of professional commitments involve giri to one's name. The Japanese requirements are often fantastic when particular circumstances bring one into the public eye and criticism might be general. There are for instance the long lists of school principals who committed suicide because fires in their schools – with which they had nothing to do – threatened the picture of the Emperor which was hung in every school.
>
> Respondent's comment: "Yes, public opinion was such that a principal would hardly dare *not* to commit suicide. You used to hear of cases like that before the war."
>
> "There are also famous stories of persons who were guilty of a slip of the tongue in ceremonious readings of one of the Imperial Rescripts . . . and who have cleared their names by committing suicide."
>
> Respondent's comment: "Yes, the stories are told of how they came home after they had committed these errors, seated themselves before their domestic shrines, and com-

mitted hara-kiri. These stories used to be told as examples
of honourable behaviour . . .' "[1]

To be sure, the answers refer to the pre-1945 period, when
the Emperor was still a god, and suicides of this particular
type no longer occur; but they do occur for other, no less
fantastic reasons, and the suicide rate is going up, not down.

[1] 'Suicide as a Communicative Act,' by S. I. Hayakawa, in *Etc. A Review of
General Semantics,* autumn 1957, Illinois, U.S.A., pp. 47-8.

The Comforts of Ambiguity

To live under such pressure would be unbearable but for a technique designed to counteract and neutralize the rigours of perfectionism. This is the technique of ambiguity and evasion, worked out to the same perfection. It is as elastic as the code is rigid. If you have to move on thin ice all your life, you are bound to become an artist in skating: you do not move in a straight line but in elegant curves, shift your weight gently from one foot to another, and never allow it to be pinned down anywhere. If you breathe deeply, you will enjoy the additional advantage of being wrapped in a cloud of mist. Sensei, writers and poets are masters of this technique; the deeper their feeling, the thicker the fog which they exhale and the more difficult it is to guess what they mean.

I have mentioned the ambiguities of the written hand. Those of the spoken language are partly inherent in the semantic structure, partly due to the logics of skating. It is a language which shuns relative pronouns and connectives designed to give a sentence coherence; it describes events that somehow float through the air without naming the subject, gender, person and number to whom they happen. Enright gives some charming, yet typical examples of the hair-raising difficulties of interpreting classic verse. The passage to be quoted describes four seventeenth-century poets conversing – and some possible interpretations of what they possibly might mean:

'YASUI   "My hermitage/nest-letting to the heron/in
(the host) vicinity"
            i.e. (possibly) "My hermitage stands in such a

place that I should like to let nests to herons"
(The host lives in such a lonely spot that he
desires the companionship even of wild birds)

BASHŌ   "Hair-growing   space-of-time/hidden   body's
situation
i.e. "(Her) situation is that of one who hides
herself from the public gaze while (her) hair is
growing"
(Bashō has taken the "host" of the preceding
stanza as a nun. For some reason – death of
husband, unhappy love affair? – she retired to
a nunnery; now she is planning to return to
the world)

JUGO   "Faithlessness/unbearable that milk/squeezes
out, throws away"
i.e. "Thinking of unbearable faithlessness, she
squeezes out her milk and throws it from her"
(Not only has the husband or lover been false
but he has taken the baby away – as was usual
in the case of divorce)

KAKEI   "In front of not-erased memorial tablet/weeps
with a heavy heart"
i.e. "With a heavy heart she weeps before the
freshly inscribed memorial tablet"
(There is no question of faithless love here; the
mother is mourning the recent death of her
child)

BASHŌ   "Shadow   (subj.)/dawn   coldly/fire   (obj.)
burning"
i.e. "In the (same?) winter dawn, a shadow is
burning fuel", or, to expand it, "In the (same?)
winter dawn, a man (?) is burning fuel (in a
vacant house?), his shadow flickering (on the
wall)"
(The man may be a mourner from the preceding verse: a close relative who must watch
through the night, after the others have left)"[1]

[1] Enright, *op. cit.*, pp. 80-1.

That was a sample of poetry in the classic vein. But modern Japanese prose is still governed by the principles of verbal skating, which demand that the point to be made should be delayed and the listener kept guessing. All qualifying clauses, however flowery and long-winded, must precede the subject and when it is necessary to come quickly to the point, as, for instance, in a telephone conversation, the sentence has to be chopped into bits and fed to the listener piecemeal. Anybody who has listened to a Japanese telephone conversation remembers the agonized, spluttering, staccato voices, struggling to make themselves understood. To quote one of the foremost living translators:

'Every few words the speaker must stop to ask whether he is being followed; and he will repeat until he has been reassured. He must ask because he is, dismembering his Japanese sentence as it would be dismembered only in the most surrealistic of poetry.

Here is the original order [of words]: "The I yesterday so you introduced from Osaka aunt tomorrow afternoon on the Sea Breeze Express is going back."

And over the telephone: "My aunt, yes? The one from Osaka, yes? The one I introduced you to, yes? Well, she's going back, yes? Tomorrow afternoon, yes? On an express, the Sea Breeze." ' [1]

This inherent semantic ambiguity is increased by deliberate evasiveness. Spaniards have the gratifying custom of putting an inverted question-mark or exclamation-mark at the beginning of the sentence to warn the reader what mood to expect. The Japanese follow the opposite principle. They leave everything in suspense until the end of the sentence, and then append an offhand 'perhaps?' 'may it not be so?' 'this is a fact', or 'this I don't believe'. But, after all, a question-mark is merely an exclamation-mark bent into a more elegant shape, and a means of avoiding the embarrassments of

[1] Edward Seidensticker, 'On Trying to Translate Japanese,' *Encounter*, London, August, 1958, p. 13.

a straightforward statement. As another tortured translator once remarked: 'You sometimes feel that you can insert a "not" into most Japanese sentences and they will still mean much the same.'[1]

Nothing could be more shocking to a Japanese than the injunction 'Let your communication be Yea, yea, Nay, nay.' He would regard it as inconceivably rude, and therefore 'insincere'. The Japanese use of the word 'sincerity' – *magokoro, magoko* – has always been a subject of puzzlement and controversy among Westerners. Thus a man may be pretending and yet be 'sincere' if his pretence comforms to the code of manners; and it is 'insincere' to be too outspoken and direct. 'Vagueness is often a virtue; a god lives in a cloud; truth cannot be put on one's finger-tip,'[2] as a Japanese writer has put it, giving a highbrow version of the old proverb against speaking out: 'Behold the frog – he opens his mouth and displays all that's inside him.'

I have spoken of the Japanese language in the singular; in fact there exist at least four languages, or styles of speech, which differ in vocabulary and grammar: the colloquial style, the slightly archaizing, epistolatory style, the literary style, and the classical style (which is almost classical Chinese); in addition, there is a court language of extreme stiltedness in which not only a spade is not called a spade, but salt also is not called salt – it is referred to as 'the flower of the wave'. This hierarchy of languages is complemented by the hierarchy of honorifics; a person will refer to himself, according to circumstances, as: 'watakushi' (selfishness), 'boku' (servant), 'sessha' (awkward person), 'shosei' (younger) or 'kono ho' (this side); while the person addressed is 'anata' (that side), 'kimi' (prince), 'o mae' (honourable in front), 'sensei' (elder), 'danna' (master) or 'nanji' (renowned), and so forth. Once more we find the now familiar dualism between hierarchic stiffness, combined with ambiguity. It is this blend of rigidity and elasticity which gives Japanese culture its specific flavour.

---

[1] Dr. Ivan Morris, translator of *The Temple of the Golden Pavilion*, and Ooka's *Fires on the Plain*, etc.
[2] Quoted by Enright, *op. cit.*, p. 81.

The comforts of ambiguity have indeed become indispensable in almost every walk of Japanese life. Revulsion against the simple and direct approach is so deeply engrained that it causes psychological blockages which otherwise would be hard to explain. I found it, for instance, almost impossible to communicate by signs. I have travelled in a good many countries whose language I knew insufficiently or not at all, but nowhere else have I met with such apparent obtuseness in interpreting a sign or gesture. My efforts were usually received with a smile, or a blank stare, or anxious attempts to oblige in any conceivable way – except the one I tried to indicate. A sign-language could evidently mean nothing to the Japanese, because gestures are too direct and therefore rude – they seem to cause a kind of mental snowblindness. The gestures of the masked Nō dancer are in a symbolic code, as it were, and hardly ever directly indicative.

A similar difficulty arose about translations of unfavourable comments about myself in Japanese papers. The nice young student acting as translator would stumble over a passage, blush, then hurriedly go on to the next. If I insisted on having the left-out bit translated, he would start to choke and stutter that it was 'insincere' or 'meant nothing' or was 'in bad Japanese'. His distress on these occasions was so painful to watch that I felt like a depraved sadist bullying a child into repeating obscene words. I would get somebody else to translate the unutterable passage, and it would turn out to be something like this: 'Mr. K. is a much respected writer, but some think that he is not yet fully acquainted with Japanese customs, perhaps'.

Super-sensitiveness to any expression of disapproval has a paralysing effect on literary and art criticism – which makes Japan into a paradise for amateur poets. More serious is its effect on academic standards, since all teachers, from the elementary school to the university level, are reluctant to inflict on their students the stigma of failure which may lead to psychological damage. Once he has passed the ordeal of gaining access to a university the student has not much to fear, and examinations, like athletic contests, usually end with everybody getting a prize. The Western mind is cast in the mould of a competitive society that teaches the child to regard life as a kind of wavy curve, a succession of small triumphs and failures, which it must take in its stride. It is taught to become a 'good loser'; that to be beaten in fair competition casts no reflection on one's honour, and that too much concern with matters of 'prestige' is a sign of unbalanced behaviour. But we tend to forget that these standards, which we take so much for granted, are of relatively recent origin, that they only emerged with the development of our liberal-capitalist-free enterprise society. In Japan, there was no comparable organic development; when the country was suddenly thrown open, 'the very idea of "competition" was strange to them, and when Western economic writings were first translated into Japanese, it was necessary to make a new word for it. It was a combination of the Japanese words for "race" and "fight", and Fukusawa, the translator, relates how shocked his colleagues were by such harsh terminology'.[1]

And so they still are – understandably. To 'fight in a race' for sport is one thing; to struggle and pant for economic survival quite another. Even in England, which started the industrial revolution, the word 'competition' was not applied to rivalry in commerce until about 1800; the Japanese never got reconciled to the idea. The manner in which they set about their own industrial revolution, in the last decades of the nineteenth century, displayed all their virtues in taking evasive action. They managed to build up an apparently capitalist society which was really feudal to the marrow – competitive in appearance, hierarchic in reality, with private industries created by State initiative. They 'reversed the normal order of the starting point and succeeding stages of capitalist production'.[2] It was the State who decided what kind of industries Japan needed, from arsenals to railroads, and then proceeded to build and run them. But once they ran smoothly the State industries were denationalized – and sold at ridiculously low prices to a few politically reliable families

[1] Sansom, *op. cit.*, p. 248.
[2] Benedict, *op. cit.*, p. 93.

of wealthy merchant bankers, who had been entrusted with trading monopolies as a feudal privilege in the days of the Shogunate. There was no question of letting a financial oligarchy develop by free competition; instead, the State oligarchy created its own finance aristocracy of railway barons and shipping magnates by the same method by which it had formerly created its feudal barons and knights. The State built a foundry or a locomotive factory and then 'sold' it to a favoured family, much as an English peerage is bestowed in the New Year's Honours List. Thus came into being the dynasties of Japanese tycoons – the Mitsui and Mitsubishi, the Sumitomo and Konoike. They were collectively known as the Zaibatsu, the financial oligarchy, which took its place next to the Hambatsu, the oligarchy of the clans. In other words, the Japanese managed to create a competitive society sans competition, and they have stuck to this principle ever since. To paraphrase an old saying, they continued to earn a precarious living by saving one another's face.

That art, too, the child begins to learn almost in the mother's pouch. The ceremonial forms of self-disparagement – 'my wretched house', 'this unworthy family', 'this lowly person' – which contrast so oddly with the emphasis on self-respect, represent another method of taking evasive action; they are a symbolic renouncement of the prestige-contest in favour of an equally symbolic contest in modesty. No Japanese will ever land himself in the awkward position of the traveller in the Latin proverb who, when watching an athletic contest in Rome and boasting how much higher his own countrymen in Rhodes could jump, was silenced by *'Hic Rhodos, his salta'* – here is Rhodes, now jump. That is the kind of situation which the Japanese will avoid at any cost – not only because of the risk of making a fool of himself, but because of the equally deadly one of making a fool of his hosts. 'Thou shalt not be laughed at', is the First Commandment of Japanese ethics.

This stubborn reluctance to compete in a competitive society, and the endless face-saving manœuvres which it entails, makes itself felt throughout the cultural life of the nation: ambiguity and evasion lie like a delicate mist over the Japanese landscape. Its effect varies: the traditional arts are surrounded by a mysterious halo like gaslights in a London fog; on the poetic muse it acts like a mild dose of tear-gas; in politics, it can sometimes become more like poison gas.

I had a faint whiff of it during a public controversy into which I became involved with the Japanese PEN Club over Boris Pasternak. The PEN Club is taken more seriously in Japan and carries more weight there than in any Western country – for writers are sensei, and their Club is part of the cultural hierarchy. Before I arrived in Japan, the PEN Club had passed a resolution on the prohibition by the Soviet censorship of *Dr. Zhivago,* whose complete text is as follows: 'The Pasternak affair draws our attention in that it is no trivial matter in regard to the question of presentation in the field of literature. We are strongly opposed that it should be utilized in the international world of power politics. Seen from a purely literary point of view and as a question of freedom of speech, we feel it as a very regrettable incident.'

This resolution was published at the time when writers everywhere protested against the muzzling of Pasternak, and its main purpose was evidently to condemn the protests as 'power politics'. A considerable number of Japanese writers disagreed with the resolution, but did not say so in public; only three foreign scholars, members of the Japan PEN, sent a letter of protest in which they pointed out that the resolution 'was so carefully worded and ambiguous that it was not clear whether it was aimed at criticizing the Soviet Government or the Swedish Academy'.[1]

To this the PEN Club replied in an official letter which said in substance:[2] 'The fact that *Dr. Zhivago* had not been published in Japan was one of the reasons we did not take a definite attitude' – thus evading the question of principle, that is, the freedom of expression; and the Executive Secre-

[1] Dr. Ivan Morris, Edward Seidensticker, both distinguished Japanese scholars, and Father Joseph Roggendorf, S.J., of Sophia University, Tokyo.
[2] *The Mainichi,* 1 March 1959.

tary of the PEN, in a Press interview, added the further statement:[1] 'The Pasternak incident may be a grave problem from the point of view of principle. But one must also think of the repercussions that might have been created if a statement were issued by us. I do not know if it is wise to stick to principles always. I believe that the PEN Club is an organization where people linked by pen, regardless of race, nationality and ideology, get together in friendly atmosphere' – and so it trailed off into the mist.

This correspondence was published a day or two before I was supposed to address a meeting of the Japanese PEN; and its effect on me was that I cancelled the meeting in an open letter, explaining that I could not accept an invitation from an organization of writers who put political considerations before the writer's freedom. Though the letter was polite, the gesture was almost inconceivably rude by Japanese standards. The PEN published an answer which ranged over a wide variety of subjects, yet omitted any reference to the fact that the publication of Pasternak's book had been prohibited in Russia. I had pointed out that millions of Russian citizens had been made to sign resolutions calling Pasternak 'a swine who befouled his own sty', and asking that he be punished for writing a book which the signatories had never been allowed to read. To this the PEN answered: 'But a member of our Club, who was in Europe during the latter part of last year has mentioned that while there he read reports stating that *Dr. Zhivago* was apparently being read by some in the Soviet Union'.[2] It was like saying 'some people in England smoke opium' without mentioning that it was prohibited by law. Regarding the PEN Executive Secretary's doubts on the wisdom of sticking to principles, the answer stated: 'What was quoted *even in Japanese*[3] might perhaps appear to those who are not familiar with our way of speech as though his stand is ambiguous on the principle of freedom of expression, since the word "gensoku", meaning "principle" is used much more broadly in Japanese than in English. Its English trans-

---

[1] *loc. cit.*
[2] *The Mainichi*, 5 March 1959.
[3] My italics.

lation completely misconveys his ideas.' What the Secretary really meant, the statement explained, was 'that whenever we make a protest it should be as effective as possible'. Since the spokesman of the PEN (the initials stand for Poets, Essayists and Novelists) managed to misconvey his ideas to that extent, not only in English but also in his native Japanese tongue, one was left to wonder how ideas ever get un-misconveyed.

'I believe in God, but I do not believe in His existence,' a Japanese theologian declared at a Round Table Conference on 'Religion and Modern Life'.[1] His statement had a certain resemblance to that classic example of logical confusion – the Oath of Abjuration which Japanese Christians had to swear when Christianity was outlawed in 1616:

> 'In denying the Christian faith . . . the converts, having abjured their religion . . . were by a curious logic made to swear by the very powers that they had just denied: "By the Father, the Son and the Holy Ghost, Santa Maria and all the Angels . . . if I break this oath may I lose the Grace of God forever and fall into the wretched state of Judas Iscariot." By an even further departure from logic all this was followed by an oath to Buddhism and Shinto deities.'[2]

But here again, there is another side to the picture:

> 'During this later and more violent phase of repression unspeakable tortures were used in efforts to secure apostasy and whole families, including infants in arms, were mercilessly destroyed. Nevertheless the Jesuit documents report a continued enrolment of new converts and an almost joyful acceptance of death by believers of all classes . . . A contemporary observer, the English trader Richard Cocks, writing of the shogun's enmity towards Christians said, "I saw 55 of them martyrized at one time at Miyako. Among them were little children of five or six years, burned alive

[1] *Bulletin of the International Institute for the Study of Religions*, Tokyo, November 1958.
[2] Sansom, *op. cit.*, pp. 186-8.

in the arms of their mothers, who cried 'Jesus, receive their souls'. There are many in prison who hourly await death, for very few return to their idolatry." ' [1]

The persecutions started in 1597, with the crucifixion of twenty-six Christians in Nagasaki. The initial cause is said to have been the boast of a captain of a Spanish galleon that the missionaries were the vanguard of a conquering armada. In 1622, evidence was alleged to have been discovered by the Shogunate, suggesting complicity of the Church in a Spanish plot to invade Japan. By 1650, some two hundred thousand Japanese Christians had perished. But an estimated hundred thousand survived, and continued to practise their faith in secret. Two centuries later, when Japan re-opened her frontiers to the world and the anti-Christian laws were rescinded, several Christian communities emerged from the underground, as it were, in various parts of the country. For two hundred years they had paid giri to their God and worshipped in concealment, all the time preserving 'the sacrament of Baptism . . . in a form of whose efficacy not even the strictest theologian could entertain a doubt'.[1] The most important surviving community was again centred on a suburb of Nagasaki, called Urakami.

After thirty years of effort, out of donations of twenty thousand Japanese Christians, a Cathedral Church was built in Urakami, and consecrated in 1914. It accommodated six thousand people and was the largest Christian place of worship in East Asia. It was destroyed by the second atomic bomb in August 1945. Though Nagasaki has been entirely rebuilt since, the authorities left the burnt-out shell of the Cathedral standing, as a memento in oblique Japanese fashion. There had been nothing oblique about that Christian bomb.

[1] Sansom, op. cit., pp. 182-3.
[2] H. McAleavy, 'The Making of Modern Japan', History Today, May 1959.

The Road to Zen

I T may be useful at this point to draw certain comparisons between India and Japan – the most traditional and the most 'modern' among the great countries of Asia.

Historically common to both are a social structure based on the family with its clan extensions, and the caste-hierarchy with its sub-divisions; the domination of male over female, of the aged over the young; the resulting authority of the Father and the Teacher; and some basic aspects of education, designed to promote conformity and to inhibit individuality in thought and action. Common to both is a type of reasoning indifferent to the 'laws' of contradiction and excluded middle, to the distinction between subject and object, between the act of perception and the thing perceived; an attitude of equanimity towards life and death, the latter being considered closer to essential Being than the former, and with a blurred boundary between the two; an approach to Reality which is intuitive and *a prioristic* rather than rational and empirical, and relies on fluid analogies rather than on well-defined concepts. Since the West regards the intuitive approach as essentially feminine, the rational approach as masculine, both Eastern cultures appear from our point of view to be dominated by men with a 'feminine' logic and sensitivity compared to the down-to-earth, matter-of-fact attitude of the women.

I shall not try to discuss which of these similarities are derived from some common Asiatic mould in the remote past and which may be due to cultural interaction – Buddhism being the most obvious example of the latter. I would like to consider instead some of the differences and contrasts within the common framework.

The caste system in India, within historical times, was rigid, in Japan, relatively fluid. A samurai was entitled to cut down without further ado any commoner who annoyed, or supposedly annoyed, him; on the other hand, a commoner could pass into the samurai class by adoption and marriage. During the Shogunate, certain rich moneylenders – who, in theory, were only one step higher up in caste than the Eta – collected rent from indebted peasants and thereby acquired the status of landed gentry, though they did not really own the land; and they bought samurai status for their sons by getting them married to daughters of samurai and simultaneously adopted into the family. The Japanese custom of adopting a son-in-law entails the erasure of his name from his own family register, and its entry on the register of his father-in-law. Originally intended to prevent the extinction of a family's male lineage, it became a method of evading the rigours of the caste system – yet another example of the Japanese genius of combining rigidity in the abstract with elasticity in practice. As a result, when the feudal economy changed into an industrial economy, the feudal aristocracy did not have to face a hostile bourgeoisie, because it had literally 'adopted' the bourgeois – either individually, or, in the case of the Zaibatsu, as a class; the new finance aristocracy was a kind of adopted son-in-law of the feudal state.

India, where the caste system rigidly survived into the modern age, had to go through a social revolution, disestablishing its Princes and their Zamindar retainers; whereas Japan was able to preserve her 'Emperor system' and build a quasi-capitalistic state on a quasi-feudal foundation. If we search for an explanation of this difference in development, we are led to a basic contrast between the two countries. In India, inter-marriage, and even inter-dining, between different castes was unthinkable because caste was ordained by divine providence and bound up with religion and rite; whereas in Japan, caste was regarded from the secular angle as a matter of rank in the social hierarchy and could be treated in a pragmatic manner.

A similar difference may be traced between the type of

authority exercised by the father, the guru, and the sensei. In India, this authority is of a religious character, in Japan a matter of social obligations and codes of behaviour. The Indian father is *ipso facto* considered a saint; the Japanese father is nothing of the sort, but a creditor to whom a vast amount of *on* is due. The guru imparts spiritual darshan by his presence; the sensei imparts wisdom, which is accepted equally uncritically, but it is a wisdom of worldly learning. The extended family in India is held together by a mystical bond reflected in the joint household; in Japan, obligations towards the more distant members of the family are limited and graded, and if a poor relative must be taken in under one's roof, he is called a 'cold rice relative' because he (or she) is last served, and treated with contempt. In India, social etiquette is vague, and the accent is on affirmations of love and affection, symbolized in the Hindu greeting of joining the palms in a smiling gesture of prayer; in Japan, it is an elaborate and watchful ritual. Exactly the reverse is true with regard to religious observances: in Japan, these are treated so nonchalantly that at the Shinto shrine you clap your hands, or pull a bell-cord, to attract the attention of the gods; in India, it is ceremonialized in a series of ablutions, purifications, recitations. The Indian is careless in his dealings with society, punctilious in his dealings with deity; in Japan, it is the reverse. In India, the beggar has a divine right to alms, and to give means to acquire darshan; in Japan, gifts are exchanged and obligations returned in the exact amount of those received. In India, education of the child starts late and remains lax, except in matters of religious and filial observance; in Japan, strict social conditioning starts early, but in all matters not covered by the social code the Japanese child and adult enjoy considerably greater freedom.

The difference between the two cultures is most pronounced in their attitudes to carnality. It goes much deeper than, for instance, the contrast between an English puritan and a French libertine. The puritan is enjoined 'to renounce the sinful lusts of the flesh' – but also to accept the Sacrament of marriage which makes 'man and wife one flesh'; the Hindu considers marriage as a necessary and passing evil during the second of the four seasons of life, and intercourse as a physical and spiritual impoverishment. The French libertine, from Sade to Genet, is always a rebel against morality, to which he pays implicit and ambivalent tribute; whereas the Japanese forms of libertinage are not anti-moral but amoral, and sex is enjoyed for its own sake – as shown by the division of labour between concubine and wife. In India, masturbation is a sin against body and spirit, leading to neurosis and hypochondria; in Japan, it is considered a solitary pastime, almost like smoking. In India, the woman – outside her role as mother – is the temptress who saps the male's strength, reflected in the image of blood-thirsty goddesses; the Japanese woman – again outside her role as mother – is a provider of manifold pleasures, skilled in dance, song, love and witty conversation. In India, accordingly, she is allowed even less individual personality than the male; in Japan, more than the male, because she is not subject to the same code of honour. The obsessional food faddism and bowel worries of the Indians are of religious origin. The Japanese, too, were vegetarians – though never teetotalers – until the disestablishment of Buddhism; but the zest with which they took to *sukiyaki* and raw fish indicates that they considered the prohibition of meat more as a secular law than a mystic commandment. Again in contrast to the Hindu pollution-phobia, the Japanese treat their fields with fresh human manure, which is put to use straight from the chamber-pot or *benjo* sink – Western housewives in Tokyo love to tell horror tales about cabbages, artistically arranged in shop-windows, and with dainty specks of excrement on them.

I like to remember and compare in retrospect some festive meals, traditional style, in India and Japan. In Japan, we would kneel in front of a low marquetry or lacquered table, manipulate with ebony chopsticks a succession of pretty and delicious miniature courses (some of which were prepared on charcoal braziers in front of us), and wash them down with thimblefuls of hot saké presented like sacrificial cups by kneeling waitresses or geisha. We would be refreshed by hot towels between dishes, and use in the course of the meal up to fifty Lilliputian plates, bowls, cups, saucers, and whatnots per guest. In India, if the meal was really in the traditional style, no plates, glasses, cups or cutlery were used. We would either squat on the floor – as in Vinoba Bhave's camps – or sit along a table, each with a palm-leaf serving as a plate in front of him, our left arms dangling lifelessly as if they had forgotten their cunning, while with three fingers of the right hand we would mix the rice, vegetables and curd into a sloppy mush and scoop it into our mouths. After the meal, the guests would each in turn move a few steps away, a servant would pour water from a jug first over his fingers, then into his cupped palm to rinse his mouth and rub his teeth, and lastly to drink a few swallows – hoping, with St. Augustine, for 'the day when Thou wilt destroy both the belly and the meat'.

Suicide in India is rare – the only cases sanctioned by tradition were widows committing suttee, and Yogis entering final samadhi; but the whole cycle of life is a detour towards death and liberation from the wheel. In Japan, even suicide is secularized, a matter of social convention, and hara-kari is treated as a fine art for connoisseurs. Aesthetic perfectionism is as alien to contemporary India as religious perfectionism to Japan. India is a country of dark, tragic grandeur, and contempt for the frills and vanities of life; the Japanese know thirty-five different ways of wrapping a gift-parcel in paper, and the worst tragedy they know is to lose face. The Indians are plagued by religious anxiety; the Japanese by worry about prestige. Ruth Benedict has suggested an interesting distinction between 'guilt cultures' and 'shame cultures', which is much to the point:

'A society that inculcates absolute standards of morality and relies on man's developing a conscience is a guilt culture . . . Shame cultures rely on external sanctions for good behaviour, not, as true guilt cultures do, on an internalized conviction of sin. Shame is a reaction to other people's criticism . . . by being openly ridiculed and rejected or by fantasying to himself that he has been made ridiculous . . . In either case it is a potent sanction. But it requires an audience or at least a man's fantasy of an audience. Guilt does not . . . Shame has the same place of authority in Japanese ethics that "a clear conscience", "being right with God", and the avoidance of sin have in Western ethics. Logically enough, therefore, a man will not be punished in the afterlife. The Japanese – except for priests who know the Indian *sutras* – are quite unacquainted with the idea of reincarnation dependent upon one's merit in this life, and – except for some well-instructed Christian converts – they do not recognize post-death reward and punishment or a heaven and a hell'.[1]

Nor do they recognize Good and Evil as absolutes; Japanese ethics is pragmatic, relativistic and situational. A man is not part good, part bad; he is part 'rough soul' and part 'gentle soul', both considered equally useful under the proper circumstances. The classical Japanese vocabulary, which had no word for 'competition' and 'civic rights', had no word for 'God' either; to the first Jesuit missionaries 'the translation of the word "God" has caused great difficulties in Japan, where it has been most inadequately represented by the word Kami, which means little more than a superior being'.[2]

Which leads us to Zen.

'Kill the Buddha'

Zen is to religion what a flat-garden is to a garden. It knows no god, no afterlife, no good and no evil, as the flat-garden knows no flowers, herbs or shrubs. It has no doctrine or holy writ, its teaching is transmitted mainly in the form of parables as ambiguous as the pebbles in the rock garden which symbolize now a mountain, now a fleeing tiger. When a disciple asks 'What is Zen?', the master's traditional answer

[1] Benedict, *op. cit.*, pp. 222-4.
[2] Sansom, *op. cit.*, p. 126.

is 'Three pounds of flax' or 'A decaying noodle' or 'A toilet stick' or a whack on the pupil's head. Zen cannot be debunked because its method is self-debunking. In its mondos and koans, Japanese ambiguity reaches its metaphysical peak; it is the ultimate evasion. And for precisely that reason it played a vital part in maintaining the balance of extremes in Japanese life.

Taken at face value and considered in itself, Zen is at best an existentialist hoax, at worst a web of solemn absurdities. But within the framework of Japanese society, this cult of the absurd, of ritual leg-pulls and nose-tweaks, made beautiful sense. It was, and to a limited extent still is, a form of psychotherapy for a self-conscious, shame-ridden society, a technique of undoing the strings which tied it into knots; in a word, Zen was the tranki of feudal Japan.

In the supposedly oldest Zen poem, attributed to Seng-Ts'an (sixth century A.D.), men are admonished:

> Saunter along and stop worrying
> If your thoughts are tied you spoil what is genuine ...
> The wise person does not strive;
> The ignorant man ties himself up ...
> If you work on your mind with your mind,
> How can you avoid an immense confusion? ...
>
> If you want to get the plain truth,
> Be not concerned with right and wrong.
> The conflict between right and wrong
> Is the sickness of the mind.[1]

From its earliest beginnings – supposedly in sixth-century China – the great masters of Zen denied that it aimed at moral improvement: 'If a man seeks the Buddha, that man loses the Buddha'.[2] According to tradition, it was a fierce-looking Indian monk, Bodhidharma, who brought Buddhism to China in the sixth century. When the Emperor asked him how much merit he, the Emperor, had acquired by supporting the new creed, Bodhidharma shouted at him: 'None what-

[1] Quoted by Alan W. Watts, *The Way of Zen*, London, 1957, pp. 89 and 115.
[2] *Ibid.*, p. 125.

soever.' The Emperor, rather shaken in his enthusiasm, then wanted to know just what the sacred doctrine of the creed was. Again Bodhidharma shouted, 'It is empty, there is nothing sacred.'

That interview set the tone for the Zen tradition, which makes a special point of being rude, abrupt, direct and sarcastic – precisely those things which, according to the Japanese code of manners, must be avoided like the plague. The founding father himself, Bodhidharma, a favourite subject of Zen painting, is invariably portrayed as a snarling tough, with eyes menacingly bulging out of his head yet at the same time twinkling with sarcastic glee. Once he fell asleep while meditating, and got so furious about it that he promptly sawed off his offending eyelids. These dropped to the ground and became the seeds of the first tea-plants – hence the saying that Zen and tea 'taste the same'. Another leg-pull story has it that the ferocious Bodhidharma persisted in meditation so long that his legs fell off.

The tradition of deliberate rudeness has, significantly, been maintained to this day, and there are endless stories to illustrate it.

'A monk asked Tosu (T'ou-tzu), a Zen master of the T'ang period: "I understand that all sounds are the voice of the Buddha. Is this right?" The master said, "That is right." The monk then proceeded: "Would not the master please stop making a noise which echoes the sound of a fermenting mass of filth?" The master thereupon struck the monk.

The monk further asked Tosu: "Am I in the right when I understand the Buddha as asserting that all talk, however trivial or derogatory, belongs to ultimate truth?" The master said, "Yes, you are in the right." The monk went on, "May I then call you a donkey?" The master thereupon struck him.' [1]

The reason why the master struck him was not the monk's rudeness – which was in the right tradition of Zen-teasing –

[1] Daisetz T. Suzuki, *Zen and Japanese Culture*, London, 1959, p. 33.

but because he was too logical – which is the one unforgiveable sin in a Zen monastery. Dr. Suzuki, the sensei of Zen senseis, comments – with a lucidity which is quite unusual in his voluminous writings:

'The masterful Tosu knew, as all Zen masters do, the uselessness of making any verbal demonstration against such a "logician". For verbalism leads from one complication to another; there is no end to it. The only effective way, perhaps, to make such a monk as this one realize the falsehood of his conceptual understanding is to strike him and so let him experience within himself the meaning of the statement, "One in All and All in One". The monk was to be awakened from his logical somnambulism. Hence Tosu's drastic measure.'[1]

A monk asked the master Ts'ui-wei for what reason Bodhidharma had come from India. The master answered: 'Pass me that chin-rest.' As soon as the monk had passed the chin-rest, the master whacked him over the head with it. That is all there is to the story. A chin-rest is a board to support the head during long meditation; and the moral of the story is evidently: don't try to reason – meditate.

'Po-chang had so many students that he had to open a second monastery. To find a suitable person as its master, he called his monks together and set a pitcher before them, saying:
"Without calling it a pitcher, tell me what it is"
The head monk said, "You couldn't call it a piece of wood."
At this the monastery cook kicked the pitcher over and walked away. The cook was put in charge of the new monastery.'[2]

Why was the cook put in charge of the new monastery? As

[1] *Ibid.*, p. 34.
[2] Watts, *op. cit.*, p. 129.

a reward, one might say, for his un-Japanese behaviour.[1] This consisted not only in the rudeness, but above all in the spontaneity and directness of his gesture: in his 'direct-pointing', as Zen calls it, in contradistinction to verbal reflection. The cook was cutting through the Gordian knot.

The whackings and teasings are a mild form of shock therapy to jolt the student out of his mental habits and to hammer it into his head that he must act spontaneously, without thinking, without self-consciousness and hesitation. This is the main purpose of the mondo – the brief, sharp dialogue between master and pupil – and the koan – the logically insoluble riddle which the pupil must try to solve. A variant of the pitcher koan, for instance, is the bath-water koan. The master suddenly springs the question at the pupil: 'When you let out the bath-water, does the eddy turn clockwise or anticlockwise?' The pupil hesitates, and the master yells at him: 'Don't think! Act!' whirling his hand in the air. Or, the master may ask: 'A girl is walking down the street. Is she the younger or the older sister?' The correct answer is apparently, for the pupil to put on a mincing walk, that is, to *become* the girl, and thereby to demonstrate that what matters is the experience of being and not its verbal description, the 'suchness' of existence and not concepts like 'older' or 'sister'.

'The truth is [says Dr. Suzuki], as Tosu declares in the following:

A monk asks, "What is the Buddha?"
Tosu answers, "The Buddha."
Monk: "What is the Tao?"
Tosu: "The Tao."
Monk: "What is Zen?"
Tosu: "Zen" '[2]

---

[1] The cook was Chinese, but let it pass. Throughout this chapter several of the stories quoted refer to the early Chinese patriarchs; but the manner of telling the story and the morale drawn from it reflect the spirit of Japanese Zen. I have used indiscriminately Chinese and Japanese terms according to which happened to occur in the texts I quoted.
[2] Suzuki, *op. cit.*, p. 34.

What is a rose? Is a rose, is a rose.

'In fact,' Dr. Suzuki informs us, 'there is no other way of illumining the monk's mind than affirming that what is is.' And what was was, perhaps.

There are said to exist some one thousand seven hundred koans, divided into various categories. In the Rinzai sect of Zen, the disciple is supposed to pass through a series of about fifty koans of increasing difficulty before his graduation as a fully Enlightened One, and the process is supposed to take about thirty years – but this need not be taken by the letter. In the classic system of Hakuin, there are five graded categories of koan; but certain Zen abbots, whom I visited in Kyoto, mentioned a different classification: according to his character, the pupil would be given either 'keen knife-edge' koans or 'gentle spring-wind' koans or 'iron ox' koans. A list of 'correct' answers has never been published since this would destroy their purpose; but most of the koans are of a type which admits of no logically correct answer, only of a symbolic rejoinder in the spirit of Zen.

The oldest-known koans are the 'Three Barriers of Hung-Lun', an eleventh-century Zen master:

'Question: Everybody has a place of birth. Where is your place of birth?

Answer: Early this morning I ate white rice gruel. Now I'm hungry again.

Question: How is my hand like the Buddha's hand?

Answer: Playing the lute under the moon.

Question: How is my foot like a donkey's foot?

Answer: When the white heron stands in the snow it has a different colour.'[1]

The first answer seems to mean that the circumstances of birth and death are mere ripples in the flow of appearances, as unimportant as the eternal cycle of hunger and satiety. The second means, perhaps: do not try to reason, but

[1] Watts, *op. cit.,* p. 106.

serenade the moon and you are the Buddha. The third I leave to the reader to meditate upon.

Some of the koans and mondos have an archetypal ring. When Yao-shan was asked, 'What is the Tao?' he pointed upwards to the sky and downwards to the water-jug before him. When pressed for an explanation, he replied, 'A cloud in the sky and water in the jug.' Other well-known classics are: 'What was your basic nature before your parents made you?' and 'What is the sound of a single-handed clap?' The last one is perhaps meant to symbolize that subject and object have no separate existence, because the act of perception is indivisible like the act of clapping. In other words, the single hand clapping is as 'exceedingly odd' as it seemed to Bishop Berkeley 'that this tree/continues to be/when there's no one about in the quad.' And there is indeed no one about in the Zen monastery's quad to answer: 'the tree/will continue to be/since observed by yours faithfully, God.'

Though submitted with the guilty knowledge that koans exist for the express purpose that they should not be logically explained, the logical explanations given above seem to be born out by the strong emphasis of Zen on the indivisibility of experience, and on the foolishness of all attempts to chop it up into dualistic or abstract categories of thought. Zen's arch-enemy, the thousand-armed hydra which it fights to destroy, is rational thinking – verbal concepts, definitions, the operations of logic, classification by categories. The more extravagant koans are designed to reduce these to absurdity, to undermine the pupil's confidence in his powers of conscious reasoning, and thus to clear away the obstacles to satori – the sudden flash of intuitive understanding which illuminates the path to Enlightenment. Hence the distrust of words, considered to be the germ-carriers of abstract thought:

> Those who know do not speak
> Those who speak do not know
>
> When you are silent 'It' speaks
> When you speak 'It' is silent.[1]

[1] *Ibid.*, pp. 77 and 145.

The philosophy of Zen is traditionally summed up in four sentences, attributed to the Second Patriarch – the pupil of Bodhidharma:

> Unteachable and unorthodox[1]
> Not founded on words and letters
> Pointing directly into the human mind
> Seeing into one's nature and attaining Buddha-hood.

The last point, by the way, is not stressed in contemporary Zen, because it holds that every man is born a Buddha anyway, though there are 'short Buddhas' and 'tall Buddhas' – or, to paraphrase Orwell, that all men are Buddha, but some are more Buddha than others. The main emphasis in the quadrain is on the rejection of 'words and letters', and on the 'direct pointing' at the intuitive faculties. Hence the deliberately absurd answer to the question, 'What is the Buddha?': 'Three pounds of flax.'

That answer it attributed to T'ung-shan, who lived in the ninth century, and a later authority comments that 'none can excel it as regards its irrationality which cuts off all passages to speculation.' The three pounds of flax remind one of the koan discussed by the mediaeval schoolmen: 'If God had chosen to be incarnated in the form of an ass or a pumpkin, could a pumpkin work miracles or be crucified?' – and of Erasmus' comment: 'They are Folly's servants.' There is something of that Erasmian attitude in Zen's contempt for the vanity of all endeavours to approach the Absolute with the yardsticks of logic.

Thus some koans do make 'sense' by their direct appeal to intuitions beyond verbal thought, while others are meant to destroy the self-imposed restraints and imaginary fetters which prevent the spontaneous exercise of the imaginative powers. Once one has entered into the spirit of the game, the answers to certain types of koan become fairly obvious. For instance, if a Zen master suddenly barked at me, 'Stop that ship on the distant ocean,' I should answer without turning a

[1] This at least is my interpretation of Alan Watts' interpretation of the four ideograms which constitute the first sentence. Watts' rendering is: 'Outside teaching; apart from tradition.' Op. cit., p. 88.

hair: 'Don't worry, I have just dropped an iceberg in front of it' – the idea being that if I am free to imagine a ship, what is there to prevent me from imagining an iceberg? When Tao-hsin asked his master how to achieve liberation, the master asked back: 'Who binds you?' 'No one binds me,' said Tao-hsin. 'Why then should you seek liberation?' And that was the moment of Tao-hsin's Enlightenment. In other words, all you need to achieve freedom is to realize that you are free – otherwise you are like the man in the Chinese proverb who was searching for the ox while he was riding on it.

To quote another proverb, the koans are 'bricks with which to knock open the door'. It is the door which leads to the 'natural man', imprisoned behind the walls of artificial restraints.

The whole teaching of Zen seems to be directed against the inhibitions and restraints imposed by the Japanese code of behaviour. Against the Spartan self-discipline demanded by the code, stands Po-chang's famous definition of Zen: 'When hungry, eat, when tired, sleep.' The traditional dread of unforeseen situations is neutralized by springing surprises and shocks on the disciple and encouraging him to reciprocate in equally eccentric fashion: the koan technique is designed to bring out just that side of a person which the social code condemns: 'the unexpected man.' In the social code, 'self-respect' is practically synonymous with cautious and circumspect behaviour, designed to avoid adverse comment; Zen bullies the pupil into throwing caution to the wind, and teaches him to respond spontaneously, 'without even the thickness of a hair between impulse and act'. Social conditioning leads to numbing self-consciousness and blushing homophobia; Zen aims at the annihilation of 'the self-observing self'. It proclaims to be the philosophy of no-mind (Wu-hsin), of no-thought (Wu-mien), no-striving (Wu-wei), no-affectation (Wu-shih), and of 'going ahead without hesitation'. In the words of Yün-men: 'When walking, just walk, when sitting, just sit, above all, don't wobble.' In the social hierarchy, the father ranks second only to the Emperor in authority; Zen debunks even paternal authority by creating a kind of psychotherapeutic transference situation, where the *roshi*, abbot, poses as a formidable father-figure of 'tigerish' appearance, but gradually induces the pupil to combine respect with spontaneity, and to respond to koan teasers with saucy counter-gambits. The cramped victim of Japanese edu-action, tangled with *giri,* crushed by his *on,* is given by the founder of the Rinzai sect this kindly advice concerning the path towards self-realization: 'Clear every obstacle out of your way . . . If on your way you meet the Buddha, kill the Buddha. When you meet your ancestor, kill your ancestor. When you meet your father and mother, kill your father and mother. When you meet your kin, kill your kin. Only thus will you attain deliverance. Only thus will you escape the trammels and become free.'[1]

Another Zen command expresses the same idea in a less fierce image: 'Let your mind go and become like a ball in a mountain stream.'

[1] There are several versions of this famous injunction; the above is Mishima's, *op. cit.,* p. 258.

Delusion and Self-Delusion

Satori and Samadhi

ZEN spontaneity became the ideal antidote to the Confucian rigidity of the social order. It was a marriage between extreme opposites, which is so characteristic of Japanese culture. But in this case the partners were destined for each other from childhood, as it were. Both came from China, where Confucianism and Taoism had from ancient times played complementary parts in the nation's life: the former determining law, order, book-learning and convention, the latter pointing to the intuitive Way – the Tao – towards the inner man and ultimate reality: the cloud in the sky and the water in the jug. Zen owes as much to Taoism as to Buddhism, and perhaps more: it has certainly remained closer to the philosophy of Lao Tse than to any Buddhist sect in other countries.

Zen was introduced into Japan in the late 12th century – more than five centuries after Confucianism and earlier forms of Buddhism. It took immediate roots; but it became radically transformed in the process, and the flower was characteristically Japanese. By a feat of mental acrobacy, of which perhaps no other nation would be capable, the gentle, non-violent doctrine of the Buddha became the adopted creed of the murderous samurai. A little later it also became the dominant influence in painting, landscape-gardening, flower arrangement, tea ceremony, firefly-hunting and similar nipponeries on the one hand – of swordsmanship, wrestling, Judo, archery, dive-bombing on the other. How was this possible? The secret is not in the Buddha's smile but in a simple formula applicable to all these diverse activities, the panacea of Zen: trust your intuition, short-circuit reflection, discard caution, act spontaneously. It is amazing what wonders this prescription can achieve, especially in a people tied in knots, conditioned to the reverse set of principles.

To make the formula take effect on the unconscious, non-verbal levels at which it was aimed, verbal admonitions were, of course, not enough. Apart from methods of developing the technical skills appropriate in each branch of activity, a mystic ritual and a special terminology were needed. Key-words in that terminology are satori, the sudden flash of insight which brings on Awakening or Enlightenment; the state of muga, which occurs when the split between the acting self and the self-observing self disappears, and the act becomes effortless, automatic, entranced – so that the painter or swordsman no longer feels that *he* is wielding the brush or making the thrust, but that a mysterious 'It' has taken charge.[1] Lastly, a man who has completed his training and reached final Enlightenment, will contiue to live zestfully and apparently unchanged, but he will *'live as one already dead'* – that is, detached and indifferent to success or failure.

Satori is a wonderfully rubbery concept. There are small satoris and big satoris. They occur when one solves a koan, or in meditation, but also through looking at peach-blossom or watching a pebble hit a bamboo. The mondos, in which the disciple who asked a too rational question is whacked on the head, usually end with the line: 'at that moment he had his satori.' Facing two famous Zen abbots in the Daitokuji Temple in Kyoto, I asked them how long a satori lasts. The first answered promptly: 'One second.' The second added as promptly: 'It might go on for days.' Dr. Suzuki defines satori as follows:

' . . . Satori finds a meaning hitherto hidden in our daily concrete particular experiences, such as eating, drinking, or business of all kinds . . .

. . . Satori is emancipation, moral, spiritual, as well as intellectual. When I am in my isness, thoroughly purged of all intellectual sediments, I have my freedom in its primary sense.

[1] *Muga* is the Japanese rendering of *Wu-mien* – No-thought.

. . . When the mind, now abiding in its isness – which, to use Zen verbalism, is not isness – and thus free from intellectual complexities and moralistic attachments of every description, surveys the world of the senses in all its multiplicities, it discovers in it all sorts of values hitherto hidden from sight.'[1]

On another occasion he says:

'. . . This supreme moment in the life of an artist, when expressed in Zen terms, is the experience of satori. To experience satori is to become conscious of the Unconscious (*mushin*, no-mind), psychologically speaking. Art has always something of the Unconscious about it.'[2]

Mr. Christmas Humphreys, Q.C., President of the Buddhist Society in London, who, like most modern exponents of Zen, is a pupil of Dr. Suzuki's, informs us in his book on Zen[3] that he had his first satori during a lesson in Judo: 'on the night when, without "thought" or feeling, I leapt to opportunity and in the fraction of time that my opponent was off his balance, threw him directly, cleanly, utterly'; but his greatest satori he had in a Turkish bath – which conjures up the image of Archimedes jumping out of the tub to shout *Eureka*. By modern Zen standards I would be quite justified to claim that I have a satori on each of the rare occasions when I manage to write down a sentence which says exactly what I mean.

Thus the phenomena covered by the term satori range from the mental click vulgarly described as 'the penny has dropped', through flashes of inspiration of a higher (artistic or mystic) order, to that lasting change of character which creates a 'living Buddha' – in our language, a well-balanced or integrated personality.

The accent is always on insight gained by intuition as opposed to cognition, and on tapping the resources of the

[1] Suzuki, *op. cit.*, pp. 16-17.
[2] *Ibid.*, p. 220.
[3] *Zen Buddhism*, London, 1949, p. 89.

unconscious; and satori could be simply translated by the word 'intuition' which is equally elastic and covers the same range of phenomena. There is not more to it, but also not less. The rest is pseudo-mystical verbiage.

Though Zen derives from Yoga and cultivates the use of Sanskrit terms, it aims in the opposite direction. Samadhi is the elimination of the conscious self in the deep sleep of Nirvana; satori is the elimination of the conscious self in the wide-awake activities of intuitive living. The Yogi strives to drown himself in the universal unconscious; the Zen practitioner strives to bring the submerged 'It' from the depths to the surface. To make the point quite clear: *literally*, samadhi means 'deep sleep', satori means 'awakening'. *Mystically*, of course, 'deep sleep' means entering into Real Life, whereas the Awakened one 'lives like one already dead'. But *cynically* speaking, it is less risky and more pleasant to choose the Zen path – to live in Nirvana rather than be dead in Nirvana. And, however sincere the Chinese Zen Patriarchs' intentions were when they reversed the direction of Indian Buddhism, the Zen way of the samurai, of the modern Flower Masters and gay abbots, seems to be more inspired by that cynical truth – not in their conscious minds, God forbid, but in the intuitive depths of their such-ness.

The Hitter and the Hit

Leaving the mumbo-jumbo aside, the special training techniques in any branch of 'applied Zen' show remarkable psychological insight and produce some equally remarkable results. Japanese wrestling, for instance, is fascinating to watch because, though the wrestlers often weigh over three hundred pounds and attain six and a half and even seven feet, which by Japanese standards makes them into giants, their movements are quick as lightning, and the contest has something of the eerie quality of a mongoose fighting a snake.

The bout itself lasts usually less than a minute, but the preliminaries take fifteen minutes and used to take up to forty-five. The purpose of these preliminary rituals is for the contestants to limber up, both mentally and physically. They approach each other, sprinkle salt on the ground by way of purification, throw water over their shoulders and perform a curious balancing act on one leg, then turn their backs and go into a kind of brooding meditation, waiting for *muga*. Part of all this may be showmanship, but one recognizes the genuine element when, the psychological moment having suddenly arrived, the two inert mountains of flesh leap at each other with lightning speed, as the mongoose leaps at the cobra's throat, as if 'It' had taken possession of them; after a few turns and twists of breathtaking nimbleness, which look as if no force were being used at all, one of the mountains crashes on the floor or is thrown clear of the ring.

The main emphasis in 'applied' Zen training is on complete indifference towards success and failure. The 'It' will only enter into action when straining and striving have ceased and the action becomes 'effortless' and automatic. The formula is, of course, quite misleading because the athlete *will* use the last ounce of his strength to win; what the training really aims at is to relieve the *mental* strain, and the resulting cramped style. But in a culture haunted by the fear of failure, the contestant must be hypnotized into the belief that he does not care about the outcome, that he is not competing but performing a mystic ritual. Hence the invariably ritualistic setting, and the mystic language employed in archery or fencing or flower arrangement, to which Western enthusiasts, unacquainted with the psychological background, are so susceptible. Mr. Christmas Humphreys, who had an Awakening because he had thrown an opponent in Judo, is a rather endearing case. But it is distressing when a book like Dr. Eugen Herrigel's *Zen in the Art of Archery*,[1] which manages to combine the more ponderous kind of Germanic mysticism with the more obvious kind of Zen hocus-pocus, is taken seriously by the public in the West. Since this is one of the few descriptions of applied Zen training, it deserves a closer look.

It starts with the inevitable Introduction by Professor Suzuki. His very first sentence informs us that the practice of

[1] London, Third Impression, 1959.

archery in Japan is 'not intended for utilitarian purposes only or for purely aesthetic enjoyment' but to bring the mind 'into contact with the ultimate reality . . . In the case of archery the hitter and the hit are no longer two opposing objects, but are one reality'. There we go; now for Herr Herrigel:

'. . . By archery in the traditional sense, which he esteems as an art and honours as a national heritage, the Japanese does not understand a sport but, strange as this may sound at first, a religious ritual. And consequently, by the "art" of archery he does not mean the ability of the sportsman which can be controlled, more or less, by bodily exercises, but an ability whose origin is to be sought in spiritual exercises and whose aim consists in hitting a spiritual goal, so that fundamentally the marksman aims at himself and may even succeed in hitting himself. . .

Should one ask, from this standpoint, how the Japanese Masters understand this contest of the archer with himself, and how they describe it, their answer would sound enigmatic in the extreme. For them the contest consists in the archer aiming at himself – and yet not at himself, in hitting himself – and yet not himself, and thus becoming simultaneously the aimer and the aim, the hitter and the hit. Or, to use some expressions which are nearest the heart of the Masters, it is necessary for the archer to become, in spite of himself, an unmoved centre. Then comes the supreme and ultimate miracle: art becomes "artless", shooting becomes not-shooting, a shooting without bow and arrow; the teacher becomes a pupil again, the Master a beginner, the end a beginning, and the beginning perfection.'[1]

Dr. Herrigel explains that he had always been attracted by mysticism; when, in the nineteen twenties, he went to Tokyo University to teach philosophy, he tried to penetrate the mysteries of Zen. But he was told that as a European he could

[1] Herrigel, *op. cit.*, pp. 14 and 16.

only succeed in this through the study of one of the arts of applied Zen. He thereupon undertook a six-year course of instruction in archery under 'one of the greatest masters of this art'. Towards this Master he soon developed the Eastern guru-father complex; the ruder the Master was the more devotedly he loved him. 'Believe me,' he quotes with approval a fellow-disciple, 'the Master knows you and each of his pupils much better than we know ourselves. He reads in the souls of his pupils more than they care to admit.'

About the technical side of the instruction we are told almost nothing – the first year was apparently spent in learning to draw the bow 'spiritually' and to control one's breathing while doing so – but all the more about the Master's sayings:

> 'We master archers say: one shot – one life! What this means, you cannot yet understand. But perhaps another image will help you, which expresses the same experience. We master archers say: with the upper end of the bow the archer pierces the sky, on the lower end, as though attached by a thread, hangs the earth . . .
>
> He who can shoot with the horn of the hare and the hair of the tortoise, and can hit the centre without bow (horn) and arrow (hair), he alone is Master in the highest sense of the word – Master of the artless art. Indeed, he is the artless art itself and thus Master and No-Master in one. At this point archery, considered as the unmoved movement, the undanced dance, passes over into Zen.'[1]

The gist of the Master's teaching, repeated in endless parables and variations, can be put into three words: Don't worry, relax. Translated into Zen jargon, they read: '. . . only by withdrawing from all attachments whatsoever, by becoming utterly egoless: so that the soul, sunk within itself, stands in the plenitude of its nameless origin . . . etc.'[2] However, on a few rare occasions, Herr Herrigel descends to earth.

[1] *Ibid.*, pp. 47 and 89.
[2] *Ibid.*, p. 52.

'If everything depends on the archer's becoming purposeless and effacing himself in the event, then its outward realization must occur automatically, in no further need of the controlling or reflecting intelligence.

It is this mastery of form that the Japanese method of instruction seeks to inculcate. Practice, repetition, and repetition of the repeated with ever increasing intensity are its distinctive features for long stretches of the way.'[1]

The key-word is 'automatically'. In the third year, the disciple underwent a spiritual crisis. It had been impressed on him that he should not loose the arrow by a conscious act of will; the shot must fall by itself from the archer 'like snow from a bamboo-leaf'. This became an *idée fixe* with him, and while on a holiday, he devised a method of cheating: he eased his grip gradually until the pressure of the bow-string loosed the shot as if this had happened spontaneously. When he demonstrated this heretic technique, 'the Master stepped up to me without a word, took the bow from my hand, and sat down on a cushion, his back towards me. I knew what that meant, and withdrew.'[2] The stern Master then refused to instruct him further, but was mollified by a distinguished Japanese go-between. In the fourth year of his training, Herrigel summoned up his courage to ask the Master: 'How can the shot be loosed if "I" do not do it?'

' "It" shoots,' he replied.[3]

More months of agony went by.

'Then one day, after a shot, the Master made a deep bow and broke off the lesson, "Just then 'It' shot!" he cried, as I stared at him bewildered.'[4]

It took, however, some time before he learnt to distinguish his own, right 'It' shots from his wrong 'I' shots. At last – whether in the fourth, or fifth year, is not made clear – he was

[1] *Ibid.*, pp. 57-8.
[2] *Ibid.*, p. 71.
[3] *Ibid.*, p. 73.
[4] *Ibid.*, p. 74.

allowed to shoot at a target. But it was not explained to him
how to take aim. Instead, the Master told him:

'If you hit the target with nearly every shot you are
nothing more than a trick archer who likes to show off. For
the professional who counts his hits, the target is only a
miserable piece of paper which he shoots to bits. The
"Great Doctrine" holds this to be sheer devilry. It knows
nothing of a target which is set up at a definite distance
from the archer. It only knows of the goal, which cannot be
aimed at technically, and it names this goal, if it names it
at all, the Buddha.'[1]

So, for the following weeks or months, he went on shooting
his arrows without taking aim. By what method he ever learnt
to aim we are again not told, but it is clearly hinted that the
method employed was telepathy.

'Thus, through deepest concentration, he transferred the
spirit of his art to his pupils, and I am not afraid to confirm
from my own experience, which I doubted long enough,
that the talk of immediate communication is not just a
figure of speech but a tangible reality. There was another
form of help which the Master communicated to us at that
time, and which he likewise spoke of as immediate transference of the spirit. If I had been continually shooting
badly, the Master gave a few shots with my bow. The
improvement was startling: it was as if the bow let itself
be drawn differently, more willingly, more understandingly.'[2]

Nevertheless, the pupil kept worrying about the Master's
contention that hitting the target had nothing to do with
aiming.

' "That is just what I cannot get into my head," I
answered. "I think I understand what you mean by the

[1] *Ibid.*, p. 78.
[2] *Ibid.*, pp. 83-4.

real, inner goal, which ought to be hit. But how it happens
that the outer goal, the disc of paper, is hit without the
archer's taking aim, and that the hits are only outward
confirmations of inner events – that correspondence is
beyond me."

"You are under an illusion," said the Master after a
while, "if you imagine that even a rough understanding of
these dark connexions would help you. These are pro-
cesses which are beyond the reach of understanding . . .
The archer hits the target without having aimed – more I
cannot say." [1]

Then, one night, the Master dispelled Dr. Herrigel's
doubts by a demonstration of two masterly shots at a target
lit only by the tiny flame of a taper. Finally, in the sixth year
of training, the author learnt to 'dance the ceremony' prescribed in the Great Doctrine of Archery 'down to the
minutest gesture', passed a public test, and was awarded a
diploma. 'The Master brought the proceedings to an end by
giving two masterly shots in robes of surpassing magnificence.
A few days later my wife, in an open contest, was awarded the
master title in the art of flower arrangement.'[2]

Just before this happy ending there is a revealing passage in
the book:

‘ "Do you now understand," the Master asked me one
day after a particularly good shot. "what I mean by "It
shoots", "It hits"?

"I'm afraid I don't understand anything more at all,"
I answered, "even the simplest things have got in a muddle.
Is it 'I' who draws the bow, or is it the bow that draws me
into the state of highest tension? Do 'I' hit the goal, or does
the goal hit me? Is 'It' spiritual when seen by the eyes of
the body, and corporeal when seen by the eyes of the spirit
– or both or neither? Bow, arrow, goal and ego, all melt
into one another so that I can no longer separate them.

---

[1] *Ibid.*, pp. 79-80.
[2] *Ibid.*, p. 88. Frau Herrigel also wrote a book – duly prefaced by Professor
Suzuki – *Zen in the Art of Flower Arrangement* (London, 1958).

And even the need to separate has gone. For as soon as I take the bow and shoot everything becomes so clear and straight-forward and so ridiculously simple . . ." '[1]

Precisely. But was that six-years' detour into the metaphysical fog really necessary before shooting an arrow was revealed as the 'ridiculously simple' act which it always had been? The answer is, of course, that every skilled performance appears hopelessly complicated until, through training, it becomes automatic and thereby 'simple'. The training has a technical and a psychological aspect. About the technical side we learn, in a passage which I quoted, that it consisted of 'practice, repetition, and repetition of the repeated with ever increasing intensity'. There is nothing new about that method; its aim is to enable the pupil to exercise his skill automatically, even 'in his sleep'. The psychological side of the training is designed to eliminate self-consciousness; its mystic verbiage and esoteric ceremonial are expected to facilitate this process by their irrational appeal to the unconscious. For a pupil brought up in traditional Japanese ways, this may be – or may have been – the proper antidote to mental cramp. On an occidental, the main effect of it is to befuddle him.

In spite of the 'Great Doctrine' and the mumbo-jumbo, the technical achievements of Japanese archery seem to be unimpressive. Dr. Herrigel writes too much in a cloud to bother about technical information; on the one occasion when he does so, we learn that the target of the two unforgettable master-shots was at twenty yards' distance.[2] In American championship tests, which consist of several rounds, the target is placed successively at sixty, eighty, and a hundred yards. But the comparison may be misleading because we do not know what kind of a bow the Master used; and I was unable to discover reports of Japanese participation in international contests. On the other hand, we know that Judo, another Zen art on behalf of which extravagant claims were made, is an excellent means of self-defence against an assailant of

[1] *Ibid.*, pp. 85-6.
[2] *Ibid.*, pp. 76 and 82.

superior physique and inferior skill, but not more – as was shown at the Olympic Games of 1928 and 1932, when Japanese champions were defeated in free-style wrestling by other teams.

If Herrigel's slim volume on Zen-archery contains little information on its proper subject, Suzuki's long treatise on 'Zen and Swordsmanship' contains no information whatsoever on swordsmanship. Neither the type of sword used, nor the technique of using it are mentioned: not even the fact that it is wielded with both hands. It is a repetitive and confused farrago of koans, mondos, poems and quotations partly on Zen in general, partly on the theme that the samurai-swordsman was fearless, indifferent to death, animated by 'It' and 'no-mind', and really a Gandhian saint, since, 'to state it more concretely, bad is good, ugly is beautiful, false is true, imperfect is perfect, and also conversely'.[1] A few more quotations are indispensable if one wishes to get a clearer idea of Zen as expounded by the undisputed contemporary authority on it:

> 'The sword is generally associated with killing, and most of us wonder how it can come into connexion with Zen, which is a school of Buddhism teaching the gospel of love and mercy. The fact is that the art of swordsmanship distinguishes between the sword that kills and the sword that gives life. The one that is used by a technician cannot go any further than killing, for he never appeals to the sword unless he intends to kill. The case is altogether different with the one who is compelled to lift the sword. For it is really not he but the sword itself that does the killing. He has no desire to do harm to anybody, but the enemy appears and makes himself a victim. It is as though the sword performs automatically its function of justice, which is the function of mercy. This is the kind of sword that Christ is said to have brought among us. It is not meant just for bringing the peace mawkishly cherished by sentimentalists . . . When the sword is expected to play this sort

[1] Suzuki, *op. cit.*, p. 33.

of role in human life, it is no more a weapon of self-defence or an instrument of killing, and the swordsman turns into an artist of the first grade, engaged in producing a work of genuine originality.[1]

. . . Tajima no kami thinks that the seeing must first take place in the mind, and then it is transmitted to the eyes, and finally to the body and limbs . . . If it is the physical organ of sight that first perceives the outside world, as our psychologists would tell us, the act that is needed to follow up the first perception will have to go through the anatomical process of transmission as we have it in our medical textbooks. This will, however, be too tortuous a procedure for the swordsman in the thick of combat involving life. He cannot afford such a luxury or refinement. He must act without intellectual jugglery or, as some would call it, tom-foolery. Hence Tajima no kami's most penetrating observation.[2]

. . . Yagyu seems to be speaking psychologically when he makes his sword see what is not visible as well as what is visible – and this simultaneously. For the visible is the invisible and conversely. In terms of logic, "A" is "not-A" and "not-A" is "A". The sword is, as it were, held at the identification point of opposites.[3]

. . . The conviction that "I am the only swordsman who has no peers in the world" . . . matches the declaration which, according to Mahayana tradition, the Buddha made at his birth: "Heavens above and earth below, I alone am the most honoured one!" This matching of the two declarations is interesting in a double sense: Ichiun applauds "infantism" as incarnating the principle of swordsmanship, while it was the infant Buddha who made the bold declaration.[4]

After swordsmanship, a brief remark on teamanship. This is not a Potterism, since Dr. Suzuki calls the master of the tea

[1] *Ibid.*, p. 145.
[2] *Ibid.*, pp. 148-9.
[3] *Ibid.*, p. 161.
[4] *Ibid.*, p. 179.

ceremony a 'teaman'. About the satori of teamanship we learn:

> 'The following is the view of the tea held by Seisetsu (1746-1820), a Japanese Zen master of the late Tokugawa era:
>
> "My Tea is No-tea, which is not No-tea in opposition to Tea. What then is this No-tea? When a man enters into the exquisite realm of No-tea he will realize that No-tea is no other than the Great Way (ta-tao) itself . . ."
>
> Seisetsu's "No-Tea" is a mysterious variation of the tea. He wants to reach the spirit of the art by the way of negation. This is the logic of Prajna philosophy, which has sometimes been adopted by the Zen masters. As long as there is an event designated as "Tea" this will obscure our vision and hinder it from penetrating into "Tea" as it is in itself.'[1]

There is one redeeming possibility: that all this drivel is deliberately intended to confuse the reader, since one of the avowed aims of Zen is to perplex and unhinge the rational mind. If this hypothesis were correct, Professor Suzuki's voluminous *oeuvre* of at least a million words, specially written for this purpose, would represent a hoax of truly heroic dimensions, and the laugh would be on the Western intellectuals who fell for it. I shall return to this point in a moment.

Decline

In spite of its remarkable achievements, Zen began to develop certain degenerative symptoms at an early stage. They seem to have started at the spiritual core of the movement, the monasteries. When St. Francis Xavier arrived in Japan in 1549 – some two hundred years after the beginning of the great Zen vogue – he made friends with a scholarly and enlightened Zen abbot named Ninjitsu.

> 'Ninjitsu one day took Xavier to the meditation hall of his monastery, where the monks were engaged in their

[1] *Ibid.*, pp. 309-310.

usual exercises of Zazen, which consists of kneeling motionless in concentrated thought upon one subject for the purpose of clearing the mind of all extraneous matters and thus approaching an intuitive grasp of truth. Xavier asked what these men were doing, and Ninjitsu replied: "Some are counting up how much they took from the faithful last month; some are considering where they can get better clothing and treatment for themselves; others are thinking of their recreations and pastimes. In short, none of them is thinking of anything that has any sense whatever.'[1]

I was reminded of that passage during a talk with an equally amiable Zen abbot in Kyoto, who, having passed through his final satori and graduated as a Buddha 'living like one already dead', had just bought himself a television set. In Mishima's novel there is another abbot, whom his devoted pupil catches out leaving a cinema, dressed in European clothes, in the company of a geisha. Their attitudes to the vanities of the world seem to be like that of the alcoholic who affirms that he is cured, and that he no longer drinks because he needs it but just for fun.

Although the practice of Zazen – sitting motionless on the wooden platform of the meditation hall – plays a dominant part in monastic routine, Zen and meditation somehow do not seem to fit together. It is the practice of a mystic technique without mystic content; if there is no God, no Moral Law, no doctrine, no teaching, what is there left to meditate about – except repeating a-rose-isarose-isarose, as a means of self-hypnosis? The same doubt was voiced more than a millennium ago by one of the great Masters, Huai-jang, when he found another Master sitting in meditation.

' "Your reverence," asked Huai-jang, "what is the objective of sitting in meditation?"

"The objective," answered Ma-tsu, "is to become a Buddha."

[1] Sansom, *op. cit.*, p. 122.

Thereupon Huai-jang picked up a floor-tile and began to polish it on a rock.

"What are you doing, master?" asked Ma-tsu.

"I am polishing it for a mirror," said Huai-jang.

"How could polishing a tile make a mirror?"

"How could sitting in meditation make a Buddha?"[1]

Yet the more dubious the object of meditation, the more rigorously it was enforced by disciplinary measures which one might call barbaric, were it not for the Japanese love of Spartan methods. The monitor in the meditation hall carries a massive staff with a sharp end, and if a disciple fidgets or becomes drowsy, he whacks him with a sharp blow across the shoulder blades. Richard Rumbold, an English Zen enthusiast, who spent about five months at the Shokokuji, a monastery in Kyoto, describes some savage beatings-up administered by the head monk and his assistant for trifling disciplinary offences. He also gives glimpses of the atmosphere in the Zendo hall:

'. . . meditation lasted normally from early evening till ten or eleven at night. But once a month there was a whole week during which we were supposed to meditate more or less continuously with only short breaks for sleep and food. These periods were a nervous ordeal since the *jitijitsu* would urge us to make a special effort to gain satori, at the same time using his stick freely; and by the middle of the week the monks had become glassy-eyed with excitement, tension and fatigue, like soldiers in the thick of battle.'[2]

The article is aptly entitled 'Catching the Mood of the Universe' . . .

Zazen meditation, unlike Yoga, holds no promise of supernatural rewards. At the risk of being repetitive, I must again mention that while both Yoga and Zazen aim at penetrating beyond the captive mind, the 'beyond' means in one

[1] Watts, *op. cit.*, pp. 96-7.
[2] *Encounter*, London, January 1959, p. 25.

case trance-sleep and death, in the other case a more intense awarenes of the Now and Here. Thus Yoga is a challenge to existence; Zen, a challenge to conventionality. The Yogi practises physical contortions to make his body acquiesce in its own annihilation; Zen uses the mental contortions of the koan to stun reason and force it to abdicate. And just as in Hatha Yoga the asanas and mudras have become physical substitutes for true meditation, thus in Rinzai Zen the koans and mondos fill the spiritual vacuum.

The koans I have so far quoted were relatively tame – like the Yoga asanas for Westerners. Here is a more advanced one, a famous classic known as Father Nansen's kitten. It appears in a thirteenth-century anthology, the *Mumonkan,* and con- cerns a famous Zen abbot, Nan Ch'uan (Nansen) – whose monks, while cutting the grass, saw a little kitten suddenly appear in a mountain temple. They caught it, but immediately the two groups inhabiting the East Hall and the West Hall of the monastery began to quarrel about its posses- sion. Father Nan Ch'uan, listening to the dispute, caught the kitten by the scruff of its neck and, putting his sickle against it, told the monks: 'If one of you can utter a "good word" (that is, a spontaneous Zen repartee), this kitten shall be saved; if not, it shall be killed.' There was a dead silence, so Father Nan Ch'uan cut the kitten into two and threw it away. Later in the day, the chief disciple, Yoshu, returned to the temple. Father Nan Ch'uan told him what had happened and asked for his opinion. 'Yoshu immediately removed his shoes, put them on his head, and left the room. At this Father Nan Ch'uan lamented sorely, saying, "Oh, if only you had been here today the kitten's life would have been saved." '[1]

My own reaction when I first read this koan was possibly good Zen, because it had nothing to do with the story itself – it brought back to my mind that in the monasteries unwanted kittens and puppies are put out and left to die of exposure because Buddhism disapproves of killing animals. It is one of the few Zen practices dictated by an ethical commandment.

To return to the koan, this is how Mishima's Zen abbot

[1] Mishima's version, *op. cit.,* p. 65.

explains its meaning in a solemn lecture to the assembled
disciples:

'The reason that Father Nansen had killed the cat was
that he had cut away the illusion of self and had eradicated
all irrelevant thoughts and fantasies from his mind. Putting his insensibility into practice, he had cut off the
kitten's head and had thus cut off all contradiction, opposition, and discord betwen self and others. This was known
as the Murdering Sword, whereas Joshu's action was called
the Life-Giving Sword. By performing an action of such
infinite magnanimity as wearing filthy and despised objects
like shoes on his head, he had given a practical demonstration of the way of the Bodhisattva.'[1]

The only appropriate comment on this is a passage by Mr.
Alan Watts, speaking in dead earnest:

'The continued practice of za-zen . . . provides the
student with a clear, unobstructed mind into which he can
toss the koan like a pebble into a pool and simply watch to
see what his mind does with it. As he concludes each koan,
the *roshi* usually requires that he present a verse from the
Zenrin Kushu which expresses the point of the koan just
solved. Other books are also used, and the late Sokeian
Sasaki, working in the United States, found that an
admirable manual for this purpose was "Alice in Wonderland." '[2]

Mr. Christmas Humphreys is equally serious in quoting an
episode from *Through the Looking-Glass,* and declaring:
'This immortal passage is the purest of Zen.'[3]
This brings me back, for almost the last time, to Professor
Suzuki and the question whether he and his disciples are trying to fool the reader or themselves. Since *Alice* is now being
used as a Zen manual, I may as well confess that I have always

[1] *Ibid.,* pp. 65-6.
[2] Watts, *op. cit.,* p. 167.
[3] *Op. cit.,* p. 113.

been puzzled by Dr. Suzuki's striking spiritual resemblance either to Tweedledum or Tweedledee, whose twin suchnesses are no doubt meant to symbolize the identity of tea and no-tea, arrow and target, author and reader, the deluding and deluded mind.

The 'It' and the Knack

The slow decline of monastic life, the voiding of Zen's spiritual core, was bound to affect the arts which had fallen under its sway. Its original impact on Japanese life had been immensely liberating and stimulating – as witnessed, for instance by the Sumi-e style of landscape painting, which had grown under Zen influence in China under the Sung dynasty and had followed Zen to Japan; or by the Haiku type of poetry; or in the Zen-inspired schools of pottery. The flourishing of the Zen arts coincided approximately with the European Renaissance, and lasted to the end of the seventeenth century. It created a style of art, and a style of life of unique flavour, a golden age whose golden fallout still lingers over the islands.

The gradual degeneration of Zen art seems to have been caused by a curious misconception inherent in Zen psychology. I mean the confusion between two different types of uninhibited 'spontaneous' responses: the spontaneous flash of creative originality, and the pseudo-sponaneity in exercising a skill which has became automatic. Both are immediate and unpremeditated; but the former is an improvisation sprung up from the creative depths of the psyche, the latter is a stereotyped reaction, either innate or impressed through learning by rote. In other words, the confusion is between intuitive response and conditioned reflex.

In a culture which rigorously suppresses the manifestation of emotions, and regards self-control as the highest of virtues, spontaneity acquires a magic aura, even if it amounts to no more than shouting in pain. Hakuin is revered as the author of the koan system in its modern form, but perhaps even more because he shouted in pain on his deathbed. In his youth, he was shocked by the story that an earlier master,

Yen-t'ou, screamed when he was killed by a robber; but when Hakuin had his satori he saw in a flash that yelling in pain was a triumph of Zen, a spontaneous manifestation of 'It'. Since Japanese women in labour are not supposed to utter a single moan, Hakuin's satori must indeed have been a revelation to him.[1] In this, as in similar Zen stories, it is impossible to say whether the 'It' is meant to convey a divine inspiration, or the natural, uninhibited play of physiological reactions: 'When walking, walk, when sitting, sit, but above all don't wobble.'[2]

Once more: in a culture where the native hue of resolution is sicklied o'er, this would be sound advice – if only it were left at that. The purpose of the koan is to make the cramped pupil answer without hesitation and reflection – but at this point the dreadful confusion sets in. Since it would need a genius to produce an intuitively inspired answer to every koan, the pupil soon learns instead the *type* of answer that is expected of him – the 'pointing' gesture, the absurd *non-sequitur*, the rude leg-pull, etc. – and the mondo becomes a game after a stereotyped pattern, another automatic skill. When the second Patriarch whacked the third Patriarch over the head and called the Buddha a noodle, they probably meant to give a new turn to mystic thought, not to create a Punch and Judy routine.

The same basic confusion, the same substitution of a ready-made formula for original intuition bedevilled all forms of

[1] To utter emotional shouts in a sword fight is an even older specifically Zen invention, which became an esoteric cult. The traditional shout is 'Katsu,' and Dr. Suzuki has explained its meaning:

' "Katsu!" is pronounced "Ho!" in modern Chinese. In Japan when it is actually uttered by the Zen people, it sounds like "Katz!" or "Kwatz!" – *tz* like *tz* in German "Blitz." It is primarily a meaningless ejaculation. Since its first use by Baso Doichi . . . it came to be extensively used by the Zen masters. Rinzai distinguishes four kinds of "Katz!" (1) Sometimes the "Katz!" is like the sword of Vajrarapa (which cuts and puts to death anything dualistic appearing before it); (2) sometimes it is like the lion crouching on the ground; (3) sometimes it is like the sounding pole or a bundle of shading grass; (4) sometimes it serves no purpose whatever . . . In Zen, what is most significant among these four "Katz!" is the fourth, when the cry ceases to serve any kind of purpose, good or bad, practical or impractical. Someone remarks that Rinzai with all his astuteness omits a fifth "Katz!" . . .' (*op. cit.*, p. 66).

[2] Next in importance among Zen slogans after Wu-mien (no-mind) is Wu-shih – i.e. that 'nothing special' is to be gained by it; at the same time Wu-shih also means 'natural, unaffected.'

applied Zen. The inspired 'It' ceded to the mechanical knack. The perfect swordsman, says Dr. Suzuki, 'becomes a kind of automaton, so to speak, as far as his own consciousness is concerned'.[1] In archery, fencing, wrestling or Judo, this automatic skill of the no-mind is, of course, infinitely preferable to self-conscious wobbling. But in poetry and painting, dancing or landscape gardening, the substitution leads to lingering death by paralysis.

The Haiku is a typical example of what happened to other Zen arts. It is a poem of seventeen syllables in three lines. It was derived from the classic form of Japanese poetry, the Waka – a succession of five-syllable and seven-syllable lines without rhyme, rhythm, stress or meter. The Waka could go on without limits, as it presumably did in early folk poetry; but from the tenth century onward, its most practised form was the Tanka – 31 syllables in lines of 5, 7, 5, 7, 7. Out of this the Haiku developed by chopping off the two last lines, leaving 5, 7, 5 syllables as its unalterable structure. Its form resembles a truncated limerick, but without rhyme or rhythmic pattern; its content is a kind of lyrical epigram – a mood caught in a butterfly net.

> With the evening breeze
> The water laps against
> The heron's legs

At its best, the Haiku is allusive and elusive like the best koans – like 'the sound of a single hand clapping'. It has 'It':

> In the dense mist
> What is being shouted
> Between hill and boat?

> The sea darkens;
> The voices of the wild ducks
> Are faintly white

> You light the fire;
> I'll show you something nice –
> A great ball of snow!

[1] Suzuki, *op. cit.*, p. 94.

But these inspired vignettes of the great Haiku masters of the sixteenth and seventeenth centuries are few and far between the mechanical turnings-out of a genre whose knack is all too easy to learn. The proof is that out of the hundreds of Haikus in Mr. Blyth's classic three-volume collection[1] it is always the same half-dozen favourites – by Basho, Buson, or Moritake[2] – that are quoted as samples. Nevertheless the seventeen-syllable Haiku and the thirty-one-syllable Tanka have remained for the last five hundred years the only forms of popular poetry in Japan. In 1956, the magazine *Haiku Research* estimated that there were at least four million Haiku poets practising the art – if that is the proper word for the tireless permutations of crows perching on a branch, frogs leaping into a pond, drops sliding off bamboo-leaves, and autumn leaves rustling in the ditch. Its stereotyped imagery and fixed number of syllables leave no scope for individuality, style, or for critical evaluation. The inquisitive Mr. Enright once asked some Japanese professors of literature, 'how they could tell a good Haiku from a bad Haiku. "We cannot," replied one of them, "the trouble is that we don't know what standards to apply. But perhaps you, from Cambridge . . ." He smiled politely. Another suggested with a strangled cough, "All Haiku are good, perhaps?" '[3]

The same degenerative process, due to the same causes, can be seen in the Zen schools of painting, from the truly 'spontaneous', powerful work of Seshu – who used not only the brush, but fistfuls of straw dipped in ink to impart to his landscapes their violent motion – through the gradual hardening of the arteries in the Zenga, Haigu and Calligraphic styles, into mannerism and aridity. Today, painting is taught much in the same manner as archery and other skilled routines. Herr Herrigel remarks admiringly: 'What is true of archery and swordsmanship also applies to all other arts. Thus, mastery in ink painting is only attained when the hand, exercising perfect control over technique, executes what hovers before the mind's eye at the moment when the

[1] R. H. Blyth, *Haiku*, Tokyo 1949, 1950, 1952.
[2] Moritake 1472-1549; Basho 11644-94; Buson 1716-84.
[3] Enright, *op. cit.*, p. 63.

mind begins to form it, without there being a hair's breadth between. Painting then becomes spontaneous calligraphy.'[1] He then goes on to quote (without saying so) George Duthuit's remark: 'He who deliberates and moves his brush intent on making a picture, misses to a still greater extent the art of painting. Draw bamboos for ten years, become a bamboo, then forget all about bamboos when you are drawing.'[2]

A surprisingly great number of Japanese have indeed the knack of drawing surprisingly pretty bamboos – and rocks, trees, cranes and butterflies; the only trouble is that the bamboos and butterflies all look the same. Zen art has declined into producing variations on a few limited themes in a few limited styles – into 'spontaneous calligraphy' as the revealing phrase reads. There are still works of greater or lesser distinction being produced, but their subjects are stereotyped and their style petrified.

Zen started as a de-conditioning cure and ended up as a different type of conditioning. The cramp of self-critical watchfulness was relieved by the self-confident ease of exercising an automatic skill. The knack became a comfortable substitute for 'It'. The autumn leaves still rustle in the ditch, but originality has gone down the drain. The water still laps against the heron's legs, but the muse lies drowned at the bottom of the ancient pond.

[1] *Op. cit.*, p. 101 f.
[2] G. Duthuit, *Chinese Mysticism and Modern Painting*, Paris 1936.

A Stink of Zen

Morita Therapy

ZEN influenced every walk of Japanese life, including psychiatry. Freud and Jung have never taken root in Japanese psychotherapy (though they are discussed among *littérateurs*), but a specifically Japanese treatment, Morita therapy, enjoyed a considerable vogue.[1]

It was founded by Shoma Morita, Professor of Psychiatry at the Jikeikai School of Medicine in Tokyo, who died one year before Freud. His biographer, Professor Shimoda, relates that the idea of the new cure came to Morita while treating a patient, a certain Miss Yatabe, who was suffering from an obsessional neurosis:

'She had been treated at the Sugamo Psychiatric Hospital for a long time, and had left the hospital without being cured. He tried at his home hypnosis, other methods of treatment, and his own method of persuasion, but could not be successful. He told me that sometimes he would lose his temper and come to strike her. To his surprise, however, the patient was cured suddenly by herself.'[2]

The therapy was developed by his disciples, among them Genya Usa, who had started as a Zen monk, and Takehisa Kora, who succeeded Morita in his Chair. Professor Kora showed me round his Tokyo clinic. He is a quiet and gentle personality, and his patients were, as usual, docile, but the treatment itself can hardly be called gentle by Western standards. It is mainly used to treat hypochondria, compulsion neurosis, chronic anxiety and 'homophobia' – all of

[1] Several Japanese psychiatrists explained to me that Freud's emphasis on sex and guilt does not apply to Japanese society 'because sex is taken for granted, and "guilt" is a concept created by Christianity'. (But what about India?)

[2] Quoted in 'Morita Therapy – A Psychotherapy in the Way of Zen', by Takehisa Kora and Koji Sato, *Psychologia*, 1, 1958, pp. 219-225.

which Morita summed up by the term 'Shinkeishitsu' (literally, 'nervousness'):

'These patients are said to be extremely punctilious, rigid, fastidious, formal, meticulous, and suffer from excessive doubt. They are so perfectionistic that nothing they do satisfies them as a job well done'.[1] We recognize what one might call the 'Confucian syndrome', and we are not surprised that its treatment was inspired by Zen.

It consists of four stages, each of them lasting on an average a week or ten days. During the first period, the patient must lie on his mat-bed in a room isolated from any stimulus or distraction. 'He is prohibited to read, to write, to talk, to smoke, to sing, to engage in any manual activity' – except eating and going to the toilet. The purpose is, roughly speaking, to let him stew in his own juice, to worry himself to a pitch followed by emotional exhaustion. After that, 'a feeling of ennui appears and he will be placed in a "stimuli-starved" state. Desire for work then becomes strong and thereby is created an extroverting mood.'[2]

During the second period, the patient is still not allowed to talk or to read, and is still isolated from human contact except with the psychiatrist; but he is allowed some light manual work, and is ordered to write a diary, which he must continue till the end of his treatment. The régime is of monastic rigidity: he must get up, go for walks, clean his room, write his diary, all according to a fixed schedule. The diary is sent in every day to the psychiatrist, who sends it back with his pithy annotations. At a later stage, brief personal exchanges take place with the psychiatrist. Thus, for instance, a patient suffering from 'anthropophobia', complains about loss of memory:

'*Patient:* "I don't remember in what way I came to this hospital."
Doctor: "If you don't remember anything you should not remember your anthropophobia." '

---

[1] 'Japanese Psychiatry and Psychotherapy,' by Avrohm Jacobson and Albert N. Berenberg, *The American Journal of Psychiatry*, November 1952.
[2] Kora and Sato, *op. cit.*

This is obviously reminiscent of the technique of the koan and mondo, during the tense, brief interviews with the roshi. The purpose of this second stage is 'to promote spontaneity of thought in the patient by forcibly restricting his physical activity';[1] or, as Professor Kora puts it: 'To the patients who are almost completely deprived of stimuli from the outer world during their bed-rest and are hungry for stimuli, the outer world has a precious charm. However, as a reaction, they often feel some sort of displeasure. Even in such cases patients are told to experience pleasure as pleasure, displeasure as displeasure, and to continue to pursue work allotted to them.'[2]

During the third period, though the patient is still barred from recreational and social activities, he is at last allowed a moderate amount of physical activity, which he has been craving. This creates a state of euphoria. Sample from a patient's diary:

' "Began to clean the cage of rabbits . . . I jumped into it and began to work. It was really interesting to clean it". *Doctor's comment:* "This attitude is wonderful".'

In the fourth and last period, the patient is allowed to pursue his normal activities, combined with heavy manual labour. The main purpose of this is to give him confidence in his own manual skill. 'Neurotics live in their imagination. You are busy handling or managing this or that. The more lively your hands the more active your mind.'[3] The patient is not only prevented from brooding, but the heavy manual work is supposed to force him to use his mind in a manner attuned to his mechanical activity—according to the principle of 'no-mind'. Among Professor Kora's hints for patients are: 'to allow the symptoms to remain as they are'; 'to accept pleasure and pain as they come as unavoidable'; 'to be always occupied with work'; 'not to grumble'; 'to adjust one's outer appearance and never act like a patient. Adjust your outward self and the inner self will adjust itself.'

[1] Jacobson and Berenberg, *op. cit.*
[2] Kora and Sato, *op. cit.*
[3] *Ibid.*

The therapy lasts from five to ten weeks. After the patient has been discharged, there is no follow-up.

During my long conversation with Professor Kora, the word 'unconscious' was not mentioned. Dreams, subconscious motivations, the causal origin of the disease do not enter into Morita therapy. Its method is not analytical, and it does not aim at unearthing the roots of the symptoms. They will either disappear, or the patient must accept them as unavoidable, and 'adjust his outward self' to the conventional pattern in the expectation that his inner self will follow suit. It is not so much a therapy as a re-conditioning based on behaviouristic principles, with special emphasis on manual skills which are expected to help the patient to acquire an automatic kind of spontaneity.

In other words, Morita therapy is a combination of Behaviourism and Zen, of the Pavlov laboratory and the doctrine of the no-mind. When Jacobson and Berenberg published their criticism of it in the *American Journal of Psychiatry*,[1] Kora and Sato replied in *Psychologia*[2] by quoting some of the American authors' most damning comments, and dismissing them with the single sentence: 'Their conclusion reveals their difficulty to understand the true nature of Morita therapy.' It echoed the sensei's innermost conviction that the Japanese can understand the Western mind, but no Westerner can ever understand the Japanese mind. I must, however, add in fairness that some of the younger psychiatrists whom I met have outgrown this attitude.

The Perils of Tolerance

Religious feeling is deader in Japan, and has been dead for a longer time, than in any of the great existing civilizations.

A poll, carried out under the auspices of UNESCO among students in Kyoto, contained the following question (from the Allport-Gillespie questionnaire): 'Of the following activities, which are the three from which you expect the greatest satis-

[1] *Loc. cit.*
[2] *Loc. cit.*

faction: your career or occupation, your family relationships, your leisure and recreational activities, your participation in activities directed towards national or international betterment, or your religious beliefs and activities?'[1] Only ten per cent of the male and fourteen per cent of the female students mentioned religion at all; and only one per cent of the males and three per cent of the females gave it first place.

In another survey, carried out by the National Public Opinion Research Institute, people were asked to mention any kind of experience which had made them happy: out of 2,761 subjects questioned, only eleven mentioned religion.[2]

Yet another official inquiry revealed that among the students in a Buddhist seminary, a declared thirty-five per cent were 'without faith in Buddha, forty-eight per cent without belief in the immortality of the soul'.[3] Stoetzel, the author of the UNESCO survey, concludes: 'What emerged quite clearly was, that, both for the group as a whole and for almost all the individual members of it, religious activities played only the most negligible part. Indeed, it appears that what we call religious needs, while not absolutely unknown to the Japanese, are an exceptional element in their psychology'.[4]

It may be argued that a culture can dispense with doctrinal religion provided it has some glimmer of that 'oceanic feeling', that spiritual awareness, which prevents the parching of the soul; and it is claimed that Zen provides just that. Thus, for instance, quoting an old Chinese text, Professor Watts says: 'As "the fish swims in the water but is unmindful of the water, the bird flies in the wind but knows not of the wind", so the true life of Zen has no need to drag in religion or spirituality as something over and above life itself.[5]

[1] Jean Stoetzel, *Without the Chrysanthemum and the Sword*, London, and UNESCO, Paris, 1955, p. 167.
[2] *Ibid.*, p. 192.
[3] J. Roggendorf, S. J., 'The Place of Religion in Modern Japan', *Japan Quarterly*, Vol. V, No. 1.
[4] Stoetzel, *op. cit.*, pp. 191-2.
[5] Watts, *op. cit.*, p. 152.

Indeed, 'to drag in religion' and engage in argument or meta-physics, is regarded in Zen circles as an abhorrent thing, which the old masters called 'to stink of Zen'. And after Fa-yung, a St. Francis-like figure, had his satori, the birds ceased to offer him flowers because his holiness 'no longer stood out like a sore thumb'.[1]

Remembering the theological disputes in the history of the Western Churches, and their dire consequences, one may be tempted to agree with this attitude – the more so as Zen keeps reassuring us that even sans theology, the mystical essence is still there – that the fish in the parable who 'swims in the water' does possess an oceanic awareness, and is not merely running after smaller fish and away from larger ones. But the boundary between an existential philosophy of Being, and the practical considerations of being, is a precarious one; and there is always the danger that Po-chung's definition of Zen 'when hungry, eat, when tired, sleep' might be taken to mean precisely what it says. We have seen how the growing spiritual void in the Zen centres acted like a suction pump, draining the arts of their inspiration and reducing them to aridity – so that when the impact of the West came, they were already sterile and defenceless. This process was repeated in the field of ethics, with even more serious consequences.

At the start of this discussion of Zen, I quoted a few lines attributed to Seng-ts'an, who lived in the sixth century A.D., and was the Third Patriarch – that is, second in succession to the Bodhidharma. They are from his work *Hsin-hsin Ming*, which is regarded as the oldest Zen poem and one of its basic texts:

> Be not concerned with right and wrong
> The conflict between right and wrong
> Is the sickness of the mind.

Fourteen centuries later, the last Patriarch reaffirms the unbroken continuity of Zen's ethical relativism:

> 'Zen is . . . extremely flexible in adapting itself to almost any philosophy and moral doctrine as long as its intuitive teaching is not interfered with. It may be found wedded to

[1] *Ibid.*, p. 152.

anarchism or fascism, communism or democracy, atheism or idealism.[1]

The difference between the two statements is in their historical setting, and in their degrees of concreteness. The first comes from a Buddhist-Taoist mystic, who looks with a smiling shrug at the sententious pendantries of Confucian society. The second could come from a philosophically minded Nazi journalist, or from one of the Zen monks who became suicide pilots.

I have stressed the point, and must stress it again in concluding, that the vivifying influence of Zen, its historical and spiritual *raison d'être,* came from its function as a complement and antidote to Confucianism. The division of labour between the rigid and demanding social code of the latter, and the relaxing, amoral spontaneity of Zen, goes back to the origins of Confucianism and Taoism in China. It continued when Zen arrived in Japan, because its teachers knew that it could only flourish within the habitual partnership; and as soon as it became firmly established, the 'Five Mountains', the five oldest Zen monasteries in Kyoto, began to propagate not only Buddhism, but at the same time the Confucian doctrine. The monks at the Five Mountains edited and printed the Confucian texts, and were the chief source of their dissemination; paradoxical as it may seem, the neo-Confucian revival under the Tokugawas, which added philosophical depth to the old social code, was chiefly due to Zen influence. The great Zen masters were, after all, sages with a shrewd knowledge of character; they knew that the cosmic nihilism of their doctrine was like arsenic – in small doses a stimulant, in large doses poison. Their wisdom found an unexpected confirmation several centuries later, when Zen was exported overseas and let loose among intellectuals with a decidedly non-Confucian background. They tried hard to obey its command: 'let your mind go and become like a ball in a mountain stream;' the result was a punctured tennis-ball surrounded by garbage, bouncing down the current from a burst water main.

[1] Suzuki, *op. cit.,* p. 63.

To revert to the old koan: Zen in itself, without its historic counterpart, is like the sound of one-hand clapping. Whether a religion, or a philosophy, deserves that name if it represents only one-hand clapping, is a problem for historians and semanticists. Perhaps the credos based on the materialism of the nineteenth century, or on the catechism of the Council of Trent issued in 1566, could be called equally one-handed. But the fact remains that Zen philosophy and Zen art had been declining for a century or more when the old social system, and with it the backbone of the Confucian code, was destroyed by the Meiji reform a hundred years ago. State Shinto was created to fill the religious vacuum; and when that synthetic Baal, too, collapsed after the lost war, neither Zen, nor the older forms of Buddhism[1] were able to offer an alternative to provide guidance in the chaos of values. They were unable, and even unwilling to do so, because of the ethical relativism of their tradition, their denial of a universal moral law, and a misguided tolerance which had become indistinguishable from passive complicity.

The contemporary Zen abbots in one of the ancient Five Mountains in Kyoto, with whom we had several discussions, confirmed this impression.[2] They were emphatic in their denials that religion had any bearing on social ethics. When we asked them whether they were indifferent to the persecution of religion in totalitarian countries, one of them answered:

'A horse eats in Tokyo and a horse in Osaka is no longer hungry. A Sputnik goes up in Moscow and the shares fall in New York.'

That was in the classic koan tradition, and it got us nowhere. When we asked a question, they answered with a parable; when I countered with a parable, they begged the question. The parable I submitted was Camus' *La Chute*: the

---

[1] I have not discussed the other Buddhist sects of Japan – Tendai, Shingon, Jodo, Nichiren, etc., because, though numerically they were, and still are, stronger, they cannot compare with Zen influence on the philosophy and art of Japan.

[2] The 'we' refers to my friend Quentin Crewe (*A Curse of Blossom*, London, 1960) and Hugh Dunphy, a young man who lived for several months in a Zen temple in Kyoto. The three of us, and Quentin's wife, Martha, travelled together through Kyushu.

problem of guilt by omission, of complacency towards evil –
Camus' Phariseean hero ignored the cry of a drowning
woman, and was subsequently destroyed by guilt. After a few
meaningless exchanges, one of the abbots said: 'Guilt is a
Christian idea. Zen has no home. It is glad for converts, but
does not seek to make proselytes.' At least this was the version
given to us by one of our lamentable translators; but it fitted
the general trend of the discussion. The abbots were delightful, but after two days of talking, we felt discouraged and
dejected. The one significant remark we got out of them
was: 'When you ask these logical questions, we feel
embarrassed.'

At another discussion, arranged as a round-table talk at
International House in Tokyo, I had an opportunity to meet
Professor N., one of the greatest Japanese experts on
Buddhism, who holds the Chair for Comparative Religion at
an old university. I asked him whether he thought it possible
to have a system of ethics divorced from any transcendental
belief. He bristled at the word 'transcendental', which, he
said, meant nothing to him. One of the participants argued
that Buddhism too held certain transcendental beliefs.
Professor N. denied this, and mentioned as an example to
the contrary that Japanese Buddhism rejected the idea of
transmigration. Then what happened after death? he was
asked. 'Death,' he answered, 'is for us, unlike for you, not
the "end" of life, but its culmination, its highest fulfilment, as
shown by the value we set on suicide.' What happened past
that culminating point? we asked him, is there an after life?
'Yes, some form of continuity, though not a personal one.'
But, we argued, that continuity, in whatever form, *does*
transcend the natural realm, so Buddhism *does* have a
transcendental aspect? 'We certainly do not believe in anything supernatural,' answered N.

Somebody tried a different angle. Buddhism lays great
stress on truth. Why should a man tell the truth when it
may be to his advantage to lie? 'Because it is simpler.' Somebody else tried another tack. 'You favour tolerance towards
all religions and all political systems. What about Hitler's

gas chambers?' 'That was very silly of him.'[1] 'Just silly, not
evil?' 'Evil is a Christian concept. Good and evil exist only
on a relative scale.' 'Should not then tolerance, too, be applied
on a relative scale? Should it include those who deny tolerance?' 'That is thinking in opposite categories, which is alien
to our thought.' And so it went on, round after dreary round.

This impartial tolerance towards the killer and the killed,
a tolerance devoid of charity, makes one sceptical regarding
the contribution which Zen Buddhism has to offer to the
moral recovery of Japan – or any other country. Once a balm
for self-inflicted bruises, it has become a kind of moral nerve-
gas – colourless and without smell, but scented by all the
pretty incense sticks which burn under the smiling Buddha
statues. For a week or so I bargained with a Kyoto antique
dealer for a small bronze Buddha of the Kamakura period;
but when he came down to a price which I was able to afford,
I backed out. I realized with a shock that the Buddha smile
had gone dead on me. It was no longer mysterious, but
empty.

Although Zen is an important chapter in Japanese history,
it is only one aspect of Japan. When the fog of depression
lifted, I was again filled with a shame-faced admiration for
the courage, the miraculous powers of recovery and the charm
of this nation of Spartan hedonists whose mentality, for all
their Western ways, is so alien to us. But it is
precisely this marriage between opposite extremes – the
Lotus and the Robot, Confucius and Zen, rigid perfectionism
and elastic ambiguity – which has such a profound fascina-
tion. Unable to achieve a synthesis, they rejected compromise,
and settled for the juxtaposition of extremes – the Spartan
and the Sybarite sharing the same bed. Instead of the Middle
Way, they chose the tight-rope, balancing a bamboo-pole
excessively weighted at both ends. The reason why I called
my admiration shame-faced is that, though I cannot approve
of this solution, it has a profound appeal to me. And, though

---

[1] The Professor had spent several years in Anglo-Saxon countries and spoke
exceptionally good English.

my Japanese friends will probably resent the directness of some of my remarks, if I were exiled from Europe, Japan would be the country where I would like to live in preference to any other – although, or because, I know that I would always remain there a bug-eyed traveller from Mars among the slit-eyed citizens of Saturn.

EPILOGUE

LILIES that fester smell far worse than weeds: both India and Japan seem to be spiritually sicker, more estranged from a living faith than the West. They are at opposite ends of the Asian spectrum, whose centre is occupied by the vastness of China, one of the world's oldest cultures; yet it proved even less resistant against the impact of a materialistic ideology. The nation which had held fast for two and a half millennia to the teaching of Confucius, Lao-Tse and the Buddha, succumbed to the atheistic doctrine formulated by the son of a German lawyer, and has become the most accomplished robot state this side of science fiction. To look to Asia for mystic enlightenment and spiritual guidance has become as much of an anachronism as to think of America as the Wild West.

Asians have a tendency to lay the blame for this decline on the soul-destroying influence of the West, and Western intellectuals are inclined to accept the blame. 'As pupils we were not bad, but hopeless as teachers' – Auden's *mea culpa,* though addressed to Italy, might serve as a motto for the Western guilt complex towards Asia. Like other complexes, it consists of a mixture of fact and fantasy. The factual elements belong to a chapter of history – imperialist expansion and colonial exploitation – which, as far as Asia is concerned, is now closed. It was, no doubt, an ugly chapter of predatoriness combined with hypocrisy. But, of course, the history of Asiatic nations is an equally unedifying tale of invasions, conquests and oppression – right up to the Moslem-Hindu massacres after Independence; and it could be cynically argued that the seafaring invaders of modern times were merely returning the visit of the Mongol invaders of Europe in earlier days. If the past were admitted to weigh on its conscience, every nation would be compelled to commit hara-kiri. Instead of nursing a guilt complex derived from the crimes of our forbears, the duty of the West is to give material help to the 'underprivileged' Asian nations; and that is now being done on a larger scale than ever before in history.

Let us turn, then, to another aspect of the complex: the psychological ravages which our materialistic civilization is supposed to have caused among the spiritual values of the traditional Asiatic cultures.

An apparent digression might help to clarify the problem. On a smaller scale, but in a more concentrated form, a similar process is now taking place closer to us. One might call it the coca-colonization of Western Europe, and in this respect I feel the same resentment as the Asian traditionalist. I loathe processed bread in cellophane, processed towns of cement and glass, and the Bible processed as a comic-strip; I loathe crooners and swooners, quizzes and fizzes, neon and subtopia, the Organization Man and the *Reader's Digest*. But who coerced us into buying all this? The United States do not rule Europe as the British ruled India; they waged no Opium War against us to force their revolting 'coke' down our throats. Europe bought the whole package because it wanted it. The Americans did not americanize us – they were merely one step ahead on the road towards a global civilization with a standardized style of living which, whether we like it or not, is beginning to emerge all over the world. For we live in a state of cultural osmosis where influences percolate across the porous frontiers, native traditions wane, and the movement towards a uniform, mechanized, stereotyped culture-pattern has become irresistible. What makes it irresistible are the new media of mass-communication; and what makes the emerging pattern so vulgar is the emergence of the under-privileged classes with their undeveloped tastes as consumers of mass-culture. The result is that inevitable levelling-down of standards to the lowest common denominator, which accompanied every revolution in the past. The liquidation of slums entails a period of cultural slumming – though only transitory, one hopes.

But this process of cultural osmosis started long before the media of mass-communication were invented – it started with Alexander, it continued in the Mogul invasion of India, and it gained a new impetus with the opening up of sea communications. European rule in Asian countries was based on force, but its cultural influence was not. They bought our culture because they wanted it; because their own cultures had lost their vigour, and succumbed to European influence – as Europe succumbed in the twentieth century to American influence. The Japanese bought European Renaissance learning from the Dutch traders in Nagasaki; then nineteenth-century Science during the Meiji reform; then the robot civilization after the Second World War. The Indian *élite* became anglicized because Hindu philosophy, science and literature had come to a standstill a long time ago, and had nothing to offer to them. We ruled by rape, but influenced by seduction. And a saint who lets herself be seduced willingly and asks for more, cannot be much of a saint.

The native customs and crafts were certainly damaged in the process. There is a tribe in Assam, the Khasis, who used to weave beautiful coloured fabrics; they also used to sacrifice little boys to the gods by pushing a two-pronged stick up their nostrils and into the brain. Now they buy hideous mass-produced textiles, and sacrifice no more little boys. It would have been better if they had accepted one half of the offer without the other. But these patterns of living hang together; they go, as the Americans say, by package deal. The Indian Government is now trying to revive the native crafts, but meets with little response. The reason, *mutatis mutandis,* is the same as in Europe: the produce of the cotton mills is cheaper than homespun *khadi*. It is, of course, also much uglier, and again for the same reason: the law of the lowest common denominator in taste. But this, too, may be a transitory phenomenon: some Indian factories are beginning to turn out remarkably attractive fabrics, printed in the traditional designs; and, sentimentality apart, only a few among the weavers, potters and cabinet-makers of the past were great artists. On the other hand, there is no reason why industrial design should not evolve from Late Woolworth into Early Wedgewood.

If the Western cultural imports into Asia provide often no more than cheap, superficial frills, the reason is that the uneducated Asiatic masses are inevitably attracted by the trashiest influence and wares – as the previously under-privileged classes in Europe are attracted by the lures of coca-colonization. If we are 'hopeless as teachers' both at home and abroad, it is because literacy, culture-hunger and leisure-time are increasing even more rapidly than the birth-rate. There have never been, relatively speaking, fewer creative talents facing a vaster audience of consumers.

All this does not prove that the material poverty of Asia is a sign of its spiritual superiority in the present or in the past. Materialism as a philosophy is less than two centuries old in Europe and now on the wane; 'materialism' in the sense of a mechanical, mindless sort of living is less than half a century old, though still on the increase. Before that, religion had been the dominant chord in European philosophy, art and social life, as far back into the past as historical comparisons are meaningful.

Asian history has been as bloody and cruel as ours; and the Buddhist-Hindu version of tolerance without charity produced as much suffering and misery as Christian charity without tolerance did. Non-Violence was an abstract command, like turning the other cheek, until quite recent times when Gandhi's genius forged it into a political weapon. The great Hindu epics, the Ramayana and Mahabharata, are as full of savagery and gore as the Old Testament, and the first three chapters of the Bhagavad Gita – the nearest Hindu equivalent to the Gospels – are devoted to an eloquent refutation of the doctrine of non-violence. The Lord Krishna in person appears on the battle-field as the charioteer of his friend Arjuna, and persuades him to drop his pacifist scruples – mainly on the grounds that the indestructible atma is embodied in both the slayer and the slain, who are One; therefore Arjuna must obey the law of Karma Yoga and fight. 'There is no higher good for a Kshatriya (member of the warrior class) than a righteous war. The truly wise mourn neither for the living nor for the dead.'

Gandhi himself was never an integral pacifist; he endorsed the Congress Resolution of 1940 that India would enter the war if granted Independence, and he gave his agreement to the invasion of Kashmir. Similarly, Vinoba Bhave in 1959 advocated armed resistance against Chinese infiltration in the Himalayas 'because India is not yet spiritually prepared for a wholly non-violent resistance'. Pacifism is a philosophy which, unfortunately, only appeals to pacifists. There is always that child bashed about by a brute, a Czechoslovakia or a Himalayan province invaded; and the dilemma between active intervention and passive complicity has never been solved, either by the East or by the West.

'You have developed the head; the heart did not keep pace. With us it was the opposite – it was with the development of the heart that we have been concerned in India.' When Vinoba said that to me, I accepted it as a truism, as most guilt-ridden Westerners do. The first half of the statement is certainly true; but what evidence is there for the second? If 'heart' refers to charity, the Oriental attitude to the sick and the poor is notoriously indifferent, because caste, rank, wealth and health are pre-ordained by the laws of Karma. Welfare work in the slums and care of the poor in general was, and still is, a monopoly of the Christian missions in Asia. Gandhi's crusade for the Untouchables and Vinoba's crusade for the landless are modern developments under Western influence – Gandhi himself acknowledged that he was inspired by Christianity, Tolstoy, Ruskin and Thoreau.

If by 'heart' Vinoba meant religion, it has been in steady decline for the last fifteen hundred years. Buddhism, Confucianism and Taoism were all founded in the sixth pre-Christian century; their spiritual message is confined to the ancient texts and to the monumental works of art which they inspired. Religious thought in the East retained its archetypal character; it does not show that evolutionary progression, that combination of a firm basic doctrine with social plasticity, which lent Western monotheism its unique continuity and ethos. Each of the great Eastern religions represents a way of life rather than a self-contained metaphysical doctrine; and when that way of life is altered by changing circumstances, as in India and Japan, the spiritual values crumble away. The Sankaracharya insisted on the rigorous observance of the Hindu rites – because if the observances go, nothing of Hinduism is left. A Hindu who breaks caste, eats meat and forsakes his *lotha*, ceases, by definition, to be a Hindu. The industrial revolution in England caused a more violent uprooting of traditions than India is experiencing at present; yet the Church of England weathered the storm, while Hinduism is foundering. The only live religious tradition in India in the last thousand years was carried on by exceptional individuals – by its great swamis, from Sankara to Vinoba. But their contribution lay more in their personality than in their teaching, and they rarely left written works of value on which their successors could build.

In other words, I think that our cherished habit of contrasting the contemplative and spiritual East with the crude materialism of the West is based on a fallacy. The contrast is not between spirituality and materialism, but between two basically different philosophies; so different, in fact, that Haas, the German Orientalist, who wrote a thoughtful and stimulating book on the question,[1] suggested a new word for the Eastern approach to life: 'philousia' as opposed to Western 'philosophy'. For all the historical evidence goes to show that the East is less interested in factual knowledge – *sophia* – of the external world than in *ousia* – essential Being; that it prefers intuition to reason, symbols to concepts, self-realization through the annihilation of the ego to self-realization through the unfolding of individuality. Obviously the two attitudes ought to complement each other like the

[1] William S. Haas, *The Destiny of the Mind*, London, 1956.

principles of masculine logic and feminine intuition, the *yin* and *yang* in Taoist philosophy. And in the history of European thought they did indeed complement each other – either by simultaneously competing for supremacy or alternating in dominance. In every chapter of European history we can trace this creative polarity on various levels – the Dionysian and the Appollonian principles; the materialism of the Ionian philosophers and the mysticism of the Eleatics; Plato, Plotinus and Augustine negating the world of the senses, Aristotle, Albert and Aquinas reasserting it; Schopenhauer's Indian pessimism confronted by Nietzsche's arrogant superman; Jung's psychology of archetypes by Adler's psychology of power – through the ages the fertile opposition of *yin* and *yang* is reformulated under different aspects.

In the history of the great Asiatic cultures, the emphasis lay much more consistently on one side only – on the intuitive, subjective, mystical, logic-rejecting side. This attitude apparently arose out of the equally consistent refusal to recognize the independent reality of the external world. As a result, conceptual thinking could not develop, and *yin* had it all to herself against *yang*. When she occasionally tried to pose as *yang* – as in the pseudo-reasoning of, say, Krishna Menon about the seer and the seen, or of Dr. Suzuki about tea which is no-tea – the result was confusion.

Thus the *hubris* of rationalism is matched by the *hubris* of irrationality, and the messianic arrogance of the Christian crusader is matched by the Yogi's arrogant attitude of detachment towards human suffering. Mankind is facing its most deadly predicament since it climbed down from the trees; but one is reluctantly brought to the conclusion that neither Yoga, Zen, nor any other Asian form of mysticism has any significant advice to offer.

Thus, in a sense, I came back impoverished rather than enriched. I felt that I had been put in my place – and that my place was Europe. But at the same time, looking at this tiny Continent from the vastness of Asia, I gained a fresh impression of its compactness and coherence, and a more intense awareness of its unique history – its unity-in-variety in Space, and continuity-through-change in Time.

Concerning the first aspect I could not help regarding myself as a typical example: born in Hungary, educated in Austria, the formative years spent in France, British by naturalization – transposed into Asian terms, one would have to imagine a person born in Ankara, who studied in Benares and ended up as a Japanese writer. Though the parallel seems rather silly, it does drive home not only the smallness of Europe, but also the homogeneity of its culture. Wherever one looks, at art, science, trade, sport, architecture, the common denominators weave their fabric across territorial and racial boundaries. Leaving aside the recently colonized territories, Europe is the only continent among the ancient geographical divisions of the world where the ethnic mosaic forms a recognizable cultural pattern; and that pattern expresses the second aspect of Europe's organic coherence, its continuity-through-change, maintained through two and a half millennia of history. Egyptian culture displayed an amazing constancy over a couple of thousand years; but this happened in a society which remained essentially static. Europe, on the other hand, was in almost continual ferment and change, and yet managed to preserve a distinct identity, a historic personality, as it were.

Oddly enough, that personality emerged at the same turning-point of human history, the sixth century B.C., which gave birth to Confucius and Lao-Tse, the Buddha, the Ionian Philosophers and the Pythagorean brotherhood. It was the parting of the ways between *philousia* and *philosophia*. Out of the same Sanskrit root, *matr-*, came two key words: *maya* and *metron*, which symbolize the split. *Maya*, in both Hinduism and Buddhism, is the symbol of an attitude which regards Nature as a veil of illusions; *metron* – measure – heralded the beginning of the great European adventure which, within the next two thousand years, was to transform the human species more radically than the previous two hundred thousand had done. In the first great synthesis of European thought, the Pythagorean school brought together into a unified vision yin and yang, mysticism and science, mathematics and music; the search for Law in Nature, the analysis of the harmony of the spheres, was proclaimed to be the highest form of divine worship. And this form of worship is a specifically European discovery. There were periods in which this discovery was forgotten and denied, like a recessive gene, but it always reasserted itself.

The impressive thing about European evolution, seen from the Asian perspective, is the organic integration of the various trends that went into it. The geometry of Euclid, Plato's *Timaeus* and Aristotle's *Categories* were not just stuck on to the Ten Commandments and the Sermon on the Mount; they were united by a process of cross-fertilization, a spiritual marriage, and as its outcome the Logos became flesh. It provided the link between mysticism and logic, between the poetry of St. John of the Cross and the Jesuit astronomers' search for order and harmony in the universe. It is this synthesis which all other great cultures rejected – the Asian cultures by rejecting both the Logos, the *metron* and the reality by the outside world, the African and pre-Columban cultures by moving towards different spiritual pastures.

Greece collapsed, Alexandria was burned, the Roman Empire collapsed, yet the Logos remained incarnate, the continuity was sustained. Roman Law, Latin as the universal language and Christianity as the universal Church, gave the European *persona* its definite physical contours and spiritual profile. Whether we believe in Christian dogma or not, the tenets of Judeo-Christian ethics, of Latin *civitas* and Greek conceptual thought, which we imbibed unconsciously, almost at the mother's breast, have become integral elements in our make-up as Europeans, and are taken as much for granted as the red and white corpuscles in our blood. The migrations injected the vitality of the barbaric tribes into the tired old races around the Mediterranean basin, but Europe did not become barbarized – it was the barbarians who became europeanized.

Equally impressive is Europe's self-regenerating power – exemplified by the manner in which it pulled itself out of its longest period of stagnation. The revival of learning in the thirteenth century and the subsequent Renaissance of culture were due to Europe's regaining possession of its own past – its temporarily lost Greek heritage. But the curious thing about this is, that during the nearly five centuries in which the Arabs (and to a lesser extent the Jews of Portugal and Spain) had been the sole keepers of the treasure of Greek learning, they did little to put it to use. Their long tenure of this vast body of knowledge remained barren; it was another skin-graft which never took. Yet when the Hellenic tissue was grafted back on to the Latin culture of Europe – after nearly a thousand years – it had an immediate reviving effect; and this tends to show that Europe really has some kind of individuality of its own. We are still in the middle of the explosive development which started with that re-grafting operation.

Continuity-through-change and unity-in-diversity seem to be the pre-conditions of a living culture. Continuity without change was characteristic of some highly sophisticated Asiatic civilizations; change without a deep awareness of continuity with the past is a characteristic of new continents such as America. I started my journey in sackcloth and ashes and came back rather proud of being a European. It may be a somewhat parochial pride, but it is not smug, for, as a Hungarian-born, French-loving English writer with some experience of prisons and concentration camps, one cannot help being aware of Europe's past sins and present deadly peril. And yet a detached comparison with other continents of the way Europe stood up to its past trials, and of its contribution to man's history, leaves one with a new confidence and affection for that small figure riding on the back of the Asian bull.

December 1958 – May 1960

Index

Index

Index

About the Author

ARTHUR KOESTLER began his career as a student of science in Vienna. When he turned to writing, he was a foreign correspondent for a few years, then became science editor of the Ullstein chain of newspapers in pre-Hitler Germany, and as early as 1930 was contributing articles on interplanetary travel and the splitting of the atom. After a detour of twenty years, which made him perhaps the most widely read political novelist of our time—*Darkness at Noon* was translated into thirty languages—he gave up writing on political subjects and reverted to his earlier passion in *The Sleepwalkers* (1959), "a history of man's changing vision of the universe."

He travels extensively and spent two years in India and Japan in preparation for the writing of *The Lotus and the Robot.* Otherwise, he divides his time between his London house and his mountain hut in the Tyrol. After the Second World War he became a British subject, and since 1940 all his books have been written in English, one of his three languages—the others being Hungarian and German—in which he writes with more than native fluency.

His other books include *Dialogue with Death, The Gladiators, Scum of the Earth, Arrival and Departure, The Yogi and the Commissar, Twilight Bar, Thieves in the Night, Insight and Outlook, Promise and Fulfillment, The Age of Longing, Arrow in the Blue, The Invisible Writing, The Trail of the Dinosaur, Reflections on Hanging, Watershed: A Biography of Johannes Kepler,* and *The Act of Creation.*

COLOPHON BOOKS ON PHILOSOPHY AND RELIGION